First and Second
Thessalonians

T0340676

First and Second Thessalonians

TIMOTHY A. BROOKINS

Baker Academic

a division of Baker Publishing Group
Grand Rapids, Michigan

© 2021 by Timothy A. Brookins

Published by Baker Academic
a division of Baker Publishing Group
PO Box 6287, Grand Rapids, MI 49516-6287
www.bakeracademic.com

Printed in the United States of America

Library of Congress Cataloging-in-Publication Data
Names: Brookins, Timothy A. author.
Title: First and Second Thessalonians / Timothy A. Brookins.
Description: Grand Rapids, Michigan : Baker Academic, a division of Baker Publishing Group, [2021] |
    Series: Paideia: commentaries on the New Testament | Includes bibliographical references and index.
Identifiers: LCCN 2021011631 | ISBN 9780801031823 (paperback) | ISBN 9781493432158 (ebook)
Subjects: LCSH: Bible. Thessalonians—Commentaries.
Classification: LCC BS2725.53 .B76 2021 | DDC 227/.8107—dc23
LC record available at https://lccn.loc.gov/2021011631

Unless otherwise indicated, all Scripture quotations are the author's translation.

Baker Publishing Group publications use paper produced from sustainable forestry practices and post-consumer waste whenever possible.

21 22 23 24 25 26 27   7 6 5 4 3 2 1

To my beloved children
Adam, Ryan, and Caitlin

Contents

Figures and Tables

Figures

Tables

Foreword

Paideia: Commentaries on the New Testament is a series that sets out to comment on the final form of the New Testament text in a way that pays due attention both to the cultural, literary, and theological settings in which the text took form and to the interests of the contemporary readers to whom the commentaries are addressed. This series is aimed squarely at students—including MA students in religious and theological studies programs, seminarians, and upper-division undergraduates—who have theological interests in the biblical text. Thus, the didactic aim of the series is to enable students to understand each book of the New Testament as a literary whole rooted in a particular ancient setting and related to its context within the New Testament.

The name "Paideia" (Greek for "education") reflects (1) the instructional aim of the series—giving contemporary students a basic grounding in academic New Testament studies by guiding their engagement with New Testament texts; (2) the fact that the New Testament texts as literary unities are shaped by the educational categories and ideas (rhetorical, narratological, etc.) of their ancient writers and readers; and (3) the pedagogical aims of the texts themselves—their central aim being not simply to impart information but to form the theological convictions and moral habits of their readers.

Each commentary deals with the text in terms of larger rhetorical units; these are not verse-by-verse commentaries. This series thus stands within the stream of recent commentaries that attend to the final form of the text. Such reader-centered literary approaches are inherently more accessible to liberal arts students without extensive linguistic and historical-critical preparation than older exegetical approaches, but within the reader-centered world the sanest practitioners have paid careful attention to the extratext of the original readers, including not only these readers' knowledge of the geography, history, and other contextual elements reflected in the text but also their ability to respond correctly to the literary and rhetorical conventions used in the text. Paideia commentaries pay deliberate attention to this extratextual repertoire in order to highlight the ways in which the text is designed to persuade and move its readers. Each rhetorical unit is explored from three angles: (1) introductory matters; (2) tracing the train of thought or narrative or rhetorical flow of the argument; and (3) theological issues raised by the text that are of interest to the contemporary Christian. Thus, the primary focus remains on the text and not its historical context or its interpretation in the secondary literature.

Our authors represent a variety of confessional points of view: Protestant, Catholic, and Orthodox. What they share, beyond being New Testament scholars of national and international repute, is a commitment to reading the biblical text as theological documents within their ancient contexts. Working within the broad parameters described here, each author brings his or her own considerable exegetical talents and deep theological commitments to the task of laying bare the interpretation of Scripture for the faith and practice of God's people everywhere.

Mikeal C. Parsons
Charles H. Talbert
Bruce W. Longenecker

Preface

The letters of 1 and 2 Thessalonians are truly underappreciated. In any case, that is the opinion I have come to the more I have studied them. These letters are perhaps best known for their attention to the "end times"—the resurrection of believers, the return of Jesus, and the coming of "the Antichrist." A deeper dive into these letters, however, reveals that their significance extends far beyond their discussion of such themes. In addition to their treatment of practical issues like sex and unemployment, they offer us a valuable window into the troubled beginnings of one of history's oldest churches, and into the strategies of pastoral care that Paul used to encourage and exhort them in his absence, as they faced persecution so soon after their conversion. It is hoped that the painstaking work of historical and textual analysis that went into this commentary will increase appreciation of these letters in the one who reads it, just as it did in me in writing it.

I was honored to write what is the concluding volume to the Paideia commentary series. My sincerest thanks to the series editors—Mikeal Parsons, Charles Talbert, and Bruce Longenecker—for their vote of confidence. I thank also the many individuals who read and offered valuable feedback on my chapters, including John Barclay, Ben Blackwell, Dave Briones, Beverly Gaventa, Paul Foster, Eric Gilchrest, James Harrison, Chris Kugler, Jason Maston, Timothy Milinovich, Peter Reynolds, Jay Smith, Todd Still, Jeffrey Weima, Joel White, Adam Winn, and Richard Wright. The students in my Greek seminar during the spring 2020 session helped sharpen my thinking on many exegetical issues. I thank the editorial staff at Baker Academic, including Bryan Dyer and Wells Turner, for their diligent work at their respective stages in the publication process.

I thank my wife, Mary Mac, and my three children for letting me spend my time writing. Most of the manuscript was completed during COVID-19 quarantine, and much of it from home. I wrote as my kids attended online classes, each of us on our separate computers. I am grateful for their stoic persistence and admirable performance as they finished the 2019–20 school year, as this allowed me the focus I needed to complete the project. I am grateful for the sweet humility that they showed me when I grew impatient from interruptions as they sought help, even more so when I consider the agony of online learning they were forced to endure. In an odd way, quarantine allowed me to be "with" them in my work as I would not have been otherwise, and for that I am grateful too. It is to them that I dedicate this book: Adam, Ryan, and Caitlin.

Abbreviations

General

/	or	forthc.	forthcoming
//	parallel to	frag(s).	fragment(s)
BCE	before the Common (Christian) era	i.e.	*id est*, that is
CE	Common (Christian) era	lit.	literally
cent.	century	NT	New Testament
cf.	*confer*, compare	OT	Old Testament
chap(s).	chapter(s)	p(p).	page(s)
diss.	dissertation	pref.	preface
ed(s).	editor(s), edited by, edition	ps.-	pseudo-
e.g.	*exempli gratia*, for example	repr.	reprinted
Ep.	*Epistles*, with specific author named	rev.	revised
esp.	especially	St.	Saint
et al.	*et alii*, and others	trans.	translator(s), translated by
etc.	*et cetera*, and the rest	v(v).	verse(s)
		vol(s).	volume(s)

Biblical Texts and Versions

ℵ	Codex Sinaiticus (4th cent.)	KJV	King James Version
A	Codes Alexandrinus (5th cent.)	LXX	Septuagint, Greek Old Testament
B	Codex Vaticanus (4th cent.)	NA²⁸	*Novum Testamentum Graece.* 28th rev. ed. Edited by [E. and E. Nestle], B. and K. Aland, J. Karavidopoulos, C. M. Martini, and B. M. Metzger. Stuttgart: Deutsche Bibelgesellschaft, 2012.
D	Codex Bezae Cantabrigiensis (6th cent.)		
Eng.	English versification		
ESV	English Standard Version		

NAB	New American Bible	$\mathfrak{P}^{46}$	Chester Beatty Papyrus II, of about 200 CE, with most of Paul's Epistles
NABRE	New American Bible, revised (2010) edition	$\mathfrak{P}^{65}$	a third-century papyrus copy of some of 1 Thessalonians
NASB	New American Standard Bible		
NIV	New International Version	$\mathfrak{P}^{92}$	a third- or fourth-century papyrus copy of some of 2 Thessalonians
NKJV	New King James Version		
NRSV	New Revised Standard Version	UBS⁵	*The Greek New Testament*, United Bible Societies, 5th rev. ed. 2014
$\mathfrak{P}^{30}$	a third-century papyrus of some of 1–2 Thessalonians		

Ancient Corpora

OLD TESTAMENT

Gen.	Genesis
Exod.	Exodus
Lev.	Leviticus
Num.	Numbers
Deut.	Deuteronomy
Josh.	Joshua
Judg.	Judges
Ruth	Ruth
1–2 Sam.	1–2 Samuel
1–2 Kings	1–2 Kings
1–2 Chron.	1–2 Chronicles
Ezra	Ezra
Neh.	Nehemiah
Esther	Esther
Job	Job
Ps(s).	Psalm(s)
Prov.	Proverbs
Eccles.	Ecclesiastes
Song	Song of Songs
Isa.	Isaiah
Jer.	Jeremiah
Lam.	Lamentations
Ezek.	Ezekiel
Dan.	Daniel
Hosea	Hosea
Joel	Joel
Amos	Amos
Obad.	Obadiah
Jon.	Jonah
Mic.	Micah

Nah.	Nahum
Hab.	Habakkuk
Zeph.	Zephaniah
Hag.	Haggai
Zech.	Zechariah
Mal.	Malachi

DEUTEROCANONICAL BOOKS

Add. Esth.	Additions to Esther
1–2 Esd.	1–2 Esdras
1–4 Macc.	1–4 Maccabees
Sir. (Ecclus.)	Sirach (Ecclesiasticus)
Tob.	Tobit
Wis.	Wisdom of Solomon

NEW TESTAMENT

Matt.	Matthew
Mark	Mark
Luke	Luke
John	John
Acts	Acts
Rom.	Romans
1–2 Cor.	1–2 Corinthians
Gal.	Galatians
Eph.	Ephesians
Phil.	Philippians
Col.	Colossians
1–2 Thess.	1–2 Thessalonians
1–2 Tim.	1–2 Timothy
Titus	Titus
Philem.	Philemon
Heb.	Hebrews

James   James
1–2 Pet.   1–2 Peter
1–3 John   1–3 John
Jude   Jude
Rev.   Revelation

OLD TESTAMENT PSEUDEPIGRAPHA

Apoc. Ab.   *Apocalypse of Abraham*
Apoc. Mos. *Apocalypse of Moses*
Aristob.   *Aristobulus*
2 Bar.   *2 Baruch (Syriac Apocalypse)*
4 Bar.   *4 Baruch*
1–2 En.   *1–2 Enoch*
4 Ezra   *4 Ezra*
Jos. Asen.   *Joseph and Aseneth*
Jub.   *Jubilees*
LAB   *Liber antiquitatum biblicarum*
LAE   *Life of Adam and Eve*
Pss. Sol.   *Psalms of Solomon*
Sib. Or.   *Sibylline Oracles*
T. Ab.   *Testament of Abraham*
T. Job   *Testament of Job*
T. Levi   *Testament of Levi*
T. Naph.   *Testament of Naphtali*

DEAD SEA SCROLLS

CD   Cairo Genizah, *Damascus Document*

1QH[a]   Qumran, Cave 1, *Hodayot Scroll, Thanksgiving Hymns*[a]
1QM   Qumran, Cave 1, *War Scroll*
1QS   Qumran, Cave 1, *Community Rule*

RABBINIC WORKS

Gen. Rab.   *Genesis Rabbah*
Pesiq. Rab.   *Pesiqta Rabbati*

NEW TESTAMENT APOCRYPHA

Acts Pet.   *Acts of Peter*
Apoc. Pet.   *Apocalypse of Peter*

APOSTOLIC FATHERS

Barn.   *Barnabas*
1–2 Clem.   *1–2 Clement*
Did.   *Didache*
Diogn.   *Diognetus*
Herm. Mand.   *Shepherd of Hermas, Mandates*
Ign. *Eph.*   Ignatius, *To the Ephesians*
Ign. *Magn.*   Ignatius, *To the Magnesians*
Ign. *Pol.*   Ignatius, *To Polycarp*
Ign. *Trall.*   Ignatius, *To the Trallians*
Mart. Pol.   *Martyrdom of Polycarp*
Pol. *Phil.*   Polycarp, *To the Philippians*

Ancient Authors

APPIAN

Bell. civ.   *Bella civilia (Civil Wars)*

ARISTOTLE

Eth. Nic.   *Ethica Nicomachea (Nicomachean Ethics)*

AUGUSTINE

Civ.   *De civitate Dei (The City of God)*

CHARITON

Chaer.   *De Chaerea et Callirhoe (Chaereas and Callirhoe)*

CICERO/PSEUDO-CICERO

Amic.   *De amicitia (On Friendship)*
Att.   *Epistulae ad Atticum (Letters to Atticus)*
Fam.   *Epistulae ad familiares (Letters to Friends)*
Nat. d.   *De natura deorum (On the Nature of the Gods)*
Off.   *De officiis (On Duties)*
Rhet. Her.   *Rhetorica ad Herennium (Rhetoric for Herennius)*
Tusc.   *Tusculanae disputationes (Tusculan Disputations)*

DEMOSTHENES

Or. Orationes (*Orations*)

DIO CHRYSOSTOM

Or. Orationes (*Discourses*)

DIODORUS SICULUS

Bib. hist. Bibliotheca historica (*Library of History*)

DIOGENES LAËRTIUS

Vit. Vitae philosophorum (*Lives of the Philosophers*)

EPICTETUS

Diatr. Diatribes

EUSEBIUS

Hist. eccl. Historia ecclesiastica (*Ecclesiastical History*)

HOMER

Il. Ilias (*Iliad*)

IRENAEUS

Haer. Adversus haereses (*Against Heresies*)

JOSEPHUS

Ag. Ap. Against Apion
Ant. Jewish Antiquities
J.W. Jewish War

JUSTIN MARTYR

1 Apol. First Apology
Dial. Dialogue with Trypho

JUVENAL

Sat. Satirae (*Satires*)

LUCIAN

Fug. Fugitivi (*The Fugitives* or *The Runaways*)
Nigr. Nigrinus
Peregr. The Passing of Peregrinus
Philops. Philopseudes (*The Lover of Lies*)

LUCRETIUS

Rer. nat. De rerum natura (*On the Nature of Things*)

MARCUS AURELIUS

Med. Meditations

MUSONIUS RUFUS

Diatr. Diatribai (*Discourses*)

ORIGEN

Cels. Contra Celsum (*Against Celsus*)
Comm. Matt. Commentary on Matthew

OVID

Metam. Metamorphoses (*Transformations*)

PHILO

Abr. De Abrahamo (*On the Life of Abraham*)
Decal. De decalogo (*On the Decalogue*)
Deus Quod Deus sit immutabilis (*That God Is Unchangeable*)
Ebr. De ebrietate (*On Drunkenness*)
Fug. De fuga et inventione (*On Flight and Finding*)
Leg. Legum allegoriae (*Allegorical Interpretation*)
Legat. Legatio ad Gaium (*On the Embassy to Gaius*)
Migr. De migratione Abrahami (*On the Migration of Abraham*)
Mos. De vita Mosis (*On the Life of Moses*)
Mut. De mutatione nominum (*On the Change of Names*)
Plant. De plantatione (*On Planting*)
QG Quaestiones et solutiones in Genesin (*Questions and Answers on Genesis*)
Sobr. De sobrietate (*On Sobriety*)
Spec. De specialibus legibus (*On the Special Laws*)
Virt. De virtutibus (*On the Virtues*)

PHILOSTRATUS

Vit. Apoll.   *Vita Apollonii (Life of Apollonius)*

PLATO

Gorg.   *Gorgias*
Phaed.   *Phaedo*
Resp.   *Respublica (Republic)*
Tim.   *Timaeus*

PLINY THE ELDER

Nat.   *Naturalis historia (Natural History)*

PLUTARCH/PSEUDO-PLUTARCH

Brut.   *Brutus*
Lib. ed.   *De liberis educandis (On the Education of Children)*
Mor.   *Moralia (Morals)*
Superst.   *De superstitione (On Superstition)*
Ti. C. Gracch.   *Tiberius et Caius Gracchus (Life of Tiberius and Gaius Gracchus)*

POLYBIUS

Hist.   *Historiae (Histories)*

PSEUDO-DIONYSIUS OF HALICARNASSUS

Rhet.   *Ars rhetorica (Art of Rhetoric)*

QUINTILIAN

Inst.   *Institutio oratoria (Institutes of Oratory)*

SENECA

Ben.   *De beneficiis (On Benefits)*
Clem.   *De clementia (On Mercy)*

Const.   *De constantia sapientis (On the Firmness of the Wise Person)*
Ep.   *Epistulae morales (Moral Epistles)*
Ira   *De ira (On Anger)*
Nat.   *Naturales quaestiones (Natural Questions)*
Prov.   *De providentia (On Providence)*
Vit. beat.   *De vita beata (On the Happy Life)*

STOBAEUS (HIEROCLES)

Flor.   *Florilegium (Anthology)*

STRABO

Geogr.   *Geographica (Geography)*

SUETONIUS

Aug.   *Divus Augustus (Divine Augustus)*
Dom.   *Domitianus (Domitian)*
Jul.   *Divus Julius (Divine Julius)*

TACITUS

Ann.   *Annales (Annals)*
Hist.   *Historiae (Histories)*

TERTULLIAN

Marc.   *Adversus Marcionem (Against Marcion)*

VERGIL

Aen.   *Aeneid*

XENOPHON

Mem.   *Memorabilia*

Series, Collections, and Reference Works

ABD   *The Anchor Bible Dictionary.* Edited by D. N. Freedman et al. 6 vols. New York: Doubleday, 1992.

BDAG   W. Bauer, F. W. Danker, W. F. Arndt, and F. W. Gingrich. *A Greek-English Lexicon of the New Testament and Other Early Christian Literature.* 3rd ed. Chicago: University of Chicago Press, 2000.

BGU	*Aegyptische Urkunden aus den Königlichen/Staatlichen Museen zu Berlin, Griechische Urkunden.* 15 vols. Berlin, 1895–1983.
ID	*Inscriptions de Délos.* Edited by Félix Dürrbach et al. 7 vols. Paris: H. Champion, 1926–72.
IG	*Inscriptiones Graecae.* Editio Minor. Berlin: de Gruyter, 1924–.
LCL	Loeb Classical Library
LSJ	H. G. Liddell, R. Scott, and H. S. Jones. *A Greek-English Lexicon.* 9th ed. Oxford: Clarendon, 1996.
Miletos	*Miletos Inscriptions: Texts and List.* Edited by Donald F. McCabe and Mark A. Plunkett. The Princeton Project on the Inscriptions of Anatolia. Princeton: Institute for Advanced Study, 1984. Packard Humanities Institute CD 6, 1991.
OTP	*The Old Testament Pseudepigrapha.* Edited by J. H. Charlesworth. 2 vols. Garden City, NY: Doubleday, 1983–85.
PGiss.	*Griechische Papyri im Museum des oberhessischen Geschichtsvereins zu Giessen.* Edited by O. Eger, E. Kornemann, and P. M. Meyer. Leipzig-Berlin, 1910–12.
P.Oxy.	*The Oxyrhynchus Papyri.* 81 vols. London: Egypt Exploration Society, 1898–.
PSI	*Papiri greci e latini: Pubblicazioni della Società Italiana per la ricerca dei papiri greci e latini in Egitto.* Edited by G. Vitelli and M. Norsa. 15 vols. Florence, 1912–2008.
SBL	Society of Biblical Literature
SEG	Supplementum epigraphicum graecum
SIG	*Sylloge Inscriptionum Graecarum.* Edited by W. Dittenberger. 3rd ed. 4 vols. Leipzig, 1915–24.
TDNT	*Theological Dictionary of the New Testament.* Edited by G. Kittel and G. Friedrich. Translated and edited by G. W. Bromiley. 10 vols. Grand Rapids: Eerdmans, 1964–76.

1 Thessalonians

Introduction to 1 Thessalonians

Around the year 50 CE, the apostle Paul dispatched a letter from Corinth, in the Roman province of Achaia, to a young church in the Macedonian city of Thessalonica, some two or three weeks' journey to the north. For reasons not precisely known to us, this letter was preserved and copied.

Today it is the earliest extant document from the early Christian movement. It continues to be read as a canonical text in the Christian church. Yet the letter, now known as "1 Thessalonians," was a historical document written within a cultural world quite different from our own, and it was carried to a specific church in Macedonia with a message that they above anyone else needed to hear. This means that some study is required if one is to understand the letter's original significance. The present commentary is intended to clarify the meaning of 1 Thessalonians—first as an ancient personal *letter*. These observations will then form the basis for discussing the letter's enduring theological significance (see the sections labeled "Theological Issues").

Before commenting on the text, it is first necessary to offer some introduction. Here we will discuss (1) 1 Thessalonians as a literary composition, (2) the identity of the author(s) and audience and the history of their relationship, and (3) the background against which the letter was written. I will then provide (4) an overview of the letter's contents.

The Letter as a Literary Composition

Reception History

In comparison with other letters traditionally attributed to Paul, 1 Thessalonians has received only moderate attention. Nevertheless, the vast body of literature dedicated to 1 Thessalonians over the centuries shows that the letter has by no means been neglected. Various scholars have summarized the history of the letter's interpretation. In a recent critical introduction to the Thessalonian correspondence, Nijay Gupta reviews its reception in the ancient and medieval periods (2019, 155–60), in the Reformation and post-Reformation periods (2019, 161–65), and in early modern scholarship (2019, 166–71). Gupta's introduction also reviews modern scholarship through the present (2019, 172–81), complementing reviews by Wolfgang Trilling (1987) and Raymond Collins (1984), which cover scholarship through the mid-1980s. R. Collins (1984, 385–401) has also produced a bibliography of studies published between 1956 and 1983, which discusses more than fifty commentaries written during this period. A more recent bibliography of modern scholarship can be found in Richard Ascough (2015). Two newly released volumes view the Thessalonian letters against the background of the urban environment of first-century Thessalonica. One (Harrison and Welborn forthc.) will be volume 7 of a multivolume work titled *The First Urban Churches*; the other (Harrison and Schliesser forthc.) will be volume 14 of a multivolume work titled *New Documents Illustrating Early Christianity*.

Text History

Surviving copies of 1 Thessalonians and references to the work by ancient writers provide a starting point for dating the document as a literary composition. First Thessalonians is included in the oldest surviving collection of Paul's letters, the papyrus manuscript $\mathfrak{P}^{46}$, which was produced around 200 CE. Several other copies of 1 Thessalonians dating to the third ($\mathfrak{P}^{30}$, $\mathfrak{P}^{65}$) and fourth centuries ($\aleph$, B) have also survived. Possible allusions to the letter appear in several Christian writings produced around 110 CE (Ign. *Pol.* 1.3//1 Thess. 5:17; Pol. *Phil.* 3.2–3//1 Thess. 1:3) or earlier (*Did.* 16.6//1 Thess. 4:16). Writing during the last quarter of the second century, Irenaeus provides the earliest extant citation of the letter (*Haer.* 5.30.2//1 Thess. 5:3), though according to Tertul-

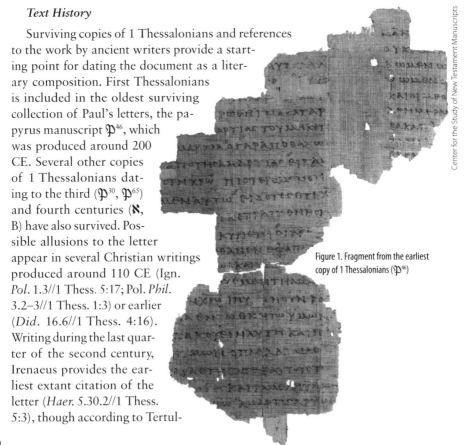

Figure 1. Fragment from the earliest copy of 1 Thessalonians ($\mathfrak{P}^{46}$)

Center for the Study of New Testament Manuscripts

lian, 1 Thessalonians had formed part of Marcion's canon, the list of NT texts Marcion compiled as early as the 140s (Tertullian, *Marc.* 5.15; cf. Irenaeus, *Haer.* 3.12.12). The letter was also included in the Muratorian list of canonical books (controversially dated to the final third of the second century); by the early fourth century, it was universally considered to be an authentic letter of the apostle Paul and was thus included among the church's "recognized" books (Eusebius, *Hist. eccl.* 3.3, 25).

The letter as preserved in the manuscript tradition appears to reflect the integrity of the original composition, though this point has been contested. Some have proposed that our "1 Thessalonians" consisted originally of two or more letters, later compiled into one (most recently, Richard [1995, 11–19] has argued in favor of a two-letter view). Others have proposed that some material may be interpolated, including 5:1–11 (Friedrich 1976) and, more seriously, 2:13–16 (on which, see comments). Some, moreover, have viewed the letter as a compilation of letters joined together by multiple interpolations (for interpreters prior to 1985, see Jewett 1986, 42–45). Apart from the few who have registered doubts, scholars today are virtually unanimous in the opinion that the letter as we have it reflects its original integrity; despite the doubts of a few about the originality of 2:13–16, scholarship as a whole has turned decidedly toward the view that the letter contains no substantial interpolations (see summary in Gupta 2019, 24–27).

Author, Date, and Provenance

The opening lines of the letter identify Paul as its author, and apart from only a few exceptions (Schrader 1836, 85–97; Baur 1845, 480–85; Scott 1909; Morton and McLeman 1964; Crüsemann 2010), no one over the last two centuries has doubted that he is. The letter's address line, however, also names two other individuals, "Silvanus and Timothy" (v. 1), who are also listed as cosenders in 2 Thessalonians.

In Acts, Silvanus is known by the name Silas (15:22, 27, 32; etc.; this is perhaps also the Silvanus meant in 1 Pet. 5:12), a Greek transliteration of the Aramaic name *šəʾîlaʾ*. Acts calls him a "prophet" (15:32) and identifies him as a leader in the Jerusalem church (15:22) and as a companion of Paul during his missions in both Thessalonica (17:4, 10) and Corinth (18:5). In 1 Thess. 2, Paul calls him an "apostle" (2:6), likely implying—according to the criteria applied in 1 Corinthians (9:1)—that Silvanus had seen the risen Jesus.

According to Acts (16:1–3), Timothy joined Paul at Lystra on his second missionary journey. Although Acts is silent about Timothy's presence in Thessalonica during Paul's ministry there (17:1–10), the reference to Timothy in 1 Thess. 1:1 and Paul's choice to send him to the Thessalonians as his surrogate (3:1–5) suggest that the Thessalonians knew Timothy.

Although Paul names at least one cosender in most of his letters—Timothy (2 Cor. 1:1, Phil. 1:1, Col. 1:1, Philem. 1), Silvanus and Timothy (2 Thess. 1:1), Sosthenes (1 Cor. 1:1), and "all the brothers with me" (Gal. 1:2)—his inclusion of Silvanus and Timothy in the address line of this letter raises at least two puzzling questions. These issues will be discussed at the appropriate points in the commentary, but here it is fitting to introduce the issues.

First, in other letters where Paul names cosenders, he speaks in the first-person singular (I) in the letter itself. In contrast, 1 Thessalonians has the first-person plural almost exclusively—forty-nine instances compared with only three instances of the first-person singular (2:18; 3:5; 5:27). Scholars are divided on how to interpret this. Some maintain that the plural is genuine and refers to Timothy and Silvanus alongside Paul (R. Collins 1984, 180), perhaps implying joint authorship (Donfried 2002, 55); others claim that the plural is merely "literary" and refers to Paul alone (Malherbe 2000, 88). In the present commentary I espouse the view that, except in cases where Paul uses it to speak of believers as a whole (3:3, 4; 4:7; 5:5, 6, 8, 10), the first-person plural throughout the letter is authentic, but only in a "weak" sense. That is, Paul's inclusion of Silvanus and Timothy in the authorial identity should be understood only to indicate that the letter's contents were endorsed by unanimous consent (cf. Klauck 2006, 359). Paul is the executive member of the authorial identity. He speaks for himself and thus sometimes only *of* himself (2:18; 3:5; 5:27).

The second relevant issue is that the plural in 3:1, if genuine, creates an apparent contradiction with the book of Acts. At 3:1 Paul recounts: "*We* thought it best to be left *alone* in Athens." If the plural implies that Silvanus was present with him, this assertion seems to conflict with Acts (17:10–15), where, by all appearances, Paul remains alone in Athens, while Timothy and Silvanus remain in Macedonia.

As to where and when the letter was written, the evidence points clearly in the direction of Corinth. Those who view Acts as providing a basically reliable historical framework for reconstructing Paul's career generally think Paul wrote from Corinth on his "second missionary journey" (15:36–18:22); others, however, propose that he wrote from Ephesus some years later (Lütgert 1909; Schmithals 1960). Some who regard Acts as an unreliable source for reconstructing Paul's career believe that the letter was written much earlier, in the late 30s or early 40s (Knox 1954, 86; Lüdemann 1984, 162; Richard 1995, 7–8; Donfried 2002, 69–117; Campbell 2014, 190–253). However, the basic reliability of the chronology of Acts has been ably demonstrated by Rainer Riesner (1994), and a preponderance of scholars continue to prefer a later date for the letter, agreeing also that the letter was most likely written from Corinth. If the majority judgment is correct, then the letter would date most likely to the year 50, just months after Paul's (first) visit to Thessalonica, described in Acts 17:1–9.

Genre and Style

It might seem pointless to state that 1 Thessalonians is a letter, but it is not always read as such. Although 1 Thessalonians has served as a canonical text for the church for millennia and in that capacity has generally been read as addressing the church across the ages, the contents of 1 Thessalonians were originally contextualized for a small foundling church in first-century Thessalonica, a group facing a new world of difficulties after their conversion to the faith from "idolatry" (1:9) and the departure of their founder from their midst (2:15–20).

The modern reader's ability to understand 1 Thessalonians, moreover, will be immensely enhanced by recognizing what *kind* of letter it is and what purposes letters of this kind served. According to modern taxonomy, ancient letters fall into three types (Klauck 2006, 68–69): nonliterary letters (personal, written for private consumption), literary letters (written with an "audience" in view or intended for publication as literature), and diplomatic letters (written by an authoritative figure to the public in a formal style). While some of Paul's letters lean toward the literary category (Romans, 1 Corinthians), Paul's letter to the Thessalonians is better understood as an example of the nonliterary type.

By ancient taxonomy, one can be even more specific. A whole branch of scholarship dedicated to "epistolography" existed as early as the fourth century BCE (Klauck 2006, 183–227). This literature both offers a theory of what letters do *in general* and provides a taxonomy of letter types according to more *specific* rhetorical purposes.

First Thessalonians nicely illustrates the general purposes of *personal* letters (cf. Klauck 2006, 184–94). In a world without motorized transportation or electronic communication, the fastest and cheapest way to maintain relationships abroad was by letter. When people were separated by great distances, the letter itself served as a surrogate for the real author and sought to establish a "philophronetic" (*philo-*, affection + *phrēn*, heart) connection with the recipient. Such "friendly" letters developed a number of "clichés" that served friendly purposes. An abundance of these clichés occur in 1 Thessalonians: the sender is present in spirit though absent in body (2:17; 3:10); the sender longs to see the recipients (2:17; 3:6, 10); the sender prays to see the recipients (3:10); the sender expresses joy at news of the recipients' well-being (3:9).

First Thessalonians exhibits characteristics that also align it with more specific letter types. Epistolographical literature identifies a great many "pure" letter types. In his work *Epistolary Types*, Pseudo-Demetrius distinguishes twenty-one types, including such types as commendatory letters, consoling letters, praising letters, and admonishing letters. As one might expect, however, most real letters did not embody only one type of letter from beginning to end but were often "mixed" in nature (Klauck 2006, 201). First Thessalonians exhibits characteristics of several letter types, most notably the consoling letter (Tellbe 2001, 104), the thankful letter (Jewett 1986, 71–72), the friendly letter (Malherbe 2000, 96), and the paraenetic letter.

Through several publications, Abraham Malherbe (1983, 169–70; 1987, 61–94; 1992; 2000, 216) has shown that, from beginning to end, 1 Thessalonians exhibits many characteristics of the paraenetic style. He observes the following relevant characteristics.

1. In their essence, paraenetic letters were used to "exhort." Paraenetic language runs thick throughout 1 Thessalonians: "exhortation" (*paraklēsis*,

2:3), "exhorting" (*parakalein*, 2:12; 3:2, 7; 4:1, 10, 18; 5:11, 14), "encouraging" (*paramytheisthai*, 2:12; 5:14), "strengthening" (*stērizein*, 3:2, 13), "instruction" (*parangelia*, 4:2), "instructing" (*parangellein*, 4:11), "asking" (*erōtān*, 4:1; 5:12), "admonishing" (*nouthetein*, 5:12, 14), "helping" (*antechesthai*, 5:14), "being patient with" (*makrothymein*, 5:14).

2. The style of paraenetic letters was more gentle than authoritarian. Accordingly, in 1 Thessalonians Paul focuses less on his authority as an apostle and depicts himself instead in caring ways: as a nurse who nurtures her own (2:7), as a father who instructs his children (2:11), and as an orphan mourning his separation from his family (2:17).

3. Paraenetic letters emphasized the writer's desire to see the recipients (2:17; 3:6, 10) and the idea that they were separated physically but not in spirit (2:17; 3:10).

4. Paraenetic letters sought to reinforce prior instruction by reminding the audience about what they already "know" (1:5; 2:1, 2, 5, 11; 3:3, 4; 4:2; 5:2) or should "remember" (2:9), and by reviewing what was previously taught (3:4; 4:1, 2, 6, 11; cf. 5:2), even when the audience had "no need" to be reminded (4:9; 5:1).

5. Paraenetic letters encouraged the audience to continue doing what they were already doing (4:1, 9; 5:1, 11; cf. 3:2, 6, 10, 12).

6. Paraenetic letters sought to reinforce previous instruction by appealing to those individuals who embodied the lifestyle desired; often appeal was made to the teacher himself (1:5–6; 2:1–12, 14–16).

A point that has not received notice in scholarly literature on 1 Thessalonians is the distribution pattern of verb forms across the letter. One noticeable peculiarity of these forms is that Paul constantly shifts between the first-person and second-person plural. A first-person verb occurs thirty-nine times in the letter (plus two instances with the copulative implied), and a second-person verb twenty-six times (plus two instances with the copulative implied). This shifting can be explained in part by Paul's commending himself as an example for his audience to imitate, as in the following:

"You know how *we* conducted ourselves, . . . and *you* became our imitators" (1:5–6).

Paul declares that his behavior is "pleasing to God" (2:4) and later asks, "therefore," that the Thessalonians walk in a way "pleasing to God" (4:1).

Mutual suffering is described in 2:14–15.

Paul exhorts the Thessalonians to live in a "holy and just and blameless way" (2:10), perhaps as he has just described himself (2:1–9).

The common expressions "as you know," "you remember," and "you are witnesses" refer the audience back to how Paul conducted himself when he was among them (1:5; 2:1, 2, 5, 10–11).

He also urges caring "toward one another and toward all, as also we showed toward you" (3:12) and concentrates (esp. in chaps. 1–3) on his relationship with them (from "*we* became" in 2:5, 7, 10 to "*you* became" in 2:8).

Second, the letter contains nineteen imperative verbs and twelve subjunctive verbs; with the exception of a purpose subjunctive in 2:16, not one of the imperative or subjunctive verbs occurs before chapter 4. The significance of this observation is that the imperative (always) and the subjunctive (often) are used to issue commands (subjunctives are hortatory in 5:6 [3×], 8; indirect commands in 4:1) or express the purpose toward which the subject ought to strive (subjunctives are telic in 4:12 [2×], 13; 5:10 [3×]). This observation reinforces Malherbe's (1987, 74) point that, by focusing on his relationship with the Thessalonians in chapters 1–3, Paul establishes a rapport that prepares them to receive his advice/ instructions/exhortation in chapters 4–5.

One more feature of the letter's style deserves comment. While from an epistolographic perspective, the letter's style—or *epistolary type*—can be considered paraenetic, Malherbe (1987, 45–46) also shows that the letter exhibits features characteristic of a *style of instruction* advocated in the philosophical schools. Commitment to a particular philosophical school was not dissimilar to religious conversion. Due to the challenges of full assimilation to a new philosophical framework, philosophical communities were attentive to the psychological needs of their proselytes and cognizant of the need for patience with them, and developed their own methods of nurture to gently reinforce the community's precepts (Malherbe 1987, 45–46, 81–88). In philosophical language, the art of reinforcing precepts was known as *psychagogy* (from Greek *psychagōgein*, meaning "to guide the soul"). The methods of psychagogic instruction can be found throughout 1 Thessalonians and will be noted in the commentary as they are encountered.

Paul and the Thessalonians

A History of Their Relationship

What brought Paul to Thessalonica was the same thing that brought him to other cities in the west (Rabens 2017). On the one hand, he made it his aim to preach Christ "where Christ had never been named" (Rom. 15:19–20). On the other hand, he appears to have been guided by "Roman geography," concentrating strategically on the more Hellenized cities and port cities (as well as cities with Jewish diaspora communities). As a Hellenized port city in the Roman province of Macedonia, Thessalonica was a natural choice for a visit.

The details about Paul's initial visit are controversial. As presented in Acts (17:1–9), Paul established the church in Thessalonica during his second missionary tour, having moved west through Macedonia after establishing a church in Philippi (15:36–18:22). When he and Silas arrived in the city, he spent "three Sabbaths" preaching to Jews in a synagogue, the fruit of which was the conversion of "some of them," along with "a great many of the devout Greeks and not a few of the leading women" (Acts 17:1 NRSV). However, "the Jews" of the city become "jealous" of his success and, after recruiting some local "ruffians" in the marketplace (presumably including Gentiles), they set the city in an uproar and storm the house of a certain Jason. Not finding Paul and Silas there, they drag Jason before the city's authorities, accusing him and his associates of "turning the world upside down" (17:6 NRSV).

Figure 2. Paul's Macedonian ministry

The authorities request bail and set Jason and his friends free. Paul and Silas escape to Berea under cover of night.

Although Paul's letter to the Thessalonians offers no detailed narrative of his time in Thessalonica, Paul does review in outline the history of his relationship with the church (2:1–3:10). (1) When he first came to the Thessalonians, he preached the gospel and instructed them (2:1–12). (2) They received his message readily (2:13) and suffered for it (2:14–16). Finally, (3) Paul was driven away from them (2:15–16).

A great deal can be determined about how Paul instructed them while he was present, based on what seems to be assumed in the letter or what Paul explicitly says he had taught. Specifically, he taught them about the "living and true God" (1:9), about Jesus's resurrection and return (1:10; 4:14; 5:1–2), about the raising of believers (4:14), and about a final judgment (4:6; 5:9). He also instructed them on "how one should walk in a way pleasing to God" (4:1), including instruction on sexual ethics (4:2–8), "brotherly [and sisterly] love" (4:9), and living a quiet life, minding their own affairs, and working with their own hands (4:11). In addition, Paul repeatedly emphasized that believers would suffer for their faith (3:3–4).

Acts and 1 Thessalonians appear to conflict on several points. First, Acts gives the impression of a shorter stay than the letter does. Several facts in the letter suggest that Paul's visit must have extended for many weeks, if not months. He remained there long enough to establish a business and secure self-support ("working night and day," 2:9; 2 Thess. 3:7–9), while also building a church out of nothing and developing a strong relationship with it (2:7–8, 11–12, 17, 19–20) and with its individual members (2:11–12). He remained there long enough to receive support from Philippi not just once but at least twice (Phil. 4:15–16), a city several days' journey away (roughly 100 miles/160 km), and to attract enough attention from opponents to be driven out of town (2:15–16).

Second, Acts says nothing about the presence of Timothy in Thessalonica, yet the letter implies that he played a role in the founding visit (1:1; cf. 3:2). Third, while Acts mentions Paul's evangelistic efforts only in "a synagogue of the Jews" (17:1 NRSV), Paul's description of the church as having "turned from idols to serve the living and true God" (1:9), together with his vehement polemic against "the Jews" (2:15–16) and several other details in the letter, indicate that the church consisted predominantly of gentiles (see below). Finding these details irreconcilable, many interpreters therefore discount Acts' account of the visit as unreliable (e.g., Richard 1995, 6; Ascough 2003, 205–8).

Most interpreters advocate a cautious use of Acts nonetheless (e.g., Riesner 1998, 342–414; Still 1999, 81–82; De Vos 1999, 130–31, 144–47, 156–58; Malherbe 2000, 69–74; Tellbe 2001, 18). Riesner's lengthy treatment of Acts 17:1–9 concludes that Luke "stylizes" rather than "invents" his narrative about Paul's visit (1998, 343). Once we grant that Luke's account is selective in its details and told in condensed fashion, the remaining points of contention are fairly easily reconciled. Luke's narrative almost certainly implies that Timothy was present with Paul in Thessalonica despite the omission of Timothy's name from his account of the events, for Paul had picked him up in Derbe/Lystra prior to the visit (16:1). And after Paul's departure from Thessalonica, Timothy is said to be present with Paul and Silas in Berea (17:14). Even if Timothy was not present during the founding visit, the Thessalonians' acquaintance with him could have stemmed from the visit he made to them when Paul dispatched Timothy from Athens (1 Thess. 3:1–2).

Luke's narrative can also accommodate what is implied in the letter about both the length of Paul's stay and the church's composition. According to Acts, Paul converted "some" Jews but also "a great many of the devout Greeks and not a few of the leading women" (Acts 17:4 NRSV). Despite highlighting Jewish converts first (as Luke tends to do), this summary surely emphasizes, albeit subtly, that Jews made up a minority. Moreover, if Acts has indeed condensed Paul's visit, then the addition of further converts is not unlikely. In this regard, Malherbe (2000, 60–61) has proposed that Paul, after preaching in the synagogue for three Sabbaths, set himself up in the house of Jason for outreach to gentiles (1987, 13–14); then he stayed for perhaps two or three months, extending his sphere of influence to friends, family, and professionals connected with the household (1987, 18). It should not be overlooked, moreover, that Acts agrees with 1 Thessalonians on at least three other points: (1) that Paul had ministered in Philippi just before visiting Thessalonica (Acts 16:11–14; 17:1–9; 1 Thess. 2:2); (2) that Paul had been pushed out of Thessalonica by, or at least at the instigation of, Jews (Acts

17:5–8; 1 Thess. 2:15–16); and (3) that Paul's departure from Thessalonica was abrupt, premature, and left the Thessalonians in the lurch (Acts 17:10; 1 Thess. 2:17–3:5). A cautious use of Acts to supplement the details of the letter, then, is not without justification.

The Thessalonian Church

A profile of the Thessalonian church can be constructed only by means of guesses. What is most certain is that its membership consisted primarily of gentiles. Indeed, they had turned to God from "idols" (1:9); they needed to be taught that God is wrathful toward sexual immorality, which Paul affirms is rampant among gentiles ("those who do not know God," 4:5); "the Jews" appear to be considered holistically as a separate group (2:14); and the letter includes not one citation from the Jewish Scriptures (although it contains possible allusions). Moreover, all named individuals attached to the church in the book of Acts have names of non-Jewish origin (Jason, 17:5–9; Aristarchus, 20:4; 27:2; Secundus, 20:4; cf. Demas in Col. 4:14; 2 Tim. 4:10). Still, the possibility of a Jewish constituency in the church, in agreement with Acts, cannot be ruled out. While there is no firm archaeological evidence of a significant Jewish community in Thessalonica during the mid-first century, literary references and archaeological evidence are highly suggestive (Riesner 1998, 344–48; Tellbe 2001, 86–90); in any case, Jewish communities existed "in all the great cities of the ancient world" (Best 1972, 2). Giving credence to Acts, perhaps a majority of interpreters maintain that the church probably contained a minority representation of Jews alongside its gentile majority (e.g., Best 1972, 2; Jewett 1986, 119; Riesner 1998, 349; Still 1999, 64; Tellbe 2001, 90; against, e.g., Ascough 2003, 191–212).

Most of the church was of modest to low means. Paul's instructions "Live quietly and mind your own affairs and *work with your own hands*" (4:11) can only mean that most of them belonged to the artisan class. Paul's commitment to self-support "so as not to burden" them (2:9) probably tells us that they did not have resources to spare. A lower-class profile also squares with Paul's description elsewhere of the Macedonian Christians as abjectly poor (2 Cor. 8:2). Recent studies have proposed that probably a majority of the Thessalonian church would have lived around subsistence level, with some exceptions tending a little higher or lower (Longenecker 2009, 248).

Acts leaves a different impression, highlighting the conversion of "leading women" in the city (17:4) and giving no indication of lower-class converts. Jason is depicted as one who had resources to provide hospitality (17:5) and to post bail after being brought before the city's authorities (17:9). Still, Luke's characterization of the church may not be far from the mark. Some person must have provided accommodations for the church's meetings. Only roughly 20 percent of urban dwellers (likely the wealthiest) had homes larger than 300 square meters (Oakes 2009b, 61), which may have been necessary to accommodate the group. Moreover, Paul's recommendation that the church's members should work could imply that some had ceased from doing so (4:11) and relied on the patronage of individuals (within the church?) who had more abundant resources.

The young church cannot have been large. Estimates are constrained by the requirements of space. De Vos estimates that if the church met in tenements, its size might have been "no more than twenty to twenty-five members" (1999, 154). Richard Ascough (2003) has proposed an intriguing theory that also incorporates other apparent features of the church's profile. According to Ascough, the church consisted entirely of what had been, before Paul's arrival, an association of leather workers (175–76), which Paul converted as a group, having shared their trade (Acts 18:3; cf. 1 Thess. 2:9; 2 Thess. 3:8; cf. 2 Cor. 11:7; 12:13). Accordingly, the group would have consisted entirely of men (Ascough distrusts the account of women converts given in Acts), since men dominated the trade (186), and it would likely have been an association of average size, typically between twenty and fifty individuals (47; cf. Nigdelis 2006, 24). The theory is speculative yet worthy of consideration.

From 1 Thess. 2:9 we learn an interesting detail about how Paul nurtured the young community: he "preached the gospel" to them while "working night and day." If he and the Thessalonians plied the same trade, they likely shared a work space (cf. Acts 18:1–3), where Paul could carry out his manual work while also instructing them further in the faith (Malherbe 1987, 8–12). Sources show that Cynic philosophers often taught in workshops while plying a trade (Hock 1980, 37–41). Paul's workshop—even if it was filled with former members of an association—might now have resembled something more like a philosophical school (cf. Meeks 1983, 75–84; Stowers 2001; Adams 2009).

The possibility should be considered that, when Paul departed in haste (2:17), the church had not existed long enough for leaders to emerge or, if such was his practice, for Paul to appoint them. On the other hand, in 1 Thess. 5:12 Paul asks the church to give special regard to "those who labor among you and are set over you and admonish you," a description that seems to refer to leaders of some sort. While all the church's members would have been more or less equally young in the faith, such leaders could have emerged while Paul was still among them. They could also have emerged organically in his absence. Or Paul might have delegated new responsibilities through Timothy when Timothy visited, now reaffirming their appointed roles in the letter. This much cannot be known, and since no title is ascribed to them, there is not sufficient evidence to conclude that these people held formal church "offices."

Backgrounds

Thessalonica within the Roman Empire

The city that Paul found when he arrived in Thessalonica was a bustling metropolis of 40,000 to 80,000 people (cf. Riesner 1994, 301; 1998, 341; De Vos 1999,

129) made up mostly of Greek-speaking people native to the Macedonian region and culturally dominated by Hellenism (De Vos 1999, 140–43; Oakes 2009a; vom Brocke 2001, 99; Stefanidou-Tiveriou 2010), yet religiously diverse and probably home to a significant Jewish population (see above). The city was important for its location as much as for its size. Positioned on the Thermaic Gulf of the Aegean Sea, Thessalonica served as a port city, connecting east and west along the Egnatian Way as far as Apollonia in the east and Dyrrhachium in the west (Strabo, *Geogr.* 7.329) and routes running north and south between the Danube region and the Balkans.

Thessalonica's history intersected with Rome's in 149 BCE, when after a series of wars Rome annexed Macedonia as a Roman province. In 146 BCE Thessalonica was named the province's capital. In 42 BCE it was granted the honorable status of a "free" city in exchange for its support of Antony and Octavian in the Roman civil wars (Pliny the Elder, *Nat.* 4.36; Appian, *Bell. civ.* 4.118; Plutarch, *Brut.* 46). This status earned the city freedom to govern its own affairs by electing magistrates of its choosing (called *politarchs* in Thessalonica) and by forming an assembly of the citizens (a *dēmos*) and an advisory council of its own (a *boulē*).

Over its history the city's well-being was tied closely to its relationship with Rome. Beginning early in Rome's entanglement in the region, the city had made concerted efforts to curry Rome's favor in the most lavish ways possible (Hendrix 1984). Its relationship with Rome embodied the patron-client ethic that dominated Roman culture. Local aristocrats and magistrates conferred "benefits" on their clients (the city's citizens), and their clients returned their favors with gestures that enhanced the honor of their benefactors. Benefactions came in the form of games, festivals, and doles, for which the citizens returned thanks in the form of honorific statues, inscriptions, or even temples or cults established in their benefactors' honor. Local elites who filled the city's magistracies in turn served as "brokers" between the city and the emperor himself—the "savior," ultimate benefactor, and indeed, like the gods, the benefactor of the world (Hendrix 1992, 43). Ample evidence of cultic devotion to benefactors in Thessalonica has survived (Tellbe 2001, 83–85). As early as 95 BCE Thessalonica established a cult honoring its Roman benefactors together with "the gods" (*IG* X:2.1.4). Inscriptional evidence exists (*IG* X:2.1.31) of a temple dedicated to the "divine Caesar" in the time of Augustus (30 BCE–14 CE). A coin survives (minted in 27 BCE) whose impression seems to depict Julius Caesar as a god and his son Augustus as "son of a god." The magistrates who undertook their city's displays of honor to Rome and the emperor earned financial rewards, the honor of Roman approval, and opportunities for advancement within the political system. They also earned for the cities themselves the award of an honored status among cities who competed for Rome's approval. To Rome's benefit, the loyalty of provincial cities bound the cities to Roman interests and played a crucial role in both uniting the empire and maintaining political control (Tellbe 2001, 32).

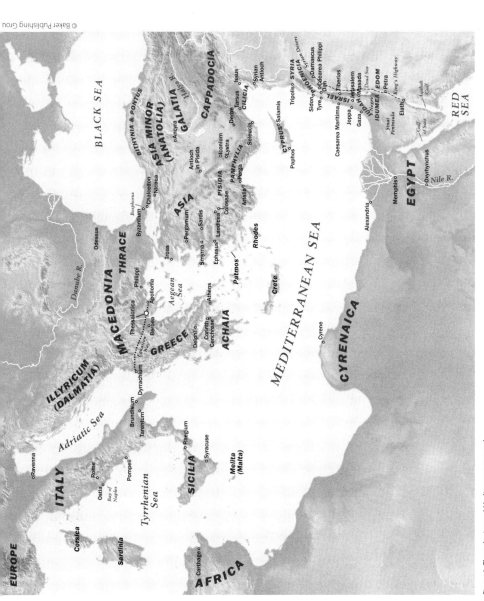

Figure 3. Thessalonica and Mediterranean travel

In this way religion was closely tied to the patron-client system. As a "client" of the emperor, Thessalonica rendered its devotion through "emperor cults" sponsored by the state and supported by its citizens. Although the initiative and costs were undertaken by the city's elites, the public participated by accepting handouts or attending the festivities provided (Oakes 2005, 311–12). Participation was not, and could not be, *officially* enforced. However, one's participation demonstrated solidarity with the city and loyalty to Rome. Anyone refusing to participate would surely be noticed by those connected with them and could be perceived as dishonoring the emperor, if not as potentially seditious (Oakes 2005, 312–14).

Figure 4. A votive to the god Osiris

Alongside the imperial cult was a great abundance of other cults, many of them dedicated to traditional Greek deities, others dedicated to deities of foreign origin. Archaeological evidence summarized by Charles Edson (1948) has revealed the existence of a cult of Dionysus, a temple of Sarapis, a society of Anubis, and a cult of Cabirus and the Dioscuri, all prior to the second century CE. More recently Helmut Koester (2010) has reviewed evidence for Egyptian religion in Thessalonica not yet available to Edson, noting inscriptions attesting to worship of Sarapis (139), Osiris (141), and Isis (144), also before the second century CE. The importance of religion in everyday social life in Thessalonica is evident in inscriptions from local clubs, or "associations," of various kinds. Pantelis Nigdelis (2006) has collected forty-four Thessalonian association inscriptions from the imperial era, twenty-four of which are religious. The bulk of these indicate devotion to the god Dionysus; a large number honor Herakles or Sarapis; and others express devotion to Aphrodite, Artemis, Asklepios, Poseidon, Cybele and Attis, or local "heroes."

In such an environment, religious scenery was omnipresent in the city's public spaces. One could look almost anywhere and catch sight of some temple or monument dedicated to the gods or statuary representing them (Stefanidou-Tiveriou 2010). Equally, one could hardly avoid participating in the city's religious life. Major civic events were inherently religious. Festivals and processions displayed the costumes and accoutrements of the gods and often culminated in sacrifices. At feasts, the public ate food sacrificed to the gods and gave thanks for their provision. Those abstaining from such activities would be perceived as highly antisocial and unpatriotic and would seriously weaken their social connections, which could ultimately lead to ostracism—all potential problems for the new Thessalonian converts.

After Paul Left Thessalonica

According to Acts, when opposition drove Paul out of Thessalonica (Acts 17:10; 1 Thess. 2:15), the "brothers" sent him and Silas immediately down to Berea. Despite success in evangelizing the local Jews there, Paul was hounded again by those who had opposed him in Thessalonica. Now pushed out of Berea, Paul came down to Athens, where he was left alone, sending instructions back to Silas and Timothy in Berea to join him as quickly as possible (17:10–15). After staying for a time in Athens (Acts 17:16–34), Paul moved on to Corinth (18:1), where Silas and Timothy joined him, having come south from Macedonia (18:5).

First Thessalonians directly confirms this basic outline: Paul was forced out of Thessalonica (2:15); the Thessalonians were left in a precarious situation (2:17–3:10); Paul is found shortly thereafter in Athens, either by himself or accompanied by only Silas (3:1); Timothy is in Macedonia while Paul is in Athens (3:2–5); and when Timothy rejoins Paul, he has come directly from Macedonia (3:6).

Acts and 1 Thessalonians appear to conflict only regarding certain movements of Silas and Timothy, though here also full reconciliation may ultimately be possible. Riesner's close examination of Paul's founding visit in Acts concludes that "of the altogether twenty-five individual pieces of information in the Lukan account of the founding, eighteen to nineteen are either directly or indirectly confirmed by 1 Thessalonians" (1998, 367).

Assuming the general reliability of Acts regarding the period between Paul's visit and Timothy's return to him from Macedonia, Acts and 1 Thessalonians can be used together to provide a fairly complete outline of Paul's circumstances following his visit: after departing from Thessalonica under duress and rather hastily (Acts 17:9; 1 Thess. 2:15), Paul developed significant anxiety over the possibility that the dangers from which he had fled had turned against his new converts (1 Thess. 2:17–3:5). In his anxiety, he tried more than once to return but was unsuccessful because he had been "hindered" by Satan (2:18). Unable to return, Paul sent Timothy to ascertain the welfare of the new converts and encourage their "faith," concerned that it might have been "shaken" by their afflictions (3:1–5). At last Timothy returned to Paul, giving him a good report about the "faith and love" of the Thessalonian converts. Paul experienced great relief and wrote the present letter (3:6–10), apparently in Corinth, where Timothy and Silas had joined him (Acts 18:1).

Several points demonstrate that the interval between Paul's departure and his composition of the letter was short. First, in 1 Thessalonians Paul creates the impression that his anxiety began immediately upon his departure and that he took steps to alleviate it as quickly as possible, first by trying to return to Thessalonica multiple times and then by sending an emissary (2:17–3:5). Second, Paul's remark that he was "hindered" from returning (2:18) suggests that the situation

© Baker Publishing Group

Figure 5. News of the Thessalonians following the founding visit

in Thessalonica had not yet cooled down and opposition still made his return impossible. Third, he describes the length of his separation from them as "the time of an hour" (2:17). Fourth, his stays in both Berea and Athens indeed appear to have been short (Acts 17:9–15, 16–34). Once Paul reached Athens, the interval of separation is lengthened only by the duration of Timothy's round trip to and from Thessalonica (1 Thess. 3:1–5), for Paul writes this letter when Timothy has "just" returned (3:6). Fifth, while Paul generally sends greetings from individuals who reside in the places from which he writes, he sends no such greetings from the Corinthian church, perhaps suggesting that he has not yet been present in Corinth long enough to establish a church.

It is generally believed that the length of time between Paul's departure from Thessalonica and his letter to the church was no longer than a few months (Riesner 1998, 366; Malherbe 2000, 73), though it must have been longer than four weeks. Paul's remark that the Thessalonians' faith had become known not only in Macedonia and Achaia but "in every place" (1:8), while not to be taken too literally, certainly implies that reports about them have had time to cross the Aegean.

But this need not have taken many months. Paul's churches were concentrated around Greece, Macedonia, and western Asia Minor, and they were very well connected, sharing contact through the frequent movement of delegates from one church to another and intermittent and sometimes urgent visits by Paul or one of his many coworkers. For the dissemination of a report about the Thessalonian church throughout these areas, an interval of many months between Paul's departure from Thessalonica and his composition of the letter is not required. The distance separating Ephesus in Asia Minor and Thessalonica in Macedonia was not three hundred miles and could be traversed in a period of thirty days or less, and the distance between Thessalonica and Corinth (where Paul resided while writing) was not much more than half of that. Moreover, it is not only possible, but should be supposed, that the crisis that led to Paul's hasty departure from Thessalonica, and that forced Jason before the authorities and left Paul's new converts vulnerable to abuse, reprisal, or legal action, would have been a matter of no small concern for the believers there and nearby, and that when it was found that the Thessalonians had endured the challenges commendably, the churches would be eager immediately to report the result to others. Meanwhile, Paul had tried twice to visit the Thessalonians, and failed twice, before sending Timothy back to them. One must suppose a period of a few weeks, then, before Timothy arrived in Thessalonica, leaving adequate time for news to have spread not only to the churches in Macedonia and Achaia (although apparently it had not yet reached Paul), but also to Ephesus and back, the report of which Timothy has now brought back to Paul, perhaps as quickly as two or three months since the crisis in Thessalonica transpired.

The Occasion of the Letter

Paul's reasons for writing 1 Thessalonians have been variously explained. Throughout the early twentieth century, scholars tended to see Paul as reacting against "opponents," who were succeeding in leading the Thessalonians astray (Lütgert 1909; Schmithals 1972). These scholars focused attention on Paul's alleged "defense" in 2:1–12, though other passages were thought to support this interpretation as well (5:12–13, 19–22).

Up until the end of the twentieth century, many interpreters believed that Paul's main reason for writing was to address eschatological concerns. The chief text of interest was the lengthy "doctrinal" section in 4:13–5:11, where Paul treats the question of the resurrection of the dead and the parousia of Jesus. In this regard, Robert Jewett (1986) argued that the Thessalonian church, thinking like "millenarian radicalists," was shocked that death was still a possibility after having received the spirit of the new age (142–47). More recently, Colin Nicholl (2004) has proposed that concerns about the "unexpected passing away of community members" was "the primary exigence of 1 Thessalonians" (112). Many interpreters have also suggested that Paul's remarks about work (4:11–12; cf. 5:14) indicate that some within the church community had stopped working due to a belief that the eschaton was imminent (Dobschütz 1909; Rigaux 1956, 519–21; Best 1972, 175–76; Jewett 1971; Bruce 1982, 91).

With a slight change of direction, Karl Donfried (1985) proposed that the letter should be read against the religious and political background of first-century Thessalonica, arguing that Paul shaped the letter with attentiveness to the specific environment in which the church was situated. Highlighting especially the importance of the local Dionysian cult, with its emphasis on the phallus, sensuality, and drunkenness, Donfried saw Paul's instructions on sexuality in 4:3–8 and his remarks about drunkenness in 5:7 as alluding to the Thessalonians' cultic environment.

Since the 1990s, treatments of the letter have explained the Thessalonians' situation almost exclusively with reference to the church's social and political context, though Jewett (1986) also connected the church's eschatology with the political situation in Thessalonica. Many scholars have argued that the Thessalonians faced significant persecution due to social conflict with those outside the believing community. John Barclay (1992) proposes that the church faced "vigorous social harassment" (52) and possibly physical opposition (53) because they had given up traditional religious practices for the "true and living God." Similarly, Craig De Vos (1999, 156–57) argues that because of their conversion, the Thessalonian believers were considered politically subversive and thus faced reprisal from the civic community. Todd Still (1999) explores the relationship between the church and outsiders through the sociological concepts of "deviance" and "conflict," arguing that the believers' ideological and social separatism, their evangelism, and their being subversive to the institutions of Greco-Roman society (267) engendered social opposition in the forms of verbal harassment, social ostracism, political sanctions, and physical abuse, possibly even martyrdom (217). These and other studies have explored how conflict between the Thessalonian believers and the civic community helped shape the church's identity (Still 1999; Tellbe 2001).

Paul's remarks about "living quietly" and "working with the hands" (4:11) have also been examined in relation to social and political concerns. Barclay (1992; 1993), among others (De Vos 1999, 161–64), sees these remarks as indicating that the Thessalonians were engaging in disruptive behavior in the public sphere due to resentment over their ill treatment. Others have seen Paul's instructions to "admonish the idlers" (5:14 NRSV) as evidence that some within the church had stopped working and were relying on support from wealthy patrons (Russell 1988; Winter 1994, 41–60).

A few studies have considered the letter in light of the possibility that the church functioned or was perceived as an "association." Richard Ascough (2000) proposes that Paul's remarks about leadership (5:12–13), disruptiveness (5:13b–14), and aspirations for honor (4:11) suggest that the church functioned like an association and reflected the kinds of problems that were common in these associations. Similarly, Callia Rulmu (2010) has proposed that, if the church was not structured like an association, it may have been perceived as one, and that Paul instructed the church to "live quietly" because associations were often considered by the Roman government to be seditious.

Reflection on the Roman political context has led many recent interpreters to see the letter as "anti-imperial." According to this view, the church faced persecution because of its refusal to participate in the imperial cult and because of a public perception of disloyalty to Caesar (on acting "contrary to the decrees of Caesar" in Acts 17:7, see Judge 1971; Tellbe 2001, 123–30). In response, Paul wrote to counter imperial propaganda about the "good news" of a Golden Age brought on by Rome and its "savior," the emperor, and asserted the lordship of Christ and the preeminence of his kingdom (Harrison 2002; 2011).

Abraham Malherbe has taken a somewhat different approach (1970; 1987; 2000; 2013). Viewing the "affliction" of the Thessalonians as their experiencing not social or physical abuse but mental stress precipitated by the crisis of conversion (1987, 47–48), Malherbe directs attention to Paul's methods of pastoral care and his moral exhortations to his new converts. Malherbe argues that the letter reflects sensitivity to the religious and intellectual dislocation (and the sense of loss of family, friends, and associates) that the community experienced due to their conversion. Paul sought to foster their personal development by clarifying the community's new identity and by inculcating a sense of belonging within a new "family" (1987, 45–46). In this regard, Malherbe stresses that the letter is thoroughly "paraenetic," being intended primarily to reinforce previous instructions and to encourage the new converts in the earliest stages of their faith.

This survey of scholarship demonstrates agreement that 1 Thessalonians was deeply shaped by the church's concrete circumstances. One of the most significant aspects of the church's situation was their recent, and perhaps still present, experience of suffering brought on by their conversion and subsequent estrangement from the wider civic community. Indeed, in the letter Paul refers to the church's "steadfastness" (1:3), as well as to "these afflictions" (3:3); he affirms that the Thessalonians received the word "with much affliction" (1:6); that they had "suffered" at the hands of their countrymen (2:14); and that, having previously been taught that believers would suffer, they now "know" it (3:4). It is evident that Paul wrote 1 Thessalonians largely to offer encouragement in the face of these experiences. The letter also makes clear that the community was at that time grieving over the (unexplained) passing of some group members (4:13). On this point Paul seeks to give comfort by clarifying the nature of the resurrection (4:13–18) and by reaffirming the community's identity as "children of light and of day" (5:1–11). Apart from these points, it is difficult to decide where Paul's remarks have been prompted by concrete circumstances and where they merely reflect generic paraenesis, applicable to all Christians at any time. Paul may have been responding to opponents (2:1–12); addressing tension with the church's leadership (5:12–13); admonishing the church about sexual deviance (4:3–8), drunkenness (5:5b–7), public disruptiveness (4:11), cessation from work (4:11; 5:14), and disparagement of prophecy (5:19–22); or answering questions put to him about the timing of the parousia (5:1–11). On the other hand, this material could make equally good sense without assuming that these issues were prompted by current exigencies. Investigating these issues can greatly enhance the reader's understanding of the letter and make it more meaningful, and the present commentary will remain attentive to these interests.

Apart from the concrete situation, it is also illuminating to read the letter with Paul's *rhetorical* purposes in view. After taking into consideration the cultural environment, the basic profile of the church, and the overall circumstances out of which Paul writes, a rhetorical approach then focuses on what Paul is trying to *accomplish* in writing to this church at this time. In this regard, attention to the conventions of ancient epistolography are greatly illuminating. Considering Paul's extensive use of *philophronetic* and *paraenetic* conventions in the letter (see above), two important purposes of the letter can be highlighted. First, Paul is anxious about his separation from the young church, wishes to assure them of his love for them, and wants to maintain a philophronetic connection with them at a time when that connection might appear to have been lost. Second, Paul wishes to strengthen the community's faith so that they can cope with the "crisis of conversion" precipitated by their estrangement from friends and family, their experience of dislocation within their religious environment, their uncertainty over their new faith, and their confusion about its expectations and the difficulty of meeting those expectations. By means of this letter, Paul seeks to reinforce his original teaching, to remind his audience of his example, to praise their progress, and to continue constructing a new sense of belonging.

The Content of 1 Thessalonians

The Theological Framework of 1 Thessalonians

Apart from Paul's treatment of the resurrection and parousia in 4:13–5:11 (and that only to some extent), 1 Thessalonians lacks any lengthy treatment of theological issues. Woven throughout the letter's lines, however, is a theological framework intended to help shape a new outlook and new behavioral expectations in Paul's new converts.

1. The letter's theological framework is intensely *apocalyptic*. A discussion of eschatology occupies the longest unit of the letter, where Paul discusses both the resurrection (4:13–18) and the parousia of Jesus (4:13–5:11). The latter is one of the letter's most prominent themes and receives attention in at least six different places (1:10; 2:19; 3:13; 4:15; 5:2, 23); in two passages the parousia is linked with the final judgment (1:10; 5:2–3, 9). The letter also envisages a dualistic opposition between the present and the future, and especially between believers and nonbelievers (see below). The recurring theme of "hope" (1:3; 2:19; 4:13; 5:8) points believers ahead to the resurrection, parousia, and final judgment. Other

apocalyptic themes include the appearance of the Messiah with his "holy ones" (3:13), Jesus as "Lord" (more than 20×), and the future kingdom of God (2:12).

John Barclay (1992) has convincingly argued that Paul's somewhat more intense emphasis on eschatology in this letter (as compared with 1 Corinthians, for instance) finds its explanation in the Thessalonians' experience of conflict with their civic environment. Although Paul likely preached an apocalyptic message in the other places that he evangelized, Barclay argues that this message resonated in a special way with the Thessalonians because they experienced immediate opposition after their conversion (2:14; 3:3–4). Among other things, Paul's original (apocalyptic) message had emphasized the separateness of the church from the world and the contrasting fates of believers and nonbelievers (4:6). Hence, when opposition fell on them, the church would have found their experience consistent with the dichotomies that Paul had already drawn. This discovery would reaffirm their sense of separateness, while the experience of opposition further confirmed their sense of estrangement from society. A stronger sense of group boundaries and increased group solidarity would result. Thus, Paul's apocalyptic emphasis appears to have been a strategic part of his rhetorical purposes.

2. Paul constructs this sense of *group identity* in several ways. He makes abundant use of kinship language to instill a new sense of family: God is their "father" (1:1; 3:11, 13), as is Paul (2:11), and they are each other's "brothers and sisters" (13× in this short letter, as opposed to 10× in Romans, 20× in 1 Corinthians, and 3× in 2 Corinthians), "beloved" by God (1:4). Paul also defines them negatively against outsiders (Barclay 2016): the Thessalonians have "turned from idols" (1:9); they should "not" capitulate to lust, like "the gentiles, who do not know God" (4:5); they should "not" be ignorant (4:13); they are "not in darkness" (5:4) and do "not belong to the night" (5:5) but "are sons of light and sons of day" (5:5); they should "not" be like "the rest" (4:13; 5:6); they should "not sleep" (5:6) and are "not destined for wrath" (5:9).

3. Complementing Paul's emphasis on eschatology is his emphasis on *what God is doing now*. Salvation is not yet complete. God has not just "called" the Thessalonians but "is calling" them (2:12; 5:24); Jesus "is delivering" them (1:10); they are destined for the "acquisition" of salvation (5:10). While God indeed "elected" them, Paul focuses on the present *proof* of their election as enabled by the Spirit's work in them (1:5). Although it is the responsibility of believers to pursue "sanctification," Paul says that the Holy Spirit enables holiness (4:7–8), and Paul prays that God will sanctify them in preparation for the parousia (3:13; 5:23).

4. Alongside emphasis on God's work in the church, Paul also puts emphasis on *Christian virtue*. The virtues of faith (1:3, 8; 3:2, 5, 6, 7, 10), love (1:3; 3:6, 12; 4:9; 5:13), and hope (1:3; 2:19; 4:13; 5:8) are each mentioned several times in the letter and sometimes in combination with each other (all three in 1:3; faith and love in 3:6). As this triad appears to have been traditional (see 1:3), these three items may be intended to summarize Christian virtue as a whole: faith is directed toward God, love is directed toward one another, and hope is directed toward

future salvation. In the midst of suffering, hope, moreover, provides grounds for joy and thanks. Paul mentions joy five times in the letter (1:6; 2:19, 20; 3:9; 5:16). He refers to his own thanks to God on three occasions (1:2–10; 2:13–16; 3:9) and at the conclusion of the letter enjoins the Thessalonians to "give thanks in everything" (5:18).

These themes anticipate major themes of Paul's later and longer letters. Absent, however, are many of the themes considered central to the theology of those letters. Missing are the themes of the law, sin, righteousness, and grace; apocalyptic distinctions such as those between flesh and spirit, freedom and slavery, life and death; and any consideration of the relationship between the gentiles and Israel. The absence of these themes could indicate that they are later developments in Paul's theology (Schnelle 1986, 207; Richard 1991, 51; Roetzel 1991, 216–17). Indeed, it is generally agreed that 1 Thessalonians is the earliest of Paul's extant letters. Assuming a date around the year 50, it was written some five to eight years prior to Paul's longer letters—1 Corinthians, 2 Corinthians, and Romans (and possibly Galatians)—leaving some time for theological development prompted by new exigencies. On the other hand, the absence of such themes may indicate that the specific occasion did not merit their treatment. Paul faced separation from a more or less completely gentile church, who were recently converted and now faced opposition because of it. He writes what this church needed to hear at the time rather than what was not immediately necessary.

Outline of 1 Thessalonians

During the 1980s and 1990s a trend developed in which Paul's letters were viewed as analogous to public "speeches." In ancient rhetorical theory, three types of speeches were identified: epideictic, deliberative, and forensic (Ps.-Cicero, *Rhet. Her.* 1.2). Aligning Paul's letters with these speech types, biblical scholars then attempted to outline his letters according to the divisions prescribed for such speeches in the ancient "rhetorical handbooks" (see outlines of 1 Thessalonians in Wanamaker 1990, 48–52; Donfried 2002, 173–76; summary of various outlines in Jewett 1986, 63–87). For a variety of reasons, over the last two decades this approach to reading Paul's letters has fallen out of favor. A main impetus for the change was an increase in attention to ancient epistolography, the ancient theory of *letter* writing. Since Paul's letters are not speeches in any conventional (or ancient) sense of the word, and since epistolography was never integrated with rhetorical theory in the ancient rhetorical tradition (Klauck 2006, 210), it is now generally agreed that outlines based on the structure of speeches are probably illegitimate. More recently scholars have taken the view that an epistolographic approach is more heuristically appropriate (Malherbe 2000; Klauck 2006, 225; Weima 2014, 55–56; alternatively, Milinovich in 2014 offers a detailed outline based on lexical criteria and a conception of the letter as an oral performance).

Greco-Roman letters typically had three parts: an opening, a body, and a closing (Klauck 2006, 18–25). Letter openings followed a common formula: a prescript, naming the sender (superscription) and addressee (adscription) and expressing greetings to the audience (salutation); next a proem, often expressing thanks (thanksgiving) for the well-being of the recipients. Then the main body of the letter commenced. If lengthy, this could contain numerous sections. Letter closings could vary but often included a wish of peace and greetings either from the author or from others. Paul structures his letter to the Thessalonians according to these typical conventions, though not rigidly. Instead, he adapts the structure to reflect his peculiar theological stance and rhetorical purposes. The outline that follows is based on a combination of epistolographic and thematic considerations.

As an alternative to the thematic outline delineated here, the letter's body could also be outlined according to its basic rhetorical purposes. As noted above, with the exception of a single purpose-subjunctive in 2:16, not one of the letter's more than thirty imperative and subjunctive verbs occurs before 4:1. This distribution is consistent with the differing rhetorical purposes of chapters 1–3 and 4–5 respectively. Chapters 1–3 provide a "history" of Paul's relationship with the

---

Outline of 1 Thessalonians

Letter opening (1:1–10)

Prescript: Superscription, adscription, and greeting (1:1)

Thanksgiving: The Thessalonians' faith and example (1:2–10)

Letter body (2:1–5:22)

Paul's ministry in Thessalonica (2:1–12)

Paul's proclamation of the gospel (2:1–2)

Paul's message and his purposes (2:3–7a)

Paul's conduct (2:7b–9)

Exhortation to walk rightly (2:10–12)

Renewed thanksgiving (2:13–16)

The Thessalonians' embrace of the gospel (2:13)

Opposition to the Thessalonians (2:14)

Opposition to Paul (2:15–16)

Paul's desire to visit again (2:17–3:13)

Paul's failed attempts to visit (2:17–20)

Paul's dispatch of Timothy (3:1–5)

The return of Timothy (3:6–10)

Prayer for a fresh visit and for strength (3:11–13)

Exhortation, part 1 (4:1–12)

Hortatory introduction (4:1–2)

Exhortation on sexual conduct (4:3–8)

Exhortation on brotherly love (4:9–12)

Exhortation, part 2 (4:13–5:11)

The general resurrection of believers at the parousia (4:13–18)

The day of the Lord (5:1–11)

Final exhortations (5:12–22)

First round of exhortations (5:12–15)

Second round of exhortations (5:16–22)

Letter closing (5:23–28)

Second wish-prayer (5:23–24)

Prayer (5:25)

Greeting (5:26)

Final instruction (5:27)

Benediction (5:28)

Thessalonians—recalling their warm reception of him and his message (2:1–14) followed by his forced separation from them (2:15–16) and then reaffirming his love for them in their separation, his eager longing to see them (2:17–3:5), and his desire to ascertain their well-being (3:6–10). In this way chapters 1–3 establish a rapport with the audience that prepares them to receive Paul's exhortations in chapters 4–5, including among its most important concerns Paul's discussion of the general resurrection and parousia (4:13–5:11). The body of the letter concludes with a series of further, though more succinct, exhortations, which appear to be generic but—as shall be seen—are almost certainly relevant to the concrete situation in Thessalonica (5:12–22).

1 Thessalonians 1:1–10

Letter Opening

Introductory Matters

When Paul's very first letter arrived after his hasty, forced departure from Thessalonica just weeks earlier (Acts 17:1–10), the Thessalonians would have seen the letter folded, tied closed with a string of papyrus fibers, and marked on the outside with an address (Klauck 2006, 13): "to *the church of the Thessalonians* from *Paul*." Unfolding the letter, they would have found what in many ways looked like a typical Greco-Roman letter (Klauck 2006, 18–25): first, a prescript, naming the sender (superscription) and addressee (adscription) and expressing greetings to the latter (salutation); then a proem, expressing thanks (thanksgiving) for their well-being.

The opening of 1 Thessalonians spans the first ten verses and includes the standard prescript (1:1–2) and proem (1:3–10). The prescript conforms essentially with the conventions of non-Christian letters, though both the adscription and the salutation exhibit unique Christian modifications. Standing out for its length, the proem runs on for nine verses (1:2–10), in which Paul tells the Thessalonians that he remembers them in prayer and explains why he gives thanks to God for them.

Topically, the expanded prescript + proem anticipates themes treated in the letter's main body: the Thessalonians' love (1:3; 3:6, 12; 4:9), their hope (1:3; 4:13–5:11), their conversion (1:10–2:12),

> ### 1 Thessalonians 1:1–10 in the Rhetorical Flow
>
> ▶ Letter opening (1:1–10)
>
> **Prescript: Superscription, adscription, and greeting (1:1)**
>
> **Thanksgiving: The Thessalonians' faith and example (1:2–10)**

their election (1:6–10; 2:12) and calling (2:12; 4:7; 5:24), their suffering persecution (1:6; 2:14–16), and the parousia (1:9; 4:13–5:11). The theme of prayer brackets the letter: Paul opens by saying that he thanks God for the Thessalonians when he prays (1:2) and closes by asking them to pray for him in return (5:25). Rhetorically, this section begins to set the letter's tone: Paul's praise for the Thessalonians communicates his deep fondness for them and establishes the letter's general hortatory purposes, thus preparing the way for his instructions in chapters 4–5.

Tracing the Train of Thought

Prescript: Superscription, Adscription, and Greeting (1:1)

1:1. First Thessalonians stands out from Paul's other letters in that Paul designates himself and his cosenders with their simple names only, forgoing any further descriptors: **Paul and Silvanus and Timothy.** Notably, Paul calls himself neither a "servant" (Phil. 1:1), a "prisoner of Christ" (Philem. 1), nor an "apostle" (Rom. 1:1; 1 Cor. 1:1; 2 Cor. 1:1; Gal. 1:1; Eph. 1:1; Col. 1:1; cf. 1 Tim. 1:1; 2 Tim. 1:1; Titus 1:1), as he does elsewhere. Where these additions do occur, they are not insignificant but serve to highlight the stance from which Paul wishes to relate to his addressees under the specific circumstances. For instance, Paul's weighty designation of himself as "an apostle not from men nor through man but through Jesus Christ and God the Father," found in Galatians (1:1), contrasts starkly with the "friendly" tone of "Paul" found here (Malherbe 2000, 101). From the start of the letter, it is evident that Paul neither wishes nor needs to exert his apostolic authority. He is pleased with the Thessalonians and is affectionately disposed toward them.

God as Father

Although the OT often designates Israel (Deut. 14:1; Jer. 3:19–20)—or more specifically, a Davidic king (2 Sam. 7:12–16)—as God's "son," "father" was not a common designation for God in the OT. This characterization of God was more common in Greco-Roman culture. In Greek and Roman mythology Jupiter (or Zeus) was known as the "Father of gods and men" (Cicero, *Nat. d.* 2.4). For many philosophical groups, God's quality as father had reference to his role as the creator of the whole human race (Seneca, *Ben.* 2.29.4; 4.8.1; Philo, *Spec.* 2.165, 198; Plato, *Tim.* 28C, referenced by Cicero in *Nat. d.* 1.30), which by implication made all people his children and also brothers and sisters of one another (Stobaeus, *Flor.* 4.27.3). Within early Christianity, the characterization of believers as "children" of God became one of the most prevalent ways of describing the community of Christ-believers, in sharp distinction from other people of the human race.

In the adscription Paul qualifies the identity of his addressees in a unique way: **to the church of Thessalonians that is in God the Father and the Lord Jesus Christ.** The word rendered "church" in English translations refers literally to an "assembly" (*ekklēsia*) of people (see Korner 2017). In the LXX, this term designates the assembly of the nation of Israel (Deut. 4:10; Judg. 20:2; 1 Kings 8:14; Ezra 2:64; etc.); at Qumran, it indicated Jews of the Dead Sea community (Donfried 2002, 139–62). In "free" Greek cities like Thessalonica (see introduction to 1 Thessalonians), the *ekklēsia* constituted a gathering of the city's citizens (all male) convened to make civic decisions. Paul employs the word but qualifies it in a way that distinguishes it from either the Jewish community or the secular assembly: it is the community "in God the Father and the Lord Jesus Christ," meaning the assembly of Thessalonian Christ-followers.

The pairing of "God the Father" with "the Lord Jesus Christ" is theologically significant. Paul often sets God/Father and Jesus/Lord parallel to one another in his letters (3:11; 1 Cor. 7:17; 8:5–6; 2 Cor. 13:13; 2 Thess. 1:2, 8; 2:16; 3:5), often also assigning them parallel actions (1 Cor. 7:17; 8:5–6; 2 Cor. 13:13; 2 Thess. 2:16; cf. 1 Cor. 12:4–6; 2 Cor. 1:21–22). In the Thessalonian letters the term "Lord" (*kyrios*) occurs as a designation for Jesus some forty-six times (as calculated by M. Smith 2013, 288; though some examples could refer to God the Father) and has definite divine resonances. In the LXX, the term applied to Yahweh. In Hellenistic politics the term denoted a king, and in Roman religion it designated the emperor; in many contexts it could imply divinity (Suetonius, *Dom.* 13; SEG 12.514; *Mart. Pol.* 8.2; 10.1). The second title used here for Jesus is a translation of the Jewish word *māšîaḥ*, "anointed one." In the OT the term could refer to a prophet (1 Kings 19:16), priest (Exod. 29:7), or king (2 Sam. 2:4–7); yet in Second Temple literature it often had divine resonances as well, especially when associated with the "Son of Man" figure (*1 En.* 52.4; 46.3; 48.2; 62.5; cf. 2 Esd. [*4 Ezra*] 12:32–33; *2 Bar.* 40.1–4).

The prescript's salutation (**grace to you and peace**) differs from the formula seen in Paul's later letters (usually "grace to you and peace from God our Father and the Lord Jesus Christ"; Rom. 1:7; 1 Cor. 1:3; 2 Cor. 1:2; Gal. 1:3; Eph. 1:2; Phil. 1:2; 2 Thess. 1:2; cf. Col. 1:2), perhaps showing that what became his standard formula had not yet crystallized. The salutation, however, does include the standard components of "grace and peace." These components reflect an adaptation of greeting formulas typically found in Hellenistic letters. By replacing *chairein* (rejoice/greetings) with *charis* (grace), Paul employs a term that shares the same semantic root as its Hellenistic counterpart while also alluding to the grace of God that is imparted through Jesus Christ. "Peace" (*eirēnē*) echoes the Hebrew greeting *šālôm* (peace), but now it refers to peace as experienced in the reconciliation of the world to God through Jesus Christ. Paul refers again to both "peace" and "grace" in the letter's closing (5:23, 28).

Thanksgiving: The Thessalonians' Faith and Example (1:2–10)

A proem commonly followed the prescript in Greco-Roman letters (Klauck 2006, 21–23). The proem was not identical to a "thanksgiving," nor did it always include a "thanksgiving" (Artz-Grabner 1994). The proem could come in many forms, including that of a health wish for the recipient (*BGU* 2:632; P.Oxy. 3:528.3–6), a thanksgiving to God or the gods (*BGU* 2:423.6–8; 2 Macc. 1:11; *4 Bar.* 6.20–21; Philem. 4), an assurance of prayer for the recipients (*BGU* 2:632.5a–10; P.Oxy. 3:528.3–6; 1 Macc. 12:11; 2 Macc. 1:6; 2 Tim. 1:3–5; Philem. 4), or some combination of these (*BGU* 2:423). In Paul's letters, however, the proem invariably comes in the form of a thanksgiving.

While forming an integral whole, the contents of the thanksgiving here can be summarized under three general headings: the Thessalonians' faith in action (vv. 2–5), the Thessalonians' imitation of Paul/Jesus and in turn their example to others (vv. 6–8), and the Thessalonians' conversion from idols to God (vv. 9–10).

1:2–5. Most of Paul's letters introduce the thanksgiving section with the formula "I/we give thanks to God" (Rom. 1:8–15; 1 Cor. 1:4–9; Phil. 1:3–11; Col. 1:3–14; Philem. 4–7; cf. 2 Thess. 1:3–12), and 1 Thessalonians is no exception: **We give thanks to God always for all of you.** In this case the thanksgiving is in fact a prayer-report: Paul thanks God *when he prays* for the Thessalonians (**making mention of you in our prayers unceasingly, as we mention before our God and Father . . .**).

> ### A Hellenistic Letter Opening
>
> *"Apion to Epimachos, his father and lord, very many greetings.*
>
> *Before all else I pray that you are well and that you may prosper in continual health, together with my sister and her daughter and my brother. I give thanks to the lord Serapis, because when I was endangered at sea, he rescued (me) immediately."* (*BGU* 2:423, trans. Klauck 2006, 10)

Among Jews, prayer was traditional after meals, at the beginning and end of the day, and on occasions of religious gatherings or festivals. These would likely be fixed prayers, as were found in liturgical hymnbooks like the Davidic Psalter. However, the Dead Sea Scrolls and the OT Apocrypha and Pseudepigrapha contain examples of informal and in some cases probably spontaneous prayers, likely reflecting private practice. Paul's affirmation that he prays constantly for the Thessalonians suggests private prayer as opposed to a liturgical setting and thus provides a window into Paul's own prayer habits or the practice of group prayer with companions such as Silvanus and Timothy (Wanamaker 1990, 74).

Paul gives thanks ("before our God and Father," v. 3) for the evidence of God's work within the church: **the work of your faith and the labor of your love and the endurance of your hope in our Lord Jesus Christ** (v. 3). The faith-love-hope triad occurs in 5:8 in the same order (in 3:6 "faith" and "love" occur without the term "hope"); it also appears in varying sequences in several other places in Paul's letters (Rom. 5:1–5; 1 Cor. 13:13; Eph. 4:2–5; Col. 1:4–5) as well as in other NT literature (Heb. 6:10–12; 10:22–24; 1 Pet. 1:3–8; 1:21–22), perhaps suggesting that the triad was pre-Pauline and already fixed in early church tradition. The constructions used here—"work *of* faith," "labor *of* love," and "endurance *of* hope"—communicate what faith, love, and hope do: "faith works, love labors, and hope endures."

1. In the ancient Mediterranean context, the root idea of *faith* (*pistis* in Greek) was loyalty toward someone or something (Morgan 2015). Thus Christian *pistis* was neither reducible to the idea of mere "belief" in the truth nor synonymous with "works." Rather, it indicated an orientation of the whole self—of both thoughts and behaviors—toward the God of Jesus Christ.
2. The word "*love*" (*agapē*) became a technical term in early Christianity for both the love of God poured out on humanity through Jesus Christ (Rom. 5:5; 8:39; 2 Cor. 13:13; 2 Thess. 3:5) and the love of believers toward their fellow brothers and sisters in Christ (4:9); in Paul's letters it rarely indicated humanity's love for God (Rom. 8:28). Here Paul may have in mind the Thessalonians' love toward other believing Macedonians, perhaps (judging from 4:9) demonstrated in the form of hospitality (Wanamaker 1990, 76, 161).
3. The expression "in our Lord Jesus Christ" applies only to the "endurance of *hope*": it is in the Lord Jesus Christ that the Thessalonians' hope is reposed (cf. 4:13). This hope refers not to a "slender chance" but to "a confident hope" (Best 1979, 69, citing Rom. 5:1–5; 1 Cor. 15:19–20). The connection made between hope and endurance here may point indirectly to the Thessalonians' endurance through suffering, which they experienced due to opposition from local nonbelievers (cf. 2:14; introduction to 1 Thessalonians).

As verse 4 indicates, Paul views the Thessalonians' faith, love, and hope as evidence of their election; that is, his certainty about their election is a *result* of the faith, love, and hope that they have demonstrated: **so that we are sure, brothers and sisters, beloved by God, of your election**. Packed into verse 4 are several items that function to shape the Thessalonians' new identity. First, their status as "brothers" (*adelphoi*) functions as an extension of their status as children of a common "Father" (1:1). Richard Ascough (2003) has argued (doubting the claim in Acts 17:4 that many "leading women" were converted) that Paul's use of the masculine "brothers" is evidence that the Thessalonian church consisted exclusively of men—perhaps an association of leather workers that he had converted as a group. However, as other ancient letters show, the masculine plural was conventionally used even where both "brothers" and "sisters" were meant (Klauck 2006, 12; citing *BGU* 2:423), so the use of the masculine (which Paul uses consistently in his letters) is not significant in itself. Moreover, if Acts 17:4 is correct and the church in Thessalonica was like Paul's churches elsewhere (Rom. 16:1, 7, 12; Phil. 4:2; Col. 4:15; Philem. 2–3), women must have been included. Thus it is appropriate to translate *adelphoi* as "brothers and sisters" as I have done in this commentary.

Although fellow Jews frequently referred to each other as "brothers" (Jer. 22:18; 1QS VI.10, 22; CD VI.20–21; Josephus, *J.W.* 2.122; *2 Bar.* 78.2), the label in 1 Thessalonians is "fictive" and refers to a bond formed not by the biology of a common ancestry but by a common identity shared among children of God through faith in Christ. This bond reinforces a sense of the group's boundaries and provides an infrastructure of moral support as they face the challenges that their new status has brought upon them. That Paul intends to place special emphasis on their kinship as *adelphoi* is shown by the relatively high frequency of this designation in the Thessalonian letters. Doubtless, this is evidence that the Thessalonian believers, perhaps more so than believers elsewhere, had suffered stressful levels of opposition and painful alienation from their kin and community due to their conversion. Through this letter Paul works to restore a sense of belonging by affirming that kinship in Christ knits them together into a new community, constituted by God as their Father and each other as brothers and sisters (Malherbe 1995, 125; repr. in 2014, 1:323).

The Thessalonians are not only "brothers and sisters"; they are also "beloved" by God. This language ("beloved") is used in the LXX for God's relationship with Israel (Pss. 60:5 [59:7 LXX]; 108:6 [107:7]). Closely related is the idea of "election." God chose Abraham (Gen. 12:1–7) and, from him, Israel (1 Chron. 16:13; Isa. 42:1; Tob. 8:15; 2 Macc. 1:25), and God gave Israel special support in the exodus and conquest. Isaiah extended the hope of election to the gentiles (19:19–25) and indeed to the whole world (45:20–25). Paul hoped to bring this promise to realization in his founding of gentile churches. Here he reassures the Thessalonians that, even if they are rejected by the world, they are children of God, "elected" by God, and "beloved" by him.

Adding to what precedes, in verse 5 Paul offers further evidence of the church's election: **that our gospel did not fix itself within you in word only but resulted in action and in the evidence of the Holy Spirit and in your full assurance.** This statement completes a mirror structure, where election sits at the center (v. 4) and is flanked on either side by proof of election, articulated in each case with a triadic formula (vv. 3, 5):

A the work of your faith *and* the labor of your love *and* the endurance of
    your hope (v. 3)
  B your election (v. 4)
A′ in power *and* in the Holy Spirit *and* in much assurance (v. 5)

In this way verse 5 states further proof of the Thessalonians' election by referring to their welcome acceptance of the gospel into their hearts and its effective power in their lives. Although Paul here refers to "our gospel" (2 Cor. 4:3; 2 Thess. 2:14; "my gospel" in Rom. 2:16; 16:25), on other occasions he refers to "the gospel of God" (2:2, 4, 8, 9; 2 Cor. 11:7), "the gospel of Christ" (3:2; Rom. 15:19; 1 Cor. 9:12; 2 Cor. 9:13), and "the gospel of his Son" (Rom. 1:9). Each expression has its own significance (Best 1979, 74): the gospel originates with God (the gospel "of God"), is about Christ (the gospel "of Christ"), and is presented by Paul and his associates ("my/our gospel"). Though Paul is the instrument of the gospel's proclamation, here he downplays the role of his preaching in producing change in the Thessalonians, instead attributing the effective power of the gospel to the Holy Spirit (Morgan 2015, 218), who makes them "holy" just as the Spirit is "holy" (4:8; Rom. 15:13; 1 Cor. 2:4–5).

The distinction that Paul makes between the "word" of his preaching and its "power" in the Thessalonians' lives parallels a commonplace of the ancient philosophers: words should be in conformity with deeds, or one's doctrines should be lived out in practice. They said that philosophy was not merely about contemplating the nature of things, but was fundamentally the "art of right living" (Cicero, *Tusc.* 4.3.5; cf. *Nat. d.* 1.7; Musonius Rufus, *Diatr.* 5; Marcus Aurelius, *Med.* 10.16; 11.29). Those who debased philosophy by touting its doctrines while contradicting those same doctrines in practice proved—or left the impression—that the doctrines of their system were useless. Paul applies the same principle here. The powerful change witnessed in the Thessalonians' lives demonstrates the validity of his message.

The final part of verse 5 makes a comparison between the Thessalonians and Paul himself, in whom the gospel has also played itself out in practice: **just like—as you are aware—*we* became among you for your sake**. Here occurs the first of many instances where Paul reminds the Thessalonians about what they "know" (2:1, 2, 5, 11; 3:3, 4; 4:2; 5:2). In its present occurrence, the device reflects a strategy that was commonly used by teachers of philosophy who, when separated from their pupils, wished to strengthen their students' commitment to what they had been taught, lest during the separation they forget the leaders' precepts and weaken in their commitment. Teachers reinforced instruction by giving persistent reminders about what their students had learned or theoretically already "knew." They advised them to continue living as if their teachers were present and to model themselves after them (Seneca, *Ep.* 32.1) or some other exemplary figure (Seneca, *Ep.* 11.9; Lucian, *Nigr.* 6–7). As Seneca remarked: "Happy is the man who can make others better, not merely when he is in their company, but even when he is in their thoughts!" (Seneca, *Ep.* 11.9).

1:6–8. Paul's self-reference becomes a hinge on which he swings attention immediately back to the Thessalonians: first, Paul and his associates had put the gospel's message into practice; as a result, the Thessalonians had done so as well: "You know what kind of people *we* became. . . . **And *you* in turn became *imitators* of us** (vv. 5–6). The theme of imitation plays an important role in Paul's letters (1 Cor. 2:2; 4:16–17; 11:1; Eph. 5:1; Phil. 3:17; 4:9). In this, Paul plays on a theme that had wide cultural currency. James Harrison (2019, 217–55) has shown that "imitation of the 'great man' was a vital dimension of civic ethics in antiquity." Paul's formulation of the theme has significant parallels with its expression within the ancient philosophical tradition. The Stoic philosophers emphasized that people learned not only through "doctrines" (*doctrinae*) and "rules" (*praecepta*), but also through imitation (*mimēsis*). It was observed that people imitate those with whom they surround themselves, whether good or bad. Hence, the Stoics constantly reminded students to choose the best models, or *exempla*, to imitate (Seneca, *Ep.* 25.6; 52.8; 104.20–33). Some philosophers said that *exempla* were generally more effective than *doctrinae* and *praecepta* at instilling ideas and behaviors, since *exempla* provided visible images and concrete instantiations of truth; in Seneca's words, "People put more trust in their eyes than in their ears" (*Ep.* 6.5). Paul's notion of imitation bore a close resemblance to that of the Stoics, who taught that the best example was set by *Natura* herself (which was identical with God), then imitated by the wise man (the perfect philosopher), who then provided a model for others. Analogously, Paul viewed Christ as the perfect example and himself as an imitator of Christ, so that he in turn became a model for others, and they for still others (Christ → Paul → the Corinthians in 1 Cor. 11:1). Paul differed from the philosophers, however, by appealing to *himself* as an example (as he does again in 2:1–12). While Seneca, for instance, pointed to the wise man as an example to imitate, he refused to consider himself such a person (*Vit. beat.* 11.1; 17.3–4) and maintained that even the best philosophers taught people to act, not as they themselves acted, but as they taught that people *ought* to act (*Vit. beat.* 18.1).

Because Paul imitated Christ, the Thessalonians by imitating Paul also imitated the Lord (**as well as of the Lord**), that is, Jesus. They were imitators of the Lord not simply in "receiving the word" (**for when you received the word**) but specifically in their receiving the word **in much affliction** and yet **with the kind of joy that flows from the Holy Spirit** (1:6). The Thessalonians' "affliction" (*thlipsis*) cannot have been limited to inner distress or anxiety (contra Malherbe 1987, 47–48). Their affliction must have included opposition from outsiders, involving social ostracization, possibly economic retaliation, and likely (since they are said to be imitating Jesus) verbal and physical abuse (see also comments on 2:14).

More remarkable is that they endured their affliction "with joy of the Holy Spirit." Their experience of affliction contradicted the political rhetoric of the day, which proclaimed good news and the arrival of "joy" (Harrison 2011, 65, citing *SIG* 797) in the happy "Golden Age" inaugurated by Rome (Vergil, *Aen.* 6.792–93). Since their experience was not one of peace or prosperity, the Thessalonians would seem to have had little reason to rejoice.

Some ancient groups affirmed the possibility of happiness despite external circumstances. The philosophical systems of the day promised to deliver happiness, whatever the circumstances, if one followed their doctrines. The ultimate test of validity was whether the devotee could be "happy on the rack": all the philosophical schools insisted that this could be so (Cicero, *Tusc.* 5.26.73; Diogenes Laërtius, *Vit.* 10.118; Lucian, *Philops.* 9). According to the philosophers, happiness was possible in such circumstances because happiness sprang from a right frame of mind, in perceiving that one already had in hand all that really mattered. For Paul, too, happiness was possible even in suffering, but not for all the same reasons. Here Paul refrains from stating the grounds of joy explicitly; yet the letter opening as a whole provides a basic theological framework that makes these grounds evident. God has called the Thessalonians into a new family, in which he is their Father (1:1, 3) and they are brothers and sisters (1:4), special to him (1:4). There is, furthermore, a prospective element in Paul's teaching, which is lacking in Greco-Roman philosophy: ahead lies the return of God's Son, bringing the completion of their deliverance and retribution on their enemies (v. 10).

The Thessalonians who imitated the example of Paul and Jesus **consequently** became **an example to all the believers in Macedonia and Achaia**: the report of their behavior had "sounded out" through Macedonia and Achaia and indeed "in every place" (**For not only did the word of the Lord ring out across Macedonia and Achaia, but also your faith in God has gone out into every place**). Apart from Macedonia and Achaia, Paul likely refers here to the other regions where he had established churches—chiefly throughout Asia Minor, and especially the Roman province of Asia, furthest to the west. Paul's remark could be taken to suggest that the Thessalonians participated in public proclamation of the gospel, or "evangelism," after the pattern of Paul. Several pieces of evidence, however, show that it is not their proclamation but the broadcast about their reputation that has "sounded out everywhere." First, while Paul routinely refers to his own proclamation of the gospel (1:5; 2:1; 2 Thess. 2:14; Rom. 2:16; 16:25; 2 Cor. 4:3), he apparently viewed this responsibility as an obligation laid upon him in his special commissioning as apostle to the gentiles (2:4; Gal. 2:16). Nowhere in either this letter or his other letters does he instruct members of his churches to engage in public evangelism (although surely he cannot have objected to it). Second, the verbal parallelism that Paul devises between "the word of the Lord has rung out" and "your faith has gone out" suggests that, just like the latter expression, the former expression concerns the report about their faith to others, as opposed to their proclamation of the gospel itself. Third, and in support of the previous point, Paul refers in verse 9 to the "*declaration*" (report) of the *other* Christians *about* the Thessalonians' warm *reception* of Paul's message. Fourth, where Paul indicates that he has "no need *to say* anything" because the word has spread so far so quickly (**so that we have no need to speak of it ourselves**), the verb "say" more naturally suggests *reporting* about their faith (he has no need to report it since it is already known everywhere) rather than *proclaiming* the gospel (he has no need to preach it as if it has already been preached everywhere).

1:9–10. In the next two verses, Paul grounds his remark about the Thessalonians' illustrious reputation among the churches by mentioning what the churches are proclaiming: the Thessalonians' warm reception of Paul and of his initial proclamation to them (**For they themselves proclaim concerning us what kind of welcome we had among you**). Paul's summary of the churches' report goes on to outline the message that he had originally proclaimed and that the Thessalonians had eagerly accepted. Verses 9–10 indicate that Paul preached to the Thessalonians during his visit about the living and true God (**and how you turned to the one God from idols, to serve the living and true God**), the resurrection and return of Jesus (**and to await his Son from the heavens, whom he raised from the dead**), the role of Christ as the instrument of salvation (**Jesus, who is delivering us**), and the final judgment (**from the wrath to come**). Beginning with "you turned," the parallel structure, succinct form, and summary nature of this section—combined with the use of numerous allegedly "non-Pauline" terms and concepts (all of which do actually occur elsewhere in Paul's letters)—has led many to conclude that this material constituted an early Christian "creed" (see also 4:14; 5:10). Perhaps it was a Christian adaptation of contemporary Jewish theology about the one true God (lifeless idols versus the living God) originating in Jewish-Christian missionary preaching, possibly in the church at Antioch (Donfried 2002, 79–80; cf. R. Collins 1984, 20–23, 54–57), where Paul inherited it. If these verses indeed recite such a creed, they constitute evidence that some of the central tenets of early Christian belief—including the resurrection and return of Jesus and several other important christological themes (e.g., Jesus's status as "Son," his role as "deliverer")—can be traced back quite early, even to a time before Paul's visit to Thessalonica in the late 40s.

All of this material recurs in some form later in the letter: gentile ignorance of God (4:5), salvation as a process that is working itself out in the present ("who is delivering us," 1:10; "is giving us his Holy Spirit," 4:8; "is calling you," 2:12; 5:24; "destined us to obtain salvation," 5:9), God's wrath (2:16; 5:9; cf. 4:6), and especially the closely associated themes of Jesus's resurrection and return. The Thessalonian letters contain no less than seventeen references to Jesus's return, and of the seven uses in Paul's letters of the term *parousia* for Christ's coming, six of them appear in the Thessalonian correspondence (1 Thess. 2:19; 3:13; 4:15; 5:23; 2 Thess. 2:1, 8; also in 1 Cor. 15:23). Paul's mention here of Jesus's resurrection and return points ahead to a longer discussion of these themes in 4:13–18.

Paul's mention of "turning" from idols to God—and indeed to a new way of viewing the world—evokes the classic idea of conversion. The LXX uses the verb "turned" (*epistrephein*) with reference to Israel's return to God (Hosea 5:4; 6:1; Joel 2:13) as well as the gentiles' turning toward God (Ps. 22:27 [21:28 LXX]; Isa. 19:22; Jer. 18:8; cf. 8:11). Both Acts (15:19; 26:18, 20) and Paul use the term to describe the "turn" of nonbelievers (apparently gentiles) to Christ (2 Cor. 3:16; Gal. 4:9). The concept of conversion is widely attested in the ancient world. It appears in the Dead Sea Scrolls with reference to Jews who join the Qumran sect (CD XV.5–6; XVI.1–5; see also I.1–II.1). In pagan religious texts such a turn refers to those who choose to commit fully to some new deity (Apuleius, *Metamorphoses*). And the concept appears in philosophical literature with reference to those

The "Son of God" and Imperial Propaganda

Paul's affirmation that Jesus is God's "Son" could be viewed as a challenge to the Roman emperor, or at least could have been perceived that way by Rome or those with pro-Roman sentiments. Despite the populace's voluntary institution of emperor cults in the eastern provinces, emperors themselves from Augustus (27 BCE–14 CE) to Vespasian (69–79 CE) generally denied that they were gods and often refused honors that treated them as such (Caligula was the main exception). Nevertheless, it was customary for emperors to be deified by decree of the Senate upon death, sometimes based on reports that the soul of the deceased had been seen ascending into heaven; the "apotheosis" of Julius Caesar is recounted in several Roman texts (Vergil, *Aen.* 1.290; Suetonius, *Jul.* 88; Ovid, *Metam.* 15.745–870). The succeeding emperor, the son of the deceased, would then fittingly be called the "son of a god." Epigraphical and numismatic evidence has survived showing that the emperors were regarded as such in ancient Thessalonica as early as the reign of Augustus. For instance, one inscription dating to his reign refers to the appointment of a priest of the "Imperator Caesar Augustus *Son of God*" (*IG* X^2 I 31,11.5–7); a series of coins minted in Thessalonica in 27 BCE depicts on one side Julius Caesar, with the legend "god" (*theos*), and on the other side an image of his son, Augustus "of the Thessalonicans," likely suggesting his status as son of the "god" (Hendrix 1984, 173). In light of the apotheosis tradition, it is evident how fundamentally Paul's eschatological gospel of Christ's lordship and imminent return conflicted with Roman ideology (Harrison 2011, 63–88).

who convert to philosophy, especially from sophistry, or from one philosophical school to another (Divjanović 2015, 22–122).

Conversion entailed a reinvention of one's worldview and way of being in the world, requiring rigorous reinforcement through instruction, or as the philosophers called them, "precepts." The art of reinforcing precepts was known as *psychagogy* (from Greek *psychagōgein*, meaning "to lead the soul"). Like the philosophers, Paul in this letter reflects awareness of his community's psychological needs and employs similar methods for dealing with them (Malherbe 1987, 45–46). Coming out of a pagan background, the Thessalonian converts required a more radical reorientation of their patterns of thought and behavior than did Jewish converts. Thus, the *paraenetic* purposes of 1 Thessalonians are evident already in the thanksgiving section. These gentiles, having recently turned to Christ out of paganism, faced serious challenges. First was that their new allegiance inevitably cut them off from or severely damaged their relationships with family, friends, and business partners, as well as from the community and city at large. Related was a danger from the watchful eye of Rome. Provincial cities were eager to magnify Rome's honor by every means possible, since this encouraged Rome's reciprocation in the form of honor and civic benevolences. Because ancient religion was embedded in the domain of politics, religious occasions were inseparable from civic life. A failure or, more extreme, a refusal of these new Christ-followers to participate in public feasts, festivals, and ceremonies would be viewed at best as an annoyance and at worse as a threat to the perceived loyalty of the city, provoking its pro-Roman constituents to take measures to silence the deviant minority. It would come as no surprise if these believers, so young in their faith, began to doubt whether their new allegiance was worth the price. Paul makes a concerted effort to form a new sense of identity within them. He emphasizes their new bond of fellowship as brothers and sisters of each other and as children of God, and he praises the steadfastness that they have already demonstrated, encouraging them to continue in their new way of life. Moreover, he assures them that the payoff is indeed worth the price: positively, Jesus will return as expected; negatively, they will be delivered from the coming wrath, which will fall upon the church's oppressors.

Theological Issues

Suffering and Joy

From the perspectives of both Paul and Rome, the good news, or "gospel," provided grounds for joy. However, the good news was different for each. The gospel of Rome was news of earthly prosperity. It announced the good news of the Roman emperor and savior, who had inaugurated a Golden Age by uniting the nations in peace and providing gifts to the people in abundance. Paul's gospel promised not prosperity but suffering. He grounded joy not in the promise of physical health, social advancement, or economic prosperity but in a new cosmic reality. From the beginning, Paul told the Thessalonians that Christ's gospel was bound to invite difficulties (3:3–4). The Thessalonians had been adopted into a new family and lived under the lordship of a benevolent, loving father, who raised Jesus from the dead and offered deliverance from final judgment. They suffer now as Christ suffered. Yet Christ was also raised from the dead; just as they have suffered like Christ, so also will they be raised like Christ (cf. 4:14). For Paul it is therefore not the absence of suffering that provides grounds for joy but the believer's hope beyond suffering. In the meantime, suffering is a true misfortune, an injustice that matters and requires eschatological remediation. Deliverance has begun, but believers wait in hope of its completion.

Words and Deeds

Though some of Paul's listeners might have heard him differently (cf. Rom. 3:8), Paul never separated faith and works. The first mention of faith found in his letters refers to a "*working* faith" (1 Thess. 1:3). Moreover, Paul declares that it was not verbal assent to his message that proved the Thessalonians' election but the "powerful" evidence in them of the gospel's acceptance: its effective work in their lives (1:5). It is this work that evinced not only the validity of their election but also the validity of the message. If it did not work, it would have held no value. A faith without effect would be of no benefit to its possessor and therefore would not be maintained for long, particularly in the face of harsh consequences such as the loss of status, resources, or health, all of which the Thessalonians are likely to have experienced. The working power of faith would be essential to maintaining the faith of those who suffered so greatly for it.

Identity and Resocialization

The degree to which the Thessalonian Christians were disintegrated from surrounding society is difficult to imagine in contexts where Christians are well assimilated in society, especially where Christianity has had a strong foothold historically, as it has had in the Western world throughout Christian history. In such contexts Christians and non-Christians live in peace under the same roofs, in the same office spaces, and in a common public arena. Seldom does a person's faith cost them their friends or family, their job, financial success, or personal well-being. For Paul's communities, by contrast, their alienation from society precipitated an acute need for a new sense of belonging. Though it alienated them from friends, family, and surrounding society, the gospel incorporated them into a new family, in which they were brothers and sisters of each other and children of God their Father, and in which they lived in hope of deliverance from impending wrath.

This new identity brought with it a new way of life, a change that was most dramatic for those converting from polytheism rather than from traditional Judaism. From a sociological perspective, such a change—or conversion—requires a deep process of "resocialization." In the first place, it requires deconstruction of fully integrated ways of seeing the world, of entire systems of belief and complex patterns of behavior that have been previously socialized into the individual by parents, teachers, and friends; by their education; and by society's many and varied institutions, which have shaped them from birth. Reorientation of one's beliefs and behaviors around a new way of life is therefore complicated by the fact that—contrary to socialization from childhood—one now needs, not to revise, but to strip away the old and then construct de novo a new way of seeing the world. For Paul, as for the philosophers, it was part of the teacher's obligation to inculcate this new reality. This required repeated instruction, constant reminders, and frequent reinforcement of what the students already "know," lest they slip into ways of thinking deeply implanted and nurtured over their long past by the chorus of voices that surrounded them, and that even now sought to pull them back into their old ways. Only by a rigorous program of resocialization, helped along by both their teacher and one another, could they build and maintain a firm sense of their new identity, separate from the dominant one that surrounded them.

1 Thessalonians 2:1–12

Paul's Ministry in Thessalonica

Introductory Matters

Paul's prolonged thanksgiving now reaches an end as he transitions to the main body of the letter (2:1–5:22). He begins by recounting the nature of his message and conduct as witnessed by the Thessalonians when he first visited them just weeks earlier (2:1–12), emphasizing that God was the source of his message (2:2, 8, 9), that he left unaltered the message with which he was entrusted (2:4), and that God is a witness (2:5, 10) of his lowly conduct among them (2:3–12).

Paul's manner of opening the letter's body may strike modern readers as odd: he simply recounts how he had conducted himself and how the Thessalonians had received him during his recent visit. Properly understanding the purpose of this section requires some decision about the "type" of letter that Paul has written (see commentary introduction above). If 1 Thessalonians is an *apologetic* letter, Paul's primary purpose in the letter is to defend himself and his message, and now he begins to fulfill that purpose in 2:1–12. Because this section consists largely of denials, interpreters for a long time assumed that Paul was responding to specific allegations made against him by a well-defined group of "opponents" (see commentary introduction), be they gnostics (Schmithals 1972), spiritual enthusiasts (Lütgert 1909), or millenarian radicals (Jewett 1986). However, in 1970 an influential article by Abraham Malherbe argued that Paul's denials were more proleptic than real and drew from stock descriptions of the ideal philosopher as distinguished from wandering Cynics and traveling figures, whom people tended to view as dishonest, insincere, and greedy. According to this interpretation, Paul was not responding to concrete charges alleged by specific opponents but was clarifying his character in anticipation that he might be misidentified with such crooked characters and specific charges might arise. While this has now become the dominant interpretation of 1 Thess. 2:1–12, some have been slow to accept it (Donfried 2002, 163–64) or have countered with further arguments for the apologetic position (J. Harrison in J. Harrison and Welborn forthc.). As a compromise between the options, it is possible that Paul was responding to specific *charges* without necessarily responding to a specific group of *opponents*. For example, he may have been responding to his general experience in Thessalonica, where many who observed him might hypothetically impugn his motives as self-serving (Still 1999, 145–49).

However, this section reflects discernible features of a *paraenetic* letter (Malherbe 2000, 134–63). First, the distinctive language of paraenesis occurs at both the beginning (*paraklēsis* in 2:3) and the end of this section (*parakalountes . . . paramythoumenoi . . . martyromenoi* in 2:12), thus creating an *inclusio* around the section. Second, characteristic of the paraenetic style, this section appeals repeatedly to what the Thessalonians "know" (2:1, 2, 5, 11) or "remember" (2:9), thereby calling to mind their initial impression of Paul and their confidence in his message. Third, the text assures the Thessalonians that Paul's message was not of human origin but that it in fact derived from God. In this way, 2:1–12 serves a hortatory function and carries on the paraenetic purposes evident in the opening thanksgiving section.

Ultimately, apologetic and paraenetic motives may be difficult to disentangle. If one sees this section primarily as self-defense, one will see Paul's attempts to instill confidence about his message as a means of solidifying the Thessalonians' support of him against those who slander him (Kim 2005). If, on the other hand, one sees this section primarily as paraenetic, Paul's review of motives is an attempt to reaffirm the divine origins of his message for the purpose of strengthening the Thessalonians' commitment to it at a time when opposition might begin to have adverse effects. As the flow of the letter will indicate, the latter appears to be a more prominent concern.

> **1 Thessalonians 2:1–12 in the Rhetorical Flow**
>
> Letter opening (1:1–10)
> Letter body (2:1–5:22)
> ▶ Paul's ministry in Thessalonica (2:1–12)
>   Paul's proclamation of the gospel (2:1–2)
>   Paul's message and his purposes (2:3–7a)
>   Paul's conduct (2:7b–9)
>   Exhortation to walk rightly (2:10–12)

Tracing the Train of Thought

The contents of this section can be broken down into four parts: Paul's proclamation of the gospel (2:1–2), Paul's message and his purposes (2:3–7a), Paul's conduct (2:7b–9), and an exhortation to walk rightly (2:10–12).

Paul's Proclamation of the Gospel (2:1–2)

2:1–2. The logical flow between 1 Thessalonians 1 and 2 shows that Paul's primary purpose in 2:1–2 is paraenetic. The word **for** (*gar*) grounds Paul's prior assertion that, as became known "in Macedonia and in Achaia and in every place" (1:7–8), the Thessalonians indeed warmly welcomed Paul and gladly received his message into their hearts. Their reception had been reported by others (1:9), and the Thessalonians know that what was said is true (2:1): **You yourselves know, brothers and sisters.** That Paul's emphasis is indeed still on the Thessalonians is confirmed by several points. First, *their* reception of his message is the topic of the immediately preceding section, where Paul emphasized the effectiveness of the gospel in their lives (1:2–10). By contrast, the word "for" cannot serve to explicate the sincerity of Paul's own conduct. For what is described in 1:2–10 (including v. 5, *pace* Best 1979, 89) is not his sincerity but the effective power of the gospel in the Thessalonians' lives ("resulted in action and in the evidence of the Holy Spirit and in your full assurance"), just as it had been powerful in his own life ("just like, as you are aware, *we* became among you for your sake"). Second, the word *kenē* in the clause **our visit was not *in vain*** (ESV, NASB, NKJV, NRSV; "not without *effect*," NAB; "not without *results*," NIV) normally refers to *effectiveness* (cf. 1 Cor. 15:10, 58; 2 Cor. 6:1; Gal. 2:2; Phil. 2:16; 1 Thess. 3:5) and not to *substance* ("empty"); thus the word refers to the Thessalonians' *reception* of Paul's message rather than to the legitimacy of his message's *content*. Third, the word *eisodos*—translated "coming" (ESV, NASB, NKJV, NRSV), "reception" (NAB), or "visit" (NIV) in modern English translations—refers just two verses earlier (1:9) to the Thessalonians' *reception* of Paul. Finally, the phrasing of 2:1 as a whole parallels and complements that of 1:9:

they *themselves* report concerning us what kind of welcome we had among you (1:9)
you yourselves know . . . what kind of arrival we had among you (2:1)

In short, Paul here further substantiates his claim that the gospel the Thessalonians received also manifested itself in *action* in their lives.

Thus in 2:1–12, the verses are oriented toward strengthening the Thessalonians' existing faith by (1) refreshing their memory as to their commitment to the message that they had not so long ago received and as to the power of the message that they had witnessed in their lives; (2) reaffirming that the message in which they had believed was not Paul's but God's (thus explaining its power); and (3) reminding them that the power of God's message was evident also in his own life, to whose example they have conformed.

This reading is confirmed as the discourse continues to unfold. The contrastive conjunction **but** (*alla*) at the beginning of verse 2 is difficult to explain if Paul's purposes are defensive, for the result would then be an uneven antithesis between the gospel's effectiveness in the Thessalonians' lives and the integrity of Paul's own character ("our visit was not in vain"; rather, **we preached boldly**). It seems better to read the contrast as one between *ineffective* proclamation (v. 1) and a message defined as **the proclamation of God** (v. 2). This latter expression, which differs in meaning from several similar expressions in Paul's letters (see "our gospel" in 1:5), refers not to Paul's message *about* God but to a message *from* God. As such, Paul suggests that the very reason for the effectiveness of his message was that it in fact originated *with God*.

Two words that appear in verse 2 strongly echo ancient philosophical commonplaces. First, in declaring his "boldness" of speech (*parrhēsiasasthai*), Paul plays on a commonplace about the popular philosophers—especially of the Cynic type (Downing 1992, 47)—who from the street corners and in the marketplace "boldly" proclaimed the virtues of philosophy, despite the fact that their audiences were unwilling to listen and even responded by reviling them as public nuisances. While the philosophers advertised their boldness as a personal virtue, Paul declares that the source of his strength is God: he spoke boldly **by God's help** (cf. Malherbe 2000, 137). Second, Paul's reference to preaching **in much opposition** (*agōn*) probably echoes a philosophical trope in which philosophers compared their lives to a "contest" against either vice (Dio Chrysostom, *Or.* 8; Seneca, *Ep.* 78.16) or those who practiced vice (4 Macc. 6:10; 17:14). That Paul presents his struggle as one braved despite recent **affliction and mistreatment in Philippi** suggests that "opposition" refers not to a "rhetorical" contest between ideological competitors in the public square (Richard 1995, 79, 92) or to an "internal" struggle against vice (Malherbe 2000, 138) or to physical exertion as an itinerant missionary but to external opposition in the form of verbal abuse and, quite possibly, physical mistreatment and incarceration (Acts 16:19–40).

Paul's Message and His Purposes (2:3–7a)

2:3–4. As in verse 1, again the initial conjunction in verse 3 offers a clue as to Paul's paraenetic purposes. **For** (*gar*) does not explicate the "boldness" of Paul in the face of opposition (*pace* Wanamaker 1990, 94) but the point that his message was **the gospel of God** (2:2, 9) and derived *from* God. Paul insists on the divine origins of his message by characterizing it first negatively and then positively: first, he denies the possibility that the message is merely a human one passed off as God's either by deception or personal error (**our kerygmatic appeal did not spring from error or from insincerity or from deceit**); second, he insists that **the very gospel message** with which he was **entrusted by God to speak** is the very message he **speaks**, unaltered and unchanged (v. 4). Paul's claim that he was "entrusted" with his message undoubtedly refers to his apostolic appointment (1 Cor. 9:16–17; Gal. 1:15). In this regard, his emphasis on motives need not be defensive. Rather, it serves to highlight the divine source of the message in order to assure the Thessalonians, as they endure present struggles, that their initial faith was not misplaced.

2:5–7a. Whereas verses 3–4 focus on the *source* of Paul's message, verses 5–6 focus on its *ends*, its purpose. Paul denies practicing flattery (**sycophancy**) and covetousness (**opportunism**)—both understood here as means of winning personal prestige. The vice of flattery was a common topic of discussion in literary treatises of the day. In two treatises on the subject (*How to Tell a Flatterer from a Friend* and *Concerning the Flatterer and Friend*), Plutarch describes the flatterer as one who uses praise of others as a means of attaining personal benefit. Paul's reference to "opportunism" likewise focuses on personal interest. Neither "sycophancy" nor "opportunism" should be understood here strictly in relation to seeking financial benefit. Since Paul's denials serve as evidence that he did not seek human **renown** (*doxa*), these items should be understood rather in relation to the honorific culture of his and the Thessalonians' milieu. In the Greco-Roman world, honor was not only to be sought but was to be sought unapologetically. Philosophers, poets, and rhetoricians sought glory through their literary achievements. Honorary statues, monuments, and inscriptions filled the urban landscape, acclaiming those who funded public buildings and renovations, sponsored public feasts and festivals, and supplied resources to the public. The lower classes, even slaves, played the game, striving for public honors, however insignificant, and seeking advance by attaching themselves to the most prominent patrons (Finney 2010, 28). It is this ethic that Paul here repudiates.

The question of whether these remarks indeed refer to a desire for *honor*, as opposed strictly to *greed* for financial gain, has important bearing on the meaning of 2:7a: **although we were able to . . .** Conceivably, this remark alludes to Paul's right as an apostle to impose a "burden" (*en barei*) on his churches, to receive financial support from them: "We were able to demand the *burden* of support from you." In favor of this reading is 1 Cor. 9:6–18, where Paul appeals

---

Literature and Eternal Glory

"My name shall be never forgotten.
Wherever the might of Rome extends in the lands she has conquered,
the people shall read and recite my words. Throughout all ages,
if poets have vision to prophesy truth, I shall live in my fame."
(Ovid, *Metam.* 15.871–79, trans. Raeburn 2004, 636)

"'If,' said Epicurus, 'you are attracted by fame, my letters will make you more renowned than all the things which you cherish and which make you cherished.' . . . That which Epicurus could promise his friend, this I promise you, Lucilius. I shall find favour among later generations." (Seneca, *Ep.* 21.3, 5, trans. Gummere, LCL)

"I have not been moved by hope of gain or desire for glory, as the rest have been, in undertaking to write." (Ps.-Cicero, *Rhet. Her.* 1, trans. Caplan, LCL)

---

to Jesus's teaching (9:14) that ministers of the gospel have a right to receive remuneration. Also supporting this reading are Paul's remarks just a few verses *later* (1 Thess. 2:9): while he was in Thessalonica, he had earned his own keep so as "not to *burden*" any of them (using the same *bar-* root). If this financial interpretation is correct, then the contrast that Paul poses here is one between his *right to earn money through his ministry* on the one hand, and his *decision not to act on the opportunity* on the other: "not being covetous, . . . although we were able to impose the *burden* of support." This reading, however, is likely not correct. If flattery and covetousness apply strictly to financial greed, then a conceptual break occurs between 2:6 and 2:7a—shifting from financial greed (v. 6) to lust for honor (v. 7a)—and the sentence's syntax is ruined. Instead, 2:6a uses a present participle (*zētountes*) to ground Paul's claim that he was neither sycophantic nor opportunistic, that is, that he had not sought *social advancement*: **Never at any time did we become sycophantic (as you well know), nor opportunistic (as God is our witness), nor did we seek renown from any human being**. As such, Paul describes not his choice to refrain from imposing the *burden* of financial support but his willingness to forgo others' recognition of the *importance, weight,* or *dignity* he is due by virtue of his apostleship (although we were able to **call attention to our *importance* as apostles of Christ**). This is an admissible rendering of *baros* (BDAG 167.2) and should be preferred here.

Paul's Conduct (2:7b–9)

2:7b–9. After defining his conduct negatively by using a series of denials, Paul now defines his conduct positively. Three interrelated issues complicate interpretation of this section. (1) The nature of the contrast introduced by the conjunction *alla* in 2:7b is not clear. (2) In connection with what precedes, 2:7b–8 could be punctuated in several different ways. (3) Manuscripts disagree as to whether the text should read "young children" (NIV) or "gentle" (ESV, NRSV). A decision about the third issue helps to elucidate the other two issues, so this one will be treated first.

Early in the history of the text's transmission, a textual variant emerged and was handed down together with the original reading. The two readings look and sound almost identical, differing by only a single letter: *nēpioi* (young children) and *ēpioi* (gentle). Both readings were known during the patristic period, although each was more or less unique to its own geographical area. From the rise of textual criticism during the Reformation until modern scholarship of the present day, the preferred reading has alternated multiple times between the two options. Until the late nineteenth century, critics preferred *ēpioi*. During the late nineteenth and early twentieth, *nēpioi* prevailed, only for the consensus to shift back to *ēpioi* during the second half of the twentieth. Since the turn of the twenty-first century, however, most interpreters have come again to prefer *nēpioi* (Gupta 2019, 110).

Considering the strength of manuscript support, transcriptional probabilities, and the rhetorical coherence of the passage (Sailors 2000; Weima 2000), *nēpioi* is indeed the more probable reading. While Paul's subsequent characterization of himself as a "nurse" introduces an abrupt change of metaphor, such combining of figures is not uncharacteristic of Paul (e.g., the church as "God's field, God's building" in 1 Cor. 3:9b–15); here it is but the first in a series of changes between conceptually inconsistent metaphors ("children," v. 7b; "nurse," v. 7c; "father," v. 11; "orphaned," v. 17). No doubt the combination highlights the complex nature of his and his converts' relationship, which could not be captured by a single idea (Gaventa 1998, 29).

The question of which reading is correct has bearing on the function of the conjunction in 2:7b: "but/rather" (*alla*). (1) If *ēpioi* is the original reading, then Paul poses a contrast between his having "weight" as an apostle on the one hand (2:6–7a) and the "gentleness" with which he treated his audience on the other (2:7b). Thus, a period would be placed after "apostles of Christ" at the end of 2:7a: ". . . although we were able to impose the *weight of our authority*, as apostles of Christ. *But instead* we became *gentle* . . ." (2) If *nēpioi* is the original reading, then two alternative interpretations are possible. In either case, a period should be placed at the end of 2:7b. (a) One interpretation locates the contrast between Paul's denial of *guile* on the one hand (2:5–6) and his childlike *innocence* on the other (2:7b): "*Rather*, we became innocent as children in your midst." (b) The other locates the contrast in the disparity between Paul's weighty apostolic *status* on the one hand (2:6–7a) and his childlike *lowliness* on the other (2:7b): "Rather, we became *lowly* children in your midst."

Several points argue in favor of interpretation 2b: **Rather, we became lowly children in your midst**. First, Paul's choice to characterize himself **just as a nurse cares for her own children** (cf. Gal. 4:19; 1 Cor. 3:1–2), against the background of his patriarchal culture, exudes an attitude contrary to the conventional gender hierarchy (Gaventa 1998, 30) and to notions of status as judged by the world's standards. While Paul intends to evoke the association between nurses and nurture and affection here, besides bearing the stigma of being "women" nurses served primarily the purpose of childcare and were often deprecated as poor, uneducated, and unsophisticated (Plato, *Resp.* 2.377C.2–4; cf. Quintilian, *Inst.* 1.1.4).

Second, "children" figure in the teaching of Jesus as the greatest in the kingdom precisely because they are the "lowliest," and the form of expression Paul uses here suggests that he may even be alluding to this teaching. He uses the unusual expression "children *in your midst* [*en mesō hymōn*]," as opposed to simply "children." In the three Gospel texts that depict children as the lowliest of all, the children are said to be put "in their midst" (Matt. 18:2), to be "among them" (Mark 9:36), or to be "among all of you" (Luke 9:48).

Third, Paul reminds the Thessalonians in 2:9 that "night and day" he had worked "with his hands"; **for you remember, brothers and sisters, our labor and toil: working night and day, so as not to burden any of you.** The conjunction "for"

Elite Contempt for Manual Labor

"Now in regard to trades and other means of livelihood, which ones are to be considered becoming to a gentleman and which ones are vulgar, we have been taught, in general as follows.... Unbecoming to a gentleman, too, and vulgar are the means of livelihood of all hired workmen whom we pay for mere manual labour, not for artistic skill; for in their case the very wage they receive is a pledge of their slavery.... And all mechanics are engaged in vulgar trades; for no workshop can have anything liberal about it. Least respectable of all are those trades which cater for sensual pleasures: 'Fishmongers, butchers, cooks, and poulterers, and fisherman,' as Terence says.... But the professions in which either a higher degree of intelligence is required or from which no small benefit to society is derived— medicine and architecture, for example, and teaching—these are proper for those whose social position they become." (Cicero, *Off.* 1.150–51, trans. Miller, LCL)

(*gar*) most likely serves to support Paul's assertion that he had "given his life" (v. 8) by now explaining how he had done so: through the self-sacrifice of work as opposed to dependence on the financial resources of the Thessalonians. In his letters Paul frequently draws attention to the fact that he supported himself by manual labor throughout his ministry (1 Thess. 2:9; 2 Thess. 3:8–9; cf. 1 Cor. 9:6, 14; 2 Cor. 11:7, 9; 12:13). Acts 18:3 describes him specifically as a "tentmaker" (*skēnopoios*) by trade. Though manual labor was the way most of the population earned their livelihood (including day laborers, artisans, and slaves), it was denigrated among the literate as mere "skill" (*technē*), requiring no measure of intelligence and as being beneath the dignity of the educated (Xenophon, *Mem.* 2.4.22).

While the elite view was generally shared among the philosophers (Hock 1980, 39), some philosophers established schools in workshops where they could earn their livelihood while instructing their students at the same time, and others elected a life of farming so that they could support themselves and instruct their students while working (Hock 1980, 41–45; Malherbe 1987, 19–20). For the most part, philosophers took on manual labor, however, either out of necessity or as a way of demonstrating the virtue of self-sufficiency (*autarkeia*). Paul's reasons for working were different. Although his choice was driven by a desire not to "burden" the church, it should not be missed that he intended this as a demonstration of *self-sacrifice*, involving damage to his social status along with the physical wear and tear. Just as he became a "child" in their midst and he became their "nursing" mother, so also he voluntarily subjected himself to the contempt shown menial laborers *for the Thessalonians' benefit*. Above all, this pattern of behavior reflected his driving motivation to imitate Christ and to offer himself as an example to the Thessalonians.

Fourth, the words **We were pleased to share with you . . . our very lives** (2:8) share language similar to Christ's saying in Matt. 20:28//Mark 10:45 about the

---

Origen on Paul as a "Lowly Child"

"But another might say that the perfect man is here called little, applying the word, 'For he that is least among you all, the same is great.' He [Paul in 1 Thess. 2:7] will affirm that he who humbles himself and becomes a child in the midst of all that believe, though he be an apostle or a bishop, and becomes such 'as when a nurse cherishes her own children,' is the little one pointed out by Jesus. . . . [For] 'He that is least among you all, the same is great.'" (*Comm. Matt.* 13.29, Gorday 2000, 65–66)

Son of Man (who "gave" his "life" for others), and they may, though with less certainty, allude to Jesus's renunciation of honor in order to sacrifice himself for the sake of others.

Fifth, while the term *nēpios* is often used negatively both in Paul's letters and in other ancient literature, Paul uses the term positively in 1 Cor. 14:20 and, as Timothy Sailors (2000, with abundant examples on 90–92) has demonstrated, the term was also frequently used in a positive sense in Christian, Jewish, and Greco-Roman literature.

Finally, this interpretation finds precedent in the church fathers. Origen, for instance, interprets Paul's self-description as a "child" here as a reference to his lowliness (see sidebar).

Verses 7–8 unmistakably reflect paraenetic intentions. In contrast with Paul's later self-description as "father" (v. 11), the nurse metaphor highlights his "maternal" side (see also Gal. 4:19) as he aims to console and nurture his young community amid their affliction and distress (McNeel 2013; 2014). These verses overflow with expressions of affection and intimacy: "cares for her own children . . . longing for you . . . were pleased to share with you . . . our very lives . . . dear to us." Such language serves to strengthen the community's sense of belonging and, in the face of their alienation from the surrounding society, to reaffirm their new identity as a community of Christ. Finally, insofar as Paul regards himself as a model to imitate (1:5–6), his self-characterization as one who abased himself for the benefit of others implicitly serves as a further example to the Thessalonians of the ethic that the gospel encapsulates.

Exhortation to Walk Rightly (2:10–12)

2:10–12. In the final portion of the unit, Paul reminds the Thessalonians how he behaved (v. 10) and how he taught while he was among them (v. 11), reminding them that his purpose was to produce in them a life pleasing to God (v. 12). While verses 10–12 could include an element of self-defense, strong paraenetic intentions continue to be evident. In this respect Paul's purposes are less to offer "proof" of his motives than to communicate a desire to strengthen his new converts in their faith. Each of this section's components dovetail with this reading.

First, in the manner of a teacher reviewing what he has taught his students, Paul *reminds* the Thessalonians of what they had witnessed: **You yourselves and God are our witnesses**. Second, Paul appeals to his personal character as an *example* for the Thessalonians to imitate: after describing his conduct (**We conducted ourselves in a holy and righteous and blameless way**), he states that his purpose was to produce similar conduct in them (**so that you might walk worthily of God**). Third, with another change of metaphor (cf. lowly children, 2:7; nurse, 2:8), Paul now characterizes himself as the Thessalonians' father (**like a father [does with] his children**), a designation often used in Paul's letters to capture his role as the spiritual father of his converts (1 Cor. 4:15; 2 Cor. 12:14; Phil. 2:22; Philem. 10). In using the metaphor in this way Paul is indebted to the Greek tradition of moral instruction, in which teachers depicted themselves as fathers of their students, instructing them as they would their children, even giving individualized instruction (**how we instructed each one of you**) adapted to the specific needs and maturity level of each student (Malherbe 2000, 150–51). Paul's description of his role may imply that he and his converts cohabited, which was not uncommon among philosophers and their students (see sidebar). Fourth, Paul describes his instruction of the Thessalonians using the specific *language* of paraenesis, piling together three essentially synonymous participles that carry such connotations (**exhorting and encouraging and invoking**). The repetition is probably intended to emphasize the repetition of his previous instructions and perhaps to remind them, now again, that instructions bear repeating (Seneca, *Ep.* 30.7, 15; 94.21). Accordingly, the words **as you know** point the Thessalonians back to Paul's previous teaching and therefore refer not to "we conducted ourselves" (which in any case is already qualified by "you are our witnesses") but rather to "exhorting . . . each one of you to walk worthily." Fifth, by using a present continuous participle to describe God's activity (**God, who is calling you into his own kingdom and glory**), Paul implies that the Thessalonians have not yet arrived at their final destination, and he seeks to encourage them to continue striving toward it. Indeed, while Paul saw the "kingdom" as having a

The Cohabiting of Teachers and Students

"For of the true lovers of philosophy, there is not one who would not be willing to live with a good man in the country, even if the place be very rude, since he would be bound to profit greatly from this sojourn by living with his teacher night and day, by being away from the evils of the city, which are an obstacle to the study of philosophy, and from the fact that his conduct, whether good or bad, cannot escape observation—a great advantage to those who are learning." (Musonius Rufus, *Diatr.* 11, trans. Lutz 1947, 54)

Citizens of the World and Children of God

"Well, then, anyone who has attentively studied the administration of the universe and has learned that 'the greatest and most authoritative and most comprehensive of all governments is this one, which is composed of men and God, and that from Him have descended the seeds of being, not merely to my father or to my grandfather, but to all things that are begotten and that grow upon earth, and chiefly to rational beings, seeing that by nature it is theirs alone to have communion in the society of god, being intertwined with him through the reason,'—why should not such a man call himself a citizen of the universe? Why should he not call himself a son of God?" (Epictetus, *Diatr.* 1.9.4–6, trans. Oldfather, LCL)

present dimension (Rom. 14:17; 1 Cor. 4:20), he also saw the kingdom as a future reality (1 Cor. 15:24, 50), as something yet to be inherited (1 Cor. 6:9–10). Sixth, 2:10–12 is shown to serve a paraenetic purpose in that these verses re-characterize the Thessalonians as a special people. Rather than addressing them simply with the second-person pronoun (you), Paul employs the over-specifying label "you who believe," thus communicating something *about* them through what he *calls* them. Moreover, he draws attention to the Thessalonians' ultimate and unique destination—God's kingdom. Paul's use of a reflexive pronoun rather than a personal pronoun (not "into his kingdom" but "into his *own* kingdom") is significant and implies a contrast between God's kingdom and other kingdoms. In some sense, Paul must have had the Roman Empire in mind. Most people in the empire lacked citizen status, either in their cities of residence or in the commonwealth of Rome. Considering their disenfranchised status within the body politic, it would be a source of consolation to the Thessalonians not only that they belonged to *God's* kingdom, but also that this was a special status not enjoyed by everyone.

Among the disenfranchised of the world, some people may have found a sense of belonging in the Stoics' idea that the world was one city and that all people—not just the privileged few—were its citizens (see sidebar). However, within Paul's apocalyptic worldview, God's kingdom, in contrast with the philosophers' "world-city," consisted only of those in Christ and excluded those without faith, who not only lived in ignorance of God but would also be subject to his wrath (4:5–6). Paul reminds the Thessalonians also that they are being called into God's "*own*" glory. The qualifying pronoun echoes the wording of 2:6: "glory from *humans*." "*God's own* glory" now stands in direct contrast. Thus the Thessalonians' status as kingdom people who will share in God's glory, though they have been marginalized within the realm of society, marks them off as unique and special to God.

Theological Issues

Human Glory versus the Glory of God

Paul's antithetical self-description in this passage highlights, not so much his need to defend himself from direct personal attacks, as the firmness with which the values of his day were entrenched. He could not simply state what he *is* but had to define himself in terms that *challenged* contemporary values. His was a world that valued esteem in the eyes of human beings, won through extraordinary wealth, glorious exploits, public distinction, and professional achievement, even if it meant flattering, compromising, and deceiving to get there. Little has changed in the world. A craving for validation, satisfied only when one surpasses the achievements of others, is deeply embedded in the human species. This is what makes Paul's message so radical. For Paul, the "gospel of Christ" (3:2) reversed the world's system of values, defining human ambition and achievement in the eyes of humanity as worthless in the eyes of God. Paul was *not* opportunistic, and he did *not* seek human glory. Despite the respect he deserved on account of his apostleship (2:7a), Paul became like a lowly child (2:7b), as unesteemed as a child's early nurse (2:7c), and as one who gave his life to the Thessalonians (2:8), assuming the contemptible occupation of a manual laborer, not out of necessity but out of sacrifice (2:9). The path to glory was lowliness; the way up was the way down.

1 Thessalonians 2:13–16

Renewed Thanksgiving

Introductory Matters

Paul's opening outpouring of thanksgiving (1:2–10), despite going on far longer than was typical in Hellenistic letters, has not yet given full vent to his gratitude, and as if building inside him, wells up again. He now thanks God for the Thessalonians' eager acceptance of the word and for its manifest power in their lives (v. 13). This leads him to compare the Thessalonians with the churches of Judea, whom they imitate in their suffering (v. 14). From here, the thanksgiving digresses unexpectedly into an invective against "the Jews" (vv. 15–16), who, Paul says, not only persecuted the churches in Judea, but who also killed Jesus and the prophets, who persecuted Paul, who are not pleasing to God, and who oppose all humanity by opposing Paul's gentile ministry, and whose punishment at God's hands looms.

Despite the excursus in 2:15–16, as a whole 2:13–16 shares substantial ties with 1:2–2:12. "Also" (*kai*) in verse 13 identifies this section as a renewal of the thanksgiving in 1:2–10. Verse 13 contains the same thematic focus on Paul's preaching (1:5; 2:1–2) and the Thessalonians' reception of it (1:6–8; 2:1) that was found earlier in chapter 2. Thus 2:14–15, like 1:2–10, features a parallel between the behavior or experiences of Paul and those of the Thessalonians (1:5c//1:6–7; 2:15–16//2:14). Other ties with earlier sections include reference to the gospel as God's "word" (1:6; 2:13); reference to the word's efficacy in the Thessalonians' lives (1:5; 2:1, 13); and the themes of wrath (1:10; 2:16), affliction (1:6; 2:14–15), and imitation (1:6–7; 2:14).

This passage has been the subject of no small contention among scholars. The renewal of thanksgiving in 2:13–16 after the first thanksgiving in 1:2–10 is seen by some as evidence that 1 Thessalonians is a compilation of two originally separate letters, with each contributing its own thanksgiving section to the final compilation. Many have regarded this section as a "non-Pauline interpolation." Finally, among those who accept the authenticity of these verses, most either take exception to its theological implications or feel that Paul's remarks require defense. A list of the key issues follows.

The double thanksgiving. First Thessalonians is unique in that a thanksgiving formula occurs in the letter not once (1:2) but twice (opens 1:2; 2:13; cf. 3:9; 2 Thess. 1:3–10; 2:13–14). Some modern interpreters have viewed the double thanksgiving as a "violation" of conventional epistolary form and therefore as evidence that two letters—each one with its own thanksgiving—have been conflated into one (see review in R. Collins 1984, 114–24).

> ### 1 Thessalonians 2:13–16 in the Rhetorical Flow
>
> **Letter opening (1:1–10)**
>
> **Letter body (2:1–5:22)**
>
>   Paul's ministry in Thessalonica (2:1–12)
>
> ▶ Renewed thanksgiving (2:13–16)
>
>   The Thessalonians' embrace of the gospel (2:13)
>
>   Opposition to the Thessalonians (2:14)
>
>   Opposition to Paul (2:15–16)

Ancient epistolary forms, however, were not rigidly prescribed even in theory, nor did they always work out the same way in practice. Not every typical stylistic component was included in every letter (note the absence of a thanksgiving in Galatians), and the components that were included did not always need to follow the same order (Klauck 2006, 40–41). Still, recognition of typical patterns in letter forms helps alert us to atypical patterns and thereby to recognize the uniqueness of the rhetorical situation. In that respect, the renewal of thanksgiving in 2:13–16 is indeed significant (see comments below).

On taking 1 Thess. 2:13–16 as an "interpolation." Originating in the mid-nineteenth century, the interpolation theory was adopted by many interpreters throughout the twentieth century. The most extensive case for this view was presented by B. A. Pearson in a 1971 article titled "1 Thessalonians 2:13–16: A Deutero-Pauline Interpolation," which many scholars found convincing. Although several points have been adduced in favor of the interpolation theory, strong responses can be made to each of them (for a recent overview of arguments, see Jensen 2019). Thus, the authenticity of the passage has continued to find defenders over the last two centuries, and in the last thirty years the common opinion has swung decisively in favor of authenticity (Gupta 2019, 118, whose summary statement is confirmed by a survey of the scholarship).

On taking 1 Thess. 2:13–16 as "anti-Semitic" slander. If these verses are authentic, one is left to explain their polemical tone. Luke Timothy Johnson (1989) has offered an explanation that situates 2:13–16 within the context of ancient "rhetoric of slander." In a far-reaching survey of ancient Jewish and Greco-Roman texts, Johnson demonstrates that the rhetoric of slander was commonplace in inter- and inner-group rivalries (see sidebar). It occurred, for instance, between philosophers and sophists, between competing philosophical schools, between Jews and Gentiles, and even between members of the same group. Such rhetoric commonly resorted to stereotypes—casting their opponents as stupid, blind, evil, hypocritical, and other things of an invective nature. The practice was virtually universal, the feelings usually mutual, and the intensity often shocking. Johnson concludes from his survey that, when compared with the slander of the day, NT examples are relatively mild.

Further points should also be taken into consideration. As Johnson observes, in the mid-first century neither Judaism nor Christianity was a monolithic entity: Christianity was still considered a part of Judaism, and non-Christian Jews were the more dominant group (423–30). In that context, Christians were a perse-cuted sect within Judaism, whose attitude toward their persecutors festered in the seedbed of their affliction. For Paul, the resentment expressed in 1 Thess. 2:13–16 undoubtedly flowed, at least in part, from the recent injuries he and the Thessalonians had experienced at the hands of their persecutors. Paul's troubles in Thessalonica were but one episode in a career of adversity from Jewish opponents. He had experienced opposition from this source in the past

---

The Rhetoric of Slander (from Johnson 1989, 430–41)

A philosopher about the sophists: "ignorant, boastful, self-deceived," "evil-spirited" (Dio Chrysostom, *Or.* 4.33, 38).

A rhetorician about the philosophers: "They despise others while being themselves worthy of scorn. They criticize others without examining themselves" (Aelius Aristides, *Platonic Discourses* 307.6).

An Epicurean philosopher about Academic philosophers: they are "buffoons, char-latans, assassins, prostitutes, nincompoops" (Plutarch, *Mor.* 1086E).

A Greek pagan about the Jews: they are seditious (Josephus, *Ag. Ap.* 2.68), atheists, and misanthropes (Josephus, *Ag. Ap.* 2.148); their practices are ridiculous (Josephus, *Ag. Ap.* 1.210).

A Jew to a gentile critic: Apion has "the mind of an ass and the impudence of a dog, which his countrymen are wont to worship. An outsider can make no sense of his lies" (Josephus, *Ag. Ap.* 2.86).

A Jew about the Egyptians: they are "a seedbed of evil in whose souls both the venom and the temper of the native crocodiles and wasps are reproduced" (Philo, *Legat.* 26.166).

A Jew about Zealot and Sicarii Jews: "Every dictate of religion is ridiculed by these men who scoffed at the prophets' oracles as imposter's fables" (Josephus, *J.W.* 4.385).

The Qumran Essenes declared their "hatred" of all those outside their community, including all other Jews (1QS II.4–10; IV.914; Josephus, *J.W.* 2.139).

(2 Cor. 11:22–29), and even as he wrote, he continued to experience it (1 Thess. 2:16).

Ultimately, the purpose of Paul's outburst was not just to vent his anger. Rather, his purpose was also deeply paraenetic. For those who were currently suffering, like the Thessalonians, the prospect of future final vindication would surely be encouraging.

Tracing the Train of Thought

The Thessalonians' Embrace of the Gospel (2:13)

2:13. Paul now offers a second reason for giving God thanks (**for this reason also**), thus renewing the outflow of thanks that extended for nine verses in the letter's opening (1:2–10). Further grounds for thanksgiving will continue intermittently all the way through 3:13. Some scholars therefore suggest that the thanksgiving section runs from 1:2 all the way through 2:16 (Doty 1973, 43) or even 3:13 (Schubert 1939, 26; Jewett 1986, 71–72), and some assert that the letter as a whole can be considered a "thankful letter" (Schubert 1939, 26; Jewett 1986, 71–72). Much of the material that intervenes between 1:2–10 and 2:13–16, however, cannot be considered part of the "thanksgiving" in any overt sense. Instead, Paul appears to launch into thanksgiving twice, first in 1:2–10 and then again in 2:13–16 (Best 1979, 109).

The same sequence of thought is repeated in both places. In the first thanksgiving, Paul had given God thanks that his "gospel" did not fix itself within the Thessalonians "in word only" but that it also "resulted in action" (1:5). Likewise here, Paul recalls that the Thessalonians had received his gospel **not as a word of human beings but—as it truly is—as a word of God, who is also at work** in them.

The continuative conjunction **and** in 2:13 shows how closely this section connects with the previous one. Verses 1–12 present a tight connection between the gospel's efficacy in the Thessalonians' lives, on the one hand, and its origins from God, on the other. This connection is now further elaborated on in 2:13. Specifically, verse 13 points back to and expands on the observation made in 2:1, that the gospel the Thessalonians received ("what kind of arrival we had among you") also manifested itself in their lives ("was not in vain"). Thus, in all three sections encountered so far (1:2–10; 2:1–12, 13–16), Paul affirms (1) that the Thessalonians earnestly welcomed the gospel and (2) that it resulted in their action (1:5; 2:1, 13). But 2:1–12 and now 2:13–16 make another, closely related point: (3) the message the Thessalonians received was a message from God. This point, however, turns out to be virtually synonymous with the point about the message's efficacy ("was not in vain," 2:1; "a word of God, who is also at work in you," 2:13). That is, the nature of the message as God's *implies* its efficacy, just as the "word" (*logos*) itself functions synonymously with "power" (*dynamis*; 2 Cor. 6:7; cf. the "gospel" as God's "power" in Rom. 1:16). In this respect, Paul's emphasis in 2:1–12 on the message as having originated with God is another way of saying that the message has inherent efficacious potential.

Paul recalls that, despite receiving the gospel through human agents, the Thessalonians received the message as if it was the word of God: **although you received a word of God reported through us, you received it not as a word of human beings but—as it truly is—as a word of God, who is also at work in you who believe.** Note the contrast between "a word of God" on the one hand and what is "reported through us [humans]" on the other, and between "a word of human beings" on the one hand and "as it truly is—a word of God" on the other. In the NT, the word "received" (*paralabontes*) often designates the transmission of church traditions from one person or church to another (1 Cor. 11:23a; 15:3; Phil. 4:9; 2 Thess. 3:6); here it refers to a message received by the Thessalonians directly from Paul, and by Paul originally from God. By saying this, Paul means neither to characterize his words as verbally inspired nor to defend his message against those who might impugn it. His statement, rather, concerns *what* the message is and thus what power lies in it: his message is not a *weak* one but rather a *powerful* (i.e., effective) one. That is why it has yielded fruit in the Thessalonians.

Opposition to the Thessalonians (2:14)

2:14. The Thessalonians did indeed receive the effective word of God into their lives: for they have been put to the test and so far have withstood their trials.

Here again ties with the preceding sections are evident. "You became an example to the churches in Macedonia and Achaia" (1:7) is now distinctly echoed in **You, brothers and sisters, in turn became imitators of the churches of God in Christ Jesus that are in Judea.** The context offers no clues as to why Paul chooses the

---

Seneca on the Test of Suffering

The value of suffering as a test of virtue was frequently underscored by the philosophers, especially the Stoics. Without being tested, they emphasized, the strength of one's commitment could not be known.

"I should bestow greater praise upon those goods that have stood trial." (Seneca, *Ep.* 66.51, trans. Gummere, LCL)

"Is there any doubt that the strength that cannot be overcome is a truer sort than that which is unassailed, seeing that uncontested powers are dubious?" (Seneca, *Const.* 3.4, trans. Basore, LCL)

"It is only evil fortune that discovers a great exemplar." (Seneca, *Ep.* 3.4, trans. Gummere, LCL)

Judean churches for comparison (for other churches are also likely to have been persecuted). Perhaps it was because of the primacy of the Jerusalem church in the early Christian movement (Gal. 2:6–10), or because the Macedonian and Jerusalem churches suffered common economic misfortune (2 Cor. 8:2; cf. 1 Thess. 4:10–12), or because Paul intended to hint at the irony of the fact that he was a former persecutor of the Jerusalem church (Gal. 1:13, 22–23). In any case, his reference to the Judean churches further extends the network of churches to which he draws attention in the letter (1:8, "Macedonia, Achaia, and every place"; 2:14, churches in Judea) and thus reminds the listeners that believers elsewhere share the same experiences as theirs and can mutually embolden one another with their steadfastness.

The comparison between churches focuses on two points: first, that both churches suffered, and second, that both of them suffered at the hands of their neighbors (**You** also suffered the same things at the hands of your own countrymen as also *they* did at the hands of the Jews). The term *Ioudaioi* (usually translated "Jews") in one sense denotes *geographical* origins (those who inhabit the province of Judea), but *Ioudaioi* was also the normal term gentiles used to refer to *ethnic* Jews and the most common term used in the NT to refer to ethnic Jews. Jewish persecution against the Jerusalem church is hinted at in Galatians (4:29; 6:12) and is best known to have occurred at the hands of Paul himself in his pre-Christian days (Acts 8:3; Gal. 1:13, 22–23). Set parallel to the term "Jews," the term *symphyletēs* (usually translated "countrymen" or "compatriots") could refer here to *location* (those who live in Thessalonica), *ethnicity* (Thessalonian gentiles), or *political status* (citizens of Thessalonica). If the term carries a sense parallel to that of "Jews" (*Ioudaioi*), it would designate local residents who are specifically of gentile ethnicity. The parallel, however, need not be exact. While in Greek literature *symphetetēs* sometimes has ethnic connotations, the term could

Jewish Persecution of the Jerusalem Church

Direct evidence for Jewish persecution of the Jerusalem church is limited, but not entirely lacking. Paul confesses that he had persecuted the church (1 Cor. 15:9; Gal. 1:13; Phil. 3:6–8), as Acts also attests (7:58–8:3; 9:1–4). Acts recounts the martyrdom of Stephen (6:8–7:60) and the anxious reaction and "persecution" (*diōgmos*) of the Jerusalem Christians around 36 CE (8:1–3), as well as the martyrdom of James the son of Zebedee under Agrippa around 41 CE (12:2). Marcus Bockmuehl (2001), moreover, has proposed that the witness of a sixth-century chronicler regarding a persecution of the Jerusalem church "in the eighth year of Claudius" (48/49 CE), while shaky as a historical source on its own, would help shed light on Paul's reference in 1 Thess. 2:14 as well as the situation addressed in Galatians, where persecution of Jerusalem Christians is apparent (6:12).

also refer to fellow residents (Tellbe 2001, 115). This broader meaning opens the possibility that "countrymen" refers here to both local gentiles *and* local Jews. In either case, Paul's words seem to comport with the account given in Acts 17:5–13. Though it is "the Jews" who become jealous of Paul, instigate a plot that results in his forced departure from the city, and pursue him as far as Berea, they are assisted by local "ruffians," presumably gentiles, whom they have recruited. When Paul slipped away (17:10), the locals' enmity toward Paul is likely to have fallen on the Thessalonian believers, as it had upon Jason (17:6–9).

The language **suffered at the hands** surely suggests physical violence. This expression (*paschein hypo*) is used in only three other places in the NT. In one instance it refers to extreme physical procedures carried out at the hands of physicians (Mark 5:26); in the other two it refers to the killing of Jesus as an analogue to the killing of the prophets (Matt. 17:12; Mark 8:31; cf. 1 Kings 19:1–10, esp. 19:2; and the violent language used in 1 Thess. 2:15).

Opposition to Paul (2:15–16)

2:15–16. Mention of "the Jews" triggers a vehement digression, in which Paul piles up a litany of incriminating accusations: **who killed not only the prophets but also Jesus the Lord, and who drove us out and are not pleasing to God and who oppose all humanity, hindering us from speaking to the gentiles so that they might be saved, thereby filling up their sins continually. "And finally the wrath came upon them."** As most interpreters and English translations agree, *grammatically* the charges appear not to be restricted to a particular group of Jews (*"the Jews who* killed the prophets") but apply to Jews generally (*"the Jews,* who killed the prophets"). All the same, Paul cannot have intended to say that all Jews had done such things. In the first place, as Paul well knew, there is no specific set of Jews who could have "killed both the prophets and Jesus" as well as "hindered" Paul "from speaking to the gentiles" (though Gilliard 1989 argues that Paul is referring to several specific groups). Paul's digression, moreover, reflects patent signs of rhetorical embellishment: "killed Jesus" alleges *direct* responsibility for a crime ultimately carried out by the Roman government, and "oppose all humanity" is self-evidently hyperbolic. Other contextual indicators also show that the charges are in reality more restrictive. First, "the Jews" are made to parallel "your own countrymen," which is certainly not intended to be all-inclusive but is obviously qualitative: it refers not to *how many* people (i.e., every person who lives in Thessalonica) but to *what kind* of people were responsible for the persecution ("fellow countrymen"). Second, Paul's most immediate concerns here place a more restrictive group in view: aside from the charges that the Jews killed Jesus and the prophets, of nearest concern are the Judean Jews who persecuted the churches "in Judea"; the Jews who are presently "preventing" Paul "from speaking to the gentiles"; and apparently and very specifically, the Thessalonian Jews who "drove him out" of Thessalonica.

Though Paul initially names the Judean churches as the targets of persecution, he quickly shifts attention back to himself: "who drove us out . . . and who

Critique of the Jewish People in the OT and Early Christianity

Those who maintain that 2:13–16 reflects a post-Pauline interpolation assert that this passage reflects Christian anti-Semitic polemic characteristic of Christian rhetoric only from the postapostolic age onward. Although it was indeed common for Christian texts to blame Jews for the death of Jesus (Acts 2:33, 36; 3:15; 4:10; 7:52) and for the killing of the prophets (Matt. 23:29–38), the idea that the Jews killed the prophets was not, however, a postapostolic Christian invention but owed its origins to the OT (1 Kings 19:10; 2 Chron. 36:15–16; Jer. 2:30; cf. Neh. 9:27, 30). This accusation is also found in Second Temple literature (2 Esd. [*4 Ezra*] 1:32) and rabbinic literature (*Pesiq. Rab.* 26 [129a]). Moreover, the pronouncement of wrath upon Israel, as seen in 1 Thess. 2:16, is also an OT theme (Num. 12:9; 2 Chron. 19:2; 25:15; 28:9; Zech. 7:12). Finally, intra-Jewish critique was exceedingly common during Paul's era, and much of it was more extreme than is found here (see "The Rhetoric of Slander" sidebar above). In sum, Paul's polemic here finds precedent in both the OT and the polemics of Paul's day and is best characterized as "intra-Jewish critique."

oppose all humanity, hindering us from speaking to the gentiles so that they might be saved." The aorist-tense form shows that "drove out" refers to a specific past event. It makes good sense to see this event as Paul's recent banishment from Thessalonica (cf. 2:17–18; Acts 17:10). If this event is in view, then the letter of 1 Thessalonians confirms another point in the Acts account of Paul's founding visit in Thessalonica (see introduction to 1 Thessalonians): that Paul's departure from Thessalonica was hasty, forced, and instigated by local Jews.

As Acts hints, the concerns of the Jews in Thessalonica may have been political in nature. When they (and the local "ruffians") seized Jason and dragged him before the city's authorities, they claimed that Paul and his people "have been turning the world upside down" and "have come here also, and . . . They are all acting contrary to the decrees of the emperor, saying that there is another king named Jesus" (Acts 17:6–7 NRSV). If Acts correctly identifies the issue, then the Jews may have believed that Paul's activity could upset the relationship between local Jews and the city's authorities. Indeed, Mikael Tellbe (2001) has argued that Christians during this period were still closely associated with Jews in the public eye: thus any perception that the Christians were politically disloyal could spoil protections that the local Jews enjoyed from the Roman government. In this regard, the Jews might have been opposing Paul and the Christians in order to ensure their own safety.

As possible as this interpretation may be, Paul here identifies their opposition as being related specifically to his ministry to "the gentiles." Substantial evidence suggests that in most cases those who opposed Paul's gentile mission probably did so out of indignation with his non-requirement of the law for gentile proselytes (cf. Still 1999, 190). "Zealots" for the Mosaic law (see sidebar), who modeled themselves after Jewish heroes like Phinehas (Num. 25:1–13) and the Maccabees (1 Macc. 2:23–60), stood ready to take violent action against those who flouted the law's requirements, as Paul himself was prepared to do before his Damascus experience (Gal. 1:13–14, 22–23; Acts 8:3).

Paul's assertion that the Jews "oppose all humanity" should also be understood in connection with his gentile ministry and not with the Jews' reputation as misanthropes, as they are often alleged to be in pagan sources (e.g., Tacitus, *Hist.* 5.5; Philostratus, *Vit. Apoll.* 5.33; Juvenal, *Sat.* 14.103.4; Josephus, *Ag. Ap.* 2.121). Paul, in short, means that the Jews oppose "humanity," not in every way, but specifically *by* hindering the salvation of gentile humanity.

In a coup de grâce, Paul finishes his outburst of vitriol against the Jews by declaring the final falling of God's "wrath upon them" (2:16). Most English Bible translations render the final part of this verse in either of two ways: (1) "at last" (ESV, NIV, NRSV; or "finally," NAB) or (2) "to the uttermost" (KJV; or "to the utmost," NASB). Some scholars opt for a third meaning, translating *eis telos* as "until the end." That is, God's wrath is poured out for a time, but in the end he relents and all Israel is saved (Gaventa 1998, 37). The second and third options seem less probable. The second ("to the uttermost") misses the parallelism between the final elements of 2:16b (*pantote*) and 2:16c (*eis telos*). The third option on the other hand shifts the mood in the opposite direction from the one it has been taking at just the moment when one would expect it to come to its climax, and leaves quite a new, undeveloped thought dangling at the end of the sentence (i.e., what happens at the end?). The complementary relationship between *pantote* and *eis telos* at the end of successive clauses shows that the first sense is the correct one: the Jews fill up their sins "continually," until "finally" the wrath of God's cup overflows on them. The notion of "filling up" sins until they have reached a

---

Zealots for the Law

"When he had finished speaking these words, a Jew came forward in the sight of all to offer sacrifice on the altar in Modein, according to the king's command. When Mattathias saw it, he burned with zeal and his heart was stirred. He gave vent to righteous anger; he ran and killed him on the altar. At the same time he killed the king's officer who was forcing them to sacrifice, and he tore down the altar. Thus he burned with zeal for the law, just as Phinehas did against Zimri son of Salu. Then Mattathias cried out in the town with a loud voice, saying: 'Let every one who is zealous for the law and supports the covenant come out with me!'" (1 Macc. 2:23–27 NRSV)

"There are thousands who are watchful, zealots for the laws, strictest guardians of the ancestral institutions, merciless to those who do anything to subvert them." (Philo, *Spec.* 2.253, trans. Colson, LCL)

limit finds precedent in the OT (Gen. 15:16; Dan. 8:23) and in other Jewish texts (*LAB* 26.1–3; cf. God's determination of a final limit to evil: 2 Macc. 6:14; 2 Esd. [*4 Ezra*] 4:34–37; 7:74; *2 Bar.* 48.2–5).

The final difficulty is deciding whether "wrath" refers to judgment that occurred in the past, that is occurring in the present, or that will occur in the future. The aorist indicative (*ephthasen*) would normally indicate past action (in addition to undefined aspect; see Brookins 2018). Paul would then be equating God's wrath with some catastrophic event that had affected Jews in recent history (i.e., since Jesus's crucifixion). From Paul's vantage point, several potentially qualifying events had occurred just a few years before his visit to Thessalonica, and some perhaps within weeks. Possible events include the pogrom against Alexandrian Jews in 38 CE, the failed insurrection of Theudas in 44–46 (Acts 5:36), the famine in Judea in 46–47 (18:11), the expulsion of Jews from Rome in 49 (18:2), and the crushed Jerusalem riots in 48–51. The aorist in this instance, however, is more likely proleptic (the so-called proleptic aorist) and its action is conceived as a past event only from the vantage point of the future. At least two considerations point in this direction. First, the basis of judgment here is the persecution of God's people. Within an apocalyptic framework, God's judgment on his people's persecutors is generally regarded as occurring in the final judgment, at which point the roles of persecutor and persecuted are reversed (4 Macc. 9:8–9; Wis. 4:16–5:23; cf. *2 Bar.* 51.1–16), a pattern also explicitly reflected in 2 Thess. 1:4–7. Moreover, operating on the assumption that 1 Thess. 2:13–16 is authentic (which most interpreters now do), the proleptic aorist provides a solution to what is otherwise a historical difficulty: the catastrophic events that afflicted Jews in the 40s, while horrific, were local and do not seem like fitting retribution for the specific Jews who persecuted the Judean churches, the Thessalonians, or Paul himself.

Furthermore, the proleptic use of the aorist is both grammatically permissible and readily intelligible in the context. The proleptic aorist is indeed not uncommon in Paul's letters and occurs several times where actions are conceived from the vantage point of the eschaton (see Rom. 8:30; 1 Cor. 15:49; Phil. 2:16; see also Rev. 10:7). Yet there is also another possibility to consider. If the saying in 1 Thess. 2:16c is either a citation or proverbial, the verb tense would be fixed and the past tense retained despite the time at which the action occurred. The saying "the wrath of God came upon them" would then function similarly to something like the English pronouncement, "And so it *ended*," as is sometimes stated in the events leading *up to* a disaster. In support of a proverbial meaning here, a very close parallel to Paul's words occurs in Ps. 78:31 (77:31 LXX; cf. Ezek. 5:13; 6:12; 20:21), and although the dating is uncertain (2nd cent. BCE through the 2nd cent. CE), the exact expression occurs in the *Testament of Levi*, with only the addition of a single word (*kyriou*, "of the Lord"). Compare the following:

kai orgē tou theou anebē ep' autous, "and the wrath of God went up against them" (Ps. 77:31 LXX) *ephthasen de hē orgē kyriou ep' autous eis telos*, "and the wrath of the Lord came upon them at last" (*T. Levi* 6.11)

ephthasen de ep' autous hē orgē eis telos, "and the wrath came upon them at last" (1 Thess. 2:16)

It seems best, then, to regard Paul's words as referring to a future event and the aorist as being retained due to the fixed wording/expression of the proverb.

Theological Issues

The Testing of Faith

For the Thessalonians, as for many Christians throughout history, and still in many parts of the world today, their commitment was tested in the crucible of suffering. This is a test that most Christians in the Western world do not face; and yet to some degree commitment cannot be known until it is tested. It cannot be helped if one lives in a hospitable environment, and this could even be counted a blessing. However, the experiences of Christians like the Thessalonian believers can, for currently unthreatened believers, present a challenge to search their own commitments and to prepare themselves for the possibility of more serious trials in the future.

Vindication and Vengeance

Persecution understandably engenders feelings of resentment in the persecuted. Faced with injustice, a longing for vindication is natural. However, there is a fine line between wanting *vindication* and wanting *vengeance*. While Paul makes a series of accusations against "the Jews" in 1 Thess. 2:13–16, he does not resort to insults against them (cf. Josephus, *Ag. Ap.* 1.210; 2.68), express hatred for them (cf. 1QS I.4, 10–11; Josephus, *J.W.* 2.139), rejoice in their punishment (cf. *1 En.* 62.11–12), or beseech God to curse them (cf. 1QS II.5–10). Rather, Paul leaves judgment to God (cf. Rom. 12:19–21; Malherbe 2000, 178).

Persecutors and the Persecuted

Out of historical context, Paul's denunciation of his Jewish persecutors has frightening potential for misinterpretation and misuse. In many parts of the world, the situation of Christians has radically changed. In Paul's day, Christians represented the persecuted minority of a movement within Judaism. In this light, Paul's impassioned denunciation of "the Jews" becomes more understandable, even excusable. Yet Christians must be conscious that, at many times and places, they have become the dominant group, and Jews have themselves become the persecuted. Now, when Christian ill will is far less likely to be a response to personal injury, and when Christianity is no longer seen to be within the boundaries of

Judaism, vilification of any or all Jews on theological grounds can be considered anti-Semitic in the truest sense of the term. Such an attitude can and has engendered horrific acts of antagonism and violence. While care should be taken to place these verses within their proper historical context (as we have sought to do here), one should also bear in mind the hurtful potential of these verses for many people today and thus handle them with extreme delicacy.

1 Thessalonians 2:17–3:13

Paul's Desire to Visit Again

Introductory Matters

The section 2:17–3:10 forms a discrete unit marked off by an *inclusio*: "we made the greatest haste to see your face, with great longing" (2:17) and "praying earnestly to see your face" (3:10). When 3:11–13 is added, four subsections can be discerned: Paul's failed attempts to visit the Thessalonians (2:17–20), Paul's dispatch of Timothy to Thessalonica (3:1–5), the return of Timothy to Paul (3:6–10), and Paul's prayer for a fresh visit and for the sanctification of the Thessalonians (3:11–13).

The literary context of 1 Thess. 2:17–3:10. While many scholars think that 2:17–3:10 connects most naturally with 2:1–12 (with 2:13–16 intruding as an interpolation), this section actually makes reasonably good sense after 2:13–16. Indeed, Paul here recounts the next chapter in his "history" with the Thessalonians, so that the following sequence in the narrative is evident:

- "We preached the gospel to you when we were among you." (2:1–12)
- "You received the message readily." (2:13)
- "You imitated the churches in their suffering." (2:14)
- "We were driven away from you by the Jews." (2:15–16)
- "Although we have been separated from you, we still want to see you." (2:17–18)

In short, while 2:1–13 covers Paul's time *with* the Thessalonians, and 2:14–16 recalls his *banishment from* Thessalonica, 2:17 and following now covers his *time away from* the Thessalonians.

The style of 1 Thess. 2:17–3:13. The epistolary style of 2:17–3:13 is consistent with what precedes. Although the letter's first three chapters include two lengthy "thanksgiving" sections (1:2–10; 2:13–16) and then a final exclamation of thanks (3:9) just before a prayer commences at the close of chapter 3 (3:11–13), 2:17–3:13 shows that the category of "thankful" letter (Schubert 1939, 26; Jewett 1986, 71–72) on the whole does not fit the content of these chapters as well as the "paraenetic" category does (Malherbe 1983). Paul's "philophronetic" (friendly) purposes here are reaffirmed by his use of stock elements typical of friendly letters (Klauck 2006, 188–93; Malherbe 1983, 241; 2000, 180). These elements include reassurance that his separation from the Thessalonians is merely physical (2:17; cf. 2 Cor. 10:11; Phil. 1:27; 1 Cor. 5:3; Col. 2:5); assurance of his affection for them despite his absence (2:17); reaffirmation of his desire to see them (2:17, 18; 3:6, 11; cf. Rom. 1:11); acknowledgment of their desire to see him (3:6); mention of their mutual love for each other (3:12); mention of the Thessalonian believers as a source of joy (2:19–20); the expression of joy over their well-being (3:7–9); the connection between Paul's well-being and their own (3:8); prayer for their well-being (3:10, 12); Paul's desire to encourage them in their faith (3:2, 13); and appeal to his example (3:12).

> **1 Thessalonians 2:17–3:13 in the Rhetorical Flow**
>
> **Letter opening (1:1–10)**
>
> **Letter body (2:1–5:22)**
>
> **Paul's ministry in Thessalonica (2:1–12)**
>
> **Renewed thanksgiving (2:13–16)**
>
> ▶ **Paul's desire to visit again (2:17–3:13)**
>
> Paul's failed attempts to visit (2:17–20)
>
> Paul's dispatch of Timothy (3:1–5)
>
> The return of Timothy (3:6–10)
>
> Prayer for a fresh visit and for strength (3:11–13)

These "friendly" elements undermine the oft-cited claim of Robert Funk (1967, 258–65) that this letter, like Paul's other letters, was intended to embody his "apostolic parousia," or the presence of his *authority* even in his absence (cf. Rom. 15:14–33; 1 Cor. 4:14–21; Phil. 2:19–24; Philem. 21–22), and that the apostolic-parousia concept is illustrated in 1 Thess. 2:17–20 in particular. To the contrary, the friendly features of this section demonstrate that Paul's purpose here is not to convey authority, but rather *philophronēsis*, "goodwill."

Tracing the Train of Thought

Paul's Failed Attempts to Visit (2:17–20)

2:17–20. Paul now resumes the account of his "history" with the Thessalonians, shifting attention back to himself (**and** *we*) after having briefly discussed the Thessalonians and the Jews in 2:13–16. Paul referred to himself as a "child" (2:7), a "nurse" (2:7), and a "father" (2:11) earlier in the chapter. Now he compares himself to an **orphan** in his separation from the Thessalonians. Reading between the lines, this section confirms Acts' report that Paul's separation from the Thessalonians occurred precipitously and quite against his will (Acts 17:5–10). Paul's attempts to return **time and again** (v. 18), as he says, and desiring to do so with **the greatest haste** and **with great longing** after being separated from them **for a period of a mere hour** suggest that he had been forced out of Thessalonica under what he felt to be irresistible pressure. Though the circumstances prohibited it, his own wish (**we wanted**) was to see them **face-to-face**.

The heartfelt insistence with which he emphasizes his desire to see the Thessalonians hints at a concern that they may have questioned his affection. The very man who persuaded them to "turn from idols to the living and true God" (1:9) skips town just when the consequences of their conversion are becoming acutely evident. Would they not be resentful? Wary of this possibility, Paul underscores his deep personal affection for them by switching from the predominant first-person plural to the first-person singular (see also 3:5; 5:27), the first of only three instances of the singular in the letter: **I, Paul**. The switch could indicate that the letter's plurals are genuine and that the reference is to Paul only when the singular is used. If, however, Paul writes as the executive representative of the group (as was proposed in the introduction), the switch serves instead to *emphasize* his individuality.

After recounting at length in 1:2–2:14 the initial success of his ministry, Paul now builds on 2:15–16 by continuing to underscore how his ministry among the Thessalonians has since been frustrated. Though the Thessalonians "received" his proclamation as "a word of God" (2:14), the Jews then "drove" him out and "hindered" him from proclaiming salvation to the gentiles (2:15–16). Now **Satan** has **thwarted** him from returning. Paul's attribution of responsibility to Satan is unusual; elsewhere Paul describes his movements as being constrained either by the "will" of God (1 Cor. 4:19; 16:7; cf. 1 Thess. 3:11) or by his preoccupation in other parts of the world (Rom. 15:14–23; cf. 1:10–13). The actions attributed to Satan here are nevertheless true to the root sense of his name: "the Adversary" (from the Aramaic Śāṭān; see Job 1:6–2:7; 1 Chron. 21:1; Zech. 3:1–2). For Paul, Satan's opposition took the form of "tempting" (3:5; 1 Cor. 7:5), "deceiving" (2 Cor. 2:11; cf. 11:14), or any other activity that threatened to block or reverse the progress of his ministry.

This need not mean that Satan had intervened supernaturally—for instance, by striking Paul with illness. Rather, Paul may have discerned Satan acting through human agents. The idea that humans could serve as mediators of Satan's purposes is abundantly attested in Second Temple Jewish as well as early Christian texts. The Dead Sea Scrolls identify the unrighteous as the "sons of darkness," as the "army of Belial" (1QM I.1–17). In Rev. 13:1–18 the power of Satan is depicted as being embodied in the Roman emperor. Early Christian martyr literature often identifies humans, especially governing officials, as agents of satanic activity (cf.

Mart. Pol. 17.1–2; Origen, *Cels.* 8.65; Eusebius, *Hist. eccl.* 5.1). In 2 Corinthians, Paul refers to certain pseudo-apostles as "messengers" of Satan (11:14–15). Since Acts depicts Paul's departure as precipitated by allegations against him before the city's administration, conceivably Paul's reference to satanic opposition here indicates an embargo against his return, ordered perhaps by a specific Roman official in Thessalonica (cf. Acts 17:9) and seen from Paul's perspective as an order instigated by "the Satan." If the Thessalonians were aware that such an order existed, then Paul's indirect reference to it here could intend to clarify that it was this, and not a lack of personal affection for them, that prevented his returning.

Verse 19 further explicates why Paul longs earnestly to visit. He asks: **What is our hope or joy or crown of boasting—or is it *not* indeed you?** The second question, "*or* is it not indeed you?" indicates an implicit rejoinder to a thought that he imagines may have entered their minds: that he did not care about them. On the contrary, this is why he is eager to return: because he holds them very dear. To drive his point home, Paul continues to make abundant use of stock elements of "friendly" letters (Klauck 2006, 188–93), including reassurance that their separation is only physical (2:17; cf. Phil. 1:27; 1 Cor. 5:3; 2 Cor. 10:11; Col. 2:5; Seneca, *Ep.* 35.3; 40.1; 55.11; 67.2), reaffirmation of his desire to see them (2:17–18; *BGU* 2:385.4–6; *PSI* 10:1161.11–19; Ps.-Demetrius, *Epistolary Types* 1; cf. Rom. 1:11), and declaration that they are a source of joy to him (2:19–20; Seneca, *Ep.* 35.3).

Conventions of "Friendly" Letters

"We feel a joy over those whom we love, even when separated from them." (Seneca, *Ep.* 35.3, trans. Gummere, LCL)

"I never receive a letter from you without being in your company forthwith. If the pictures of our absent friends are pleasing to us, though they only refresh to the memory and lighten our longing by a solace that is unreal and unsubstantial, how much more pleasant is a letter, which brings us real traces, real evidences, of an absent friend!" (Seneca, *Ep.* 40.1, trans. Gummere, LCL)

"A friend should be retained in the spirit; such a friend can never be absent. He can see every day whomsoever he desires to see." (Seneca, *Ep.* 55.11, trans. Gummere, LCL)

"Whenever your letters arrive, I imagine that I am with you, and I have the feeling that I am about to speak my answer, instead of writing it. Therefore let us together investigate the nature of this problem of yours, just as if we were conversing with one another." (Seneca, *Ep.* 67.2, trans. Gummere, LCL)

"Even though I have been separated from you for a long time, I suffer this in body only." (Ps.-Demetrius, *Epistolary Types* 1)

Paul pushes the Thessalonians' importance to the highest possible level by affirming that they are, and will be, his hope and joy and crown of boasting when he stands **before our Lord Jesus upon his coming** (2:19; cf. 2 Cor. 5:10). That is, the Thessalonians hold eschatological significance for him and will stand as proof of his faithfulness at the final judgment. Paul's letters show that he viewed his communities as exhibits of his faithfulness and as critical for determining his final fate at the judgment (1 Thess. 2:19; 1 Cor. 3:11–15; 4:1–5; 9:2; 2 Cor. 3:2). Thus, in a metonymic sense the Thessalonians are the *cause* for his hope of salvation, a *cause* of the joy received therein, and a *cause* of the crown conferred upon him at the judgment.

Though the expression **crown of boasting** derives from the LXX (Ezek. 16:12; 23:42; Prov. 16:31), the concept shares resonances with athletic metaphors often employed in Greco-Roman philosophical literature, which identify the crown as the reward of virtue (Dio Chrysostom, *Or.* 8.11; Seneca, *Ep.* 78.16). The metaphor was adapted in Hellenistic-Jewish (Philo, *Mut.* 1.82; *T. Job* 4.10–11; 27.3–5; cf. Wis. 4:2) and early Christian texts (1 Pet. 5:4; James 1:12; Rev. 3:11). Paul expands the metaphor in 1 Cor. 9:24–27, where he uses it with reference to believers' eschatological reward ("running in a race," "receive the prize," "receive an incorruptible crown," etc.), not least his own ("lest somehow I be disqualified"). Here Paul's reference to a reward and his right to "boast" could be taken to suggest the merits of a human achievement, even though he decries boasting at many points

The Figurative "Crown" as a Reward

A crown for the virtuous:

"What blows do athletes receive on their faces and all over their bodies! Nevertheless, through their desire for fame they endure every torture. . . . So let us also win the way to victory in all our struggles,—for their reward is not a garland or a palm or a trumpeter who calls for silence at the proclamation of our names, but rather virtue, steadfastness of soul, and a peace that is won for all time." (Seneca, *Ep.* 78.16, trans. Gummere, LCL)

"And what garland more fitting for its purpose or of richer flowers could be woven for the victorious soul than the power which will enable him to behold the Existent with clear vision? Surely that is a glorious guerdon to offer to the athlete-soul, that it should be endowed with eyes to apprehend in bright light Him Who alone is worthy of our contemplation." (Philo, *Mut.* 1.82, trans. Colson, LCL)

A crown for the persecuted or martyred:

"Blessed is the man who remains steadfast under trial, for when he has stood the test he will receive the crown of life." (James 1:12 ESV)

in his letters (1 Cor. 1:29; 3:21; 4:7; 2 Cor. 5:12). His boast, however, shines the spotlight not on himself but on the Thessalonians.

For good measure, Paul repeats himself: the Thessalonians are his **glory and joy** (2:20). Again, the reference is eschatological. This is not the "glory" of status earned by good merit (as in 2:6) but the almost physical splendor characteristic of a glorified human body. A number of Second Temple texts describe glory as an original attribute of Adam, lost when he disobeyed by eating from the tree, but still recoverable (1QS IV.23; CD III.20; 1QH[a] IV.15; cf. *T. Ab.* 11.9). Paul's later letters make explicit that this glory derives from association with Christ (Rom. 8:17; Col. 1:27; 3:4) and will be characteristic of the resurrection body (Rom. 8:18, 21; 1 Cor. 15:43; 2 Cor. 4:16–17; Phil. 3:21; Col. 3:4). Such glory awaited Paul, thanks in part to the Thessalonians.

Paul's Dispatch of Timothy (3:1–5)

3:1–3. No longer able to bear their separation (**bearing it no longer**), Paul was forced to make a tough decision: **We thought it best to be left alone in Athens.** These remarks pose substantial historical difficulties. Since Paul continues to speak in the first-person plural, the word "alone" (*monoi*) occurs in the nominative plural in agreement with the subject ("*we* thought it best to be left *alone* in Athens"). At this point a decision about the meaning of the first-person plural is necessary in order to determine Paul's situation at the time of writing, a decision that has bearing on the question of agreement between Paul's letter and the narrative of Acts.

The plural *monoi* cannot include Timothy: it is the departure of Timothy that results in the subject's/subjects' being left "alone." Thus there are only two possible referents. Either the plural refers to Paul and Silvanus (if this is a "genuine" plural), or it refers strictly to Paul as an individual (if this is a "literary" plural). Both options present problems. If the plural is genuine, then Acts would conflict with Paul's letter by depicting him as being singularly alone in Athens while Silvanus and Timothy apparently remained in Macedonia (Acts 17:10–15). If the plural is literary, on the other hand, then Paul indicates that he was left in Athens quite alone. Although the latter scenario would comport with the account given in Acts on one point (that Paul was alone in Athens), the implication given in 1 Thess. 3:1, that Timothy had been with him before being dispatched, would not (cf. Acts 17:15).

In deciding between these options, it should be observed that in 3:5 Paul repeats the statement that he made in 3:1 about his decision to send Timothy, in virtually identical form, but now with verbs in the first-person singular. Compare "putting up with it no longer, *we* thought it best to be left alone and *we* sent" (3:1) with **I, putting up with it no longer, sent** (3:5). The use of the singular in a statement that is otherwise identical to one previously expressed in the plural suggests that the first instance was a literary plural rather than a genuine plural. So while the plural may be genuine elsewhere in the letter, at least in a "weak" sense (see introduction

> ## Comparing Travel Routes in Acts and 1 Thessalonians
>
> *According to Acts:* (1) Paul and Silas (and probably Timothy) from Thessalonica to Berea; (2) Paul from Berea to Athens, then Corinth; (3) Silas and Timothy to Corinth.
>
> *According to 1 Thessalonians:* (1) Paul (and Silvanus and Timothy?) from Thessalonica toward Achaia; (2) Paul (and Silvanus and Timothy?) in Athens; (3) Timothy to Thessalonica; (4) Timothy from Thessalonica to Paul.
>
> *If these movements could be harmonized:* (1) Paul, Silvanus, and Timothy from Thessalonica to Berea; (2) Paul to Athens; (3) Timothy and Silvanus from Berea to Athens; (4) Timothy to Thessalonica; (5) Silvanus to Macedonia; (6) Paul to Corinth; (7) Timothy and Silvanus from Macedonia to Corinth.

above), the likelihood of a genuine plural here seems to be reduced essentially to zero. This makes "alone" in 3:1 an exclusive reference to Paul. A conflict remains on the question of Timothy's presence in Athens, though one could speculate that Timothy arrived there sometime after the events described in Acts 17:15.

For Paul, Timothy was the next closest thing to himself; if he could not make a personal visit, he was often content to send Timothy as his surrogate (cf. 1 Cor. 4:17; 16:10; Phil. 2:19). Timothy's role in Paul's ministry was in many ways analogous to that of diplomatic emissary (Mitchell 1992, 645–49). Emissaries were regarded as representatives of the sender. They spoke on behalf of the sender and were expected to be received as the sender would be received. They carried not only the sender's authority but also the sentiments of the sender's goodwill. However, the emissary's role worked both ways. Besides expressing the feelings of the sender to the recipients, the emissary also carried the amicable sentiments of the recipients back to the original sender, confirming the two parties' mutual affection for one other and continuing to foster a personal relationship between them even in their separation. As couriers of written communiques, emissaries were also expected to supplement the messages they carried by conveying oral instructions, performing certain

© Baker Publishing Group

Figure 6. Travel routes before and after the founding visit (see sidebar)

requisite actions, or seeing that instructions to the recipients were carried out to completion (Klauck 2006, 63).

Paul names two reasons for sending his emissary. First, he sent **Timothy to strengthen and encourage** the Thessalonians in the **faith** so that they **might not be shaken by these afflictions.** "Faith" here refers not only to what is believed but also to the whole commitment of their lives. Evidently Paul was concerned that their affliction might even induce them to apostatize. Again, his response is paraenetic. In the NT the word "strengthen" (*stērixai*) often refers to steadying a person in the face of persecution (1 Pet. 5:10; Luke 22:32; cf. Acts 14:22). The verb "encourage" (*parakalesai*), also a key term in paraenetic discourse, now appears in its second of eight appearances in the letter (Malherbe 1987, 76). Timothy is to both "strengthen" and "encourage" the Thessalonians, lest their afflictions lead them to falter.

3:4. Here Paul identifies affliction as a general condition of life as a Christ-follower: **We are appointed for this** [kind of life]. Paul reiterates that the Thessalonians **know** this already (cf. 1:5; 2:1, 2, 5, 11; 3:3, 4; 4:2; 5:2), reminding them how he had told them repeatedly that **we** believers **were going to be afflicted** and pointing out now that his words proved to be prophetic (**as also happened and as you know only too well**). What kind of "affliction" Paul has in mind is debated, as is the question whether *these* **afflictions** belonged to Paul or to the Thessalonians. Abraham Malherbe (1987, 65) argues that the affliction was Paul's; that his affliction consisted in distress over the church; that Paul was fearful that his distress might rattle the Thessalonians' faith; and that Paul's purpose was to set the Thessalonians at ease by assuring them that he had been comforted by Timothy's good report. It seems unnecessarily complicated, however, to view Paul's intent to encourage the Thessalonians as a response to their distress over his distress rather than to view his encouragement simply as a response to their own distress.

Moreover, there is convincing evidence in both Acts and 1 Thessalonians that the Thessalonians had recently experienced persecution. Acts states that when the angry mob that collected in the forum could not find Paul, they "dragged Jason and some believers before the city authorities" (Acts 17:6 NRSV) and exacted bail from Jason (17:9). Apart from Acts, several statements made in 1 Thessalonians indicate that the church had experienced persecution. Paul has already mentioned that the Thessalonians had received the word "in much affliction" (1:6) and "suffered at the hands of their countrymen" (2:14). Here Paul reminds them that he had taught them that believers are "going to be afflicted," and now he indicates that they know the accuracy of this promise firsthand ("as also happened and as you know only too well"). Undoubtedly their persecution had a social element. Their radical realignment of social and cultic affiliations must have elicited hostility from others, or at least a degree of social alienation, resulting in significant inner anguish (Richard 1995, 150). However, the term "affliction" often has a physical dimension, as Jewish apocalyptic texts show (*2 Bar.* 27.2, 11, 12; *Jub.* 23.22–25). Moreover, Paul's earlier references to the Thessalonians' suffering after the pattern of Jesus (1:6) and their suffering "at the hands of" their countrymen (2:14) both indicate probable violence (see esp. comments on 2:14).

Paul's counseling approach here has noteworthy affinities to the methods of the philosophers. The Stoics placed heavy emphasis on "preparation" as a way of preventing shock or misjudgment when adversity struck. They said that one must prepare mentally, cultivate a proper perspective, repeat the precepts of truth, rehearse the appropriate actions, and practice willingly living them out before being forced to do so (Epictetus, *Diatr.* 2.18; 3.8.2; 3.10.1, 6–8; 3.11; 3.13.8; 3.15.1–7; 3.24.84, 103; 3.26.13, 39; 4.4.30). In this way one strengthens the mental faculty, enabling it to more accurately evaluate mental "impressions" (*phantasia*) when they occur. "Weakness" (*astheneia*; Long and Sedley 1987, §65T) of mind resulted in an improper evaluation of situations—as good or bad or indifferent—and consequently resulted in poor judgment. Any such lapse of reason was considered a "passion" (Long and Sedley 1987, §65A). Every passion was a "fluttering" (*ptoia*) of the mind because it involved mental fluctuation (Long and Sedley 1987, §65A). Latin texts describe subjects as sometimes being "shaken" by mental impressions (*agitare, quatire; perturbatio*; Seneca, *Ep.* 74.31–33; cf. *Ep.* 71.27–33; Cicero, *Tusc.* 3), implying a certain mental instability or wavering between reason and passion. It is noteworthy that "distress" (*lypē*) was counted among the passions (Cicero, *Tusc.* 3.11.24–25; 4.7.16–22; Diogenes Laërtius, *Vit.* 7.111; Long and Sedley 1987, §65): "an irrational contraction, or a fresh opinion that something bad is present" (Long and Sedley 1987, §65B; translation on p. 411). The Stoics emphasized that through mental preparation one's mind could remain unshaken when distress presented itself.

As the Thessalonians' "teacher," Paul was also their trainer. While he was with them (**also when we were with you**), he had sought to prepare them for adversity and to inculcate a proper perspective by telling them repeatedly (**we kept saying**) that believers would be persecuted (v. 4), and indeed, that they were "appointed" (by Providence?) for this. Paul reminds them of this precept now, though, giving them the benefit of the doubt, he affirms that they already "know" it (vv. 3–4). On top of this, they know it now by experience (because it has "happened" to

---

Philosophy as Preparation

"But what is philosophy? Does it not mean making preparation to meet the things that come upon us? . . . In life, if we stop the pursuit of philosophy, what good does it do? What, then, ought a man to say to himself at each hardship that befalls him? 'It was for this that I kept training, it was to meet this that I used to practise.' . . . Now it is time for your fever, let it come upon you in the right way; for thirst, bear your thirst in the right way; to go hungry, bear hunger in the right way." (Epictetus, *Diatr.* 3.10.6–8, trans. Oldfather, LCL)

them). Paul, then, has sought to imbue them with a proper perspective through constant reiteration: he has said it repeatedly, and now he says it again; as he points out, what he had warned them about has happened to them. They could face their difficulties by having expected them (cf. Seneca, *Ep.* 24.15; 91.4). They would not be "shaken" (*sainein*, 3:3) and give way to the passion of "distress."

3:5. Verse 5 rounds out the paragraph. Echoing the wording of 3:1 (**bearing our separation no longer**), Paul now states his second reason for sending Timothy: **I sent him to ascertain (the state of) your faith, (fearful) lest perhaps the Tempter had tempted you and our labor turned out to be futile.** As in 2:18, where Paul had referred to "Satan" (the Adversary), he again employs "thematic" name-calling by referring to the same entity as "the Tempter," thus highlighting a new characteristic. Yet Paul again sees Satan's efforts aimed at undermining the progress of his ministry, and he expresses concern that the Thessalonians' faith might disappear and his work amount to nothing (cf. 1 Cor. 15:10).

The Return of Timothy (3:6–10)

3:6–10. Paul continues to recount his history with the Thessalonians, moving now to the next chapter in the story: **but now, Timothy having just returned to us from you.** "Friendly" elements continue to abound (Malherbe 2000, 181) as Paul notes his and the Thessalonians' mutual desire to see each other (3:6), their mutual love for each other (3:12), his joy at their well-being (3:7–9), and the connection of their well-being with his own (3:8).

While Paul had been fearful that the Thessalonians' faith might collapse under the weight of their affliction (3:5), he now breathes a sigh of relief: Timothy has brought back a **favorable report** about their **faith and love**. Paul's coordination of faith and love recalls the letter's opening thanksgiving, where he had said that he thanks God for their "work of faith," their "labor of love," and their "endurance of hope" (1:3). The absence of hope here seems curious, given Paul's concern later that the Thessalonians might be acting as those who "have no hope" (4:13). Paul could be hinting that their hope was running short (cf. M. Smith 2013, 284). The omission of hope, however, need not have much significance. In the first place, taking 2 Thessalonians into consideration, the three terms "faith" (*pistis*), "love" (*agapē*), and "endurance" (*hypomonē*) (cf. "endurance of hope" in 1 Thess. 1:3) are there conjoined three times in various combinations. Two of the three terms occur together each time, each one being conjoined with each of the other two once: "faith" and "love" (2 Thess. 1:3), "endurance" and "faith" (1:4), and "love" and "endurance" (3:5). Second, despite the absence of hope here, Paul has already expressed thanks to God for the Thessalonians' hope (1 Thess. 1:3). Conversely, despite expressing his satisfaction with their faith and love here ("faith" in 3:2, 10; "love" in 3:12), he still seeks an increase of their love (3:12) and still sees a "deficiency" in their faith (3:10). Fourth, the pair "faith and love" seems to have been a fixed combination in early Christian tradition: Paul joins these two items several times elsewhere in his letters (2 Thess. 1:3; 1 Cor. 16:13–14; 2 Cor. 8:7;

Philem. 5), and the combination is notably prevalent in the letters of Ignatius (*Eph.* 1.1; 9.1; 14.1; 20.1; *Magn.* 1.2; 13.1; *Trall.* 8.1; etc.). The inclusion or exclusion of faith, love, or hope in various contexts, then, cannot with certainty be taken as an indication that these particular virtues were present or absent. As in the letters of Ignatius, "faith" and "love" could be understood in general terms to encompass the virtues of "faith" and "good works."

To the extent that something was **lacking** in the Thessalonians' **faith** (v. 10), the lack cannot have been significant since Paul found the report of their faith encouraging (3:7). Paul's remark about lacking could imply that, due to his forced, premature departure from Thessalonica, he had not been able to instruct the church thoroughly and see their faith through to completion. However, his departure and their deficiency need not be closely related. Elsewhere Paul prays for his churches to increase in the Christian virtues (2 Cor. 8:7; 9:8; Phil. 1:9). At two other points in 1 Thessalonians, moreover, Paul asks that the Thessalonians might "increase" in behaviors that he indicates they are already exercising (4:1, 10). Finally, Paul's dissatisfaction with his audience's progress in spite of their headway is consistent with his general attitude about the Christian life as a "contest," in which the athlete presses toward the goal without having yet reached it (cf. 1 Cor. 9:24; Gal. 5:7; Phil. 3:12–14).

In fact, so encouraging was the Thessalonians' faith to Paul (**because of this**) that he was comforted even in his **distress and affliction** (*anankē* and *thlipsis*, 3:7). The words *anankē* and *thlipsis* are somewhat synonymous and constitute a fixed pair in the language of the LXX (Job 15:24; Ps. 118:143 [119:143 Eng.]; Zeph. 1:15; cf. Ps. 24:17 [25:17 Eng.]; 2 Cor. 6:4; *diōgmos* and *thlipsis* in 2 Thess. 1:4); the pair occurs in Zephaniah for the "woes" said to characterize the "day of the LORD" (Zeph. 1:7, 15). Here the reference is to the sufferings that attend the lives of believers generally, not just in the end. While Paul's "distress and affliction" may have been partly psychological (Bruce 1982, 67), the terms *thlipsis* and *anankē* almost always indicate physical deprivation or external attack of some sort, including the experience of violence (Wanamaker 1990, 135). In 2 Corinthians Paul places the terms *thlipsis* and *anankē* side by side in a list of ten "hardships," where the other eight terms clearly describe suffering caused by either physical deprivation or violence (2 Cor. 6:4–5). These two terms can have the same connotations when they appear individually: distress/*anankē* (1 Cor. 7:26); affliction/*thlipsis* (Acts 14:22; Rev. 7:14).

This is the third time in chapter 3 that Paul has used the *thlib-* root. He used it once to refer to the afflictions of the Thessalonians (3:3) and once for the suffering that awaits believers generally (3:4); now he uses it to describe his own afflictions. While Paul's main purpose is to communicate that he was **encouraged through** the faith of the Thessalonians despite his own misfortune, mention of his afflictions serves indirectly to identify him with the Thessalonians in *their* affliction. That is, Paul comforts the Thessalonians while acknowledging the comfort he has received from them (2 Cor. 1:4).

Paul remarks that the church's well-being is closely bound up with his own: **For now we live, if you continue to stand fast in the Lord**. Statements connecting the well-being of author and recipient were conventional in "friendly" letters. Abraham Malherbe (2000, 202) cites an example: "I beg you to send for me, else I die because I do not see you daily" (PGiss. I 17). Here, however, Paul's reference may be more oriented toward eschatology. Paul viewed his status in the final judgment as contingent on his success as a minister (1 Cor. 3:13–15; cf. 9:1–2, 27; Phil. 3:11). If this idea is in play here, then Paul *lives*—attains to the resurrection (Phil. 3:11)—because of his faithfulness as a minister. The Thessalonians are living proof that he has been faithful. Yet they must be wary of lapsing: he lives "if" they continue to "stand fast in the Lord" (cf. 1 Cor. 15:2). Paul's life is in their hands. A discernible hortatory purpose lies beneath the surface.

For the time being, Paul is so elated at where things stand that he expresses despair at the possibility of thanking God adequately: **What thanks are we able**

Gift-Giving and Gift-Return in Philo of Alexandria

"And indeed though the worshippers bring nothing else, in bringing themselves they offer the best of sacrifices, the full and truly perfect oblation of noble living, as they honour with hymns and thanksgivings their Benefactor and Saviour." (Philo, *Spec.* 1.272, trans. Colson, LCL)

"It is impossible to requite even our parents with boons equal to those which we have received from them—for it is out of the question to requite by becoming their parents. How must it not be impossible to recompense or to praise as He deserves Him who brought the universe out of non-existence?" (Philo, *Leg.* 3.10, trans. Colson, LCL)

"What, then, of him who has been deemed worthy of blessings so great, so transcendent, so multitudinous? What should he do but requite his Benefactor with the words of his lips with song and with hymn? . . . For it is meet that he who has God for his heritage should bless and praise Him, since this is the only return that he can offer, and all else, strive as he will, is quite beyond his power." (Philo, *Sobr.* 1.58, trans. Colson and Whitaker, LCL)

"We take the same line and say that the work most appropriate to God is conferring boons, that most fitting to creation giving thanks, seeing that it has no power to render in return anything beyond this." (Philo, *Plant.* 1.130, trans. Colson and Whitaker, LCL)

"For to whom should we make thank-offering save to God? and wherewithal save by what He has given us? for there is nothing else whereof we can have sufficiency. God needs nothing, yet in the exceeding greatness of His beneficence to our race He bids us bring what is His own." (Philo, *Deus* 2.7, trans. Colson, LCL)

to return to God? The appropriateness of thanksgiving for God's good provision is a theme in the OT. Though this theme is reflected here, echoes of Greco-Roman conceptions of gift-giving are also manifest. The basic principles of the Greco-Roman gift system are well illustrated in the works of Seneca and Philo of Alexandria. (1) God is a "Benefactor" or gift-giver (Philo, *Spec.* 1.272; Seneca, *Ben.* 6.20.1–6.24.2). (2) A gift requires a "return" (Seneca, *Ben.* 1.4.1–1.7.3; 2.30.2). (3) One ought to "return" God's gift with the gift of gratitude (Philo, *Migr.* 142; *Virt.* 1.72; *QG* 1.64; *Spec.* 2.171; Seneca, *Ben.* 2.29.1–3; 2.30.2; 5.17.7; 6.20.1–6.24.2). (4) Where God is the giver, gratitude is the only return possible (Philo, *Leg.* 3.10; *Sobr.* 1.58; *Mos.* 2.256; *Spec.* 2.174, 180, 199, 209; *Plant.* 1.130; Stobaeus, *Flor.* 4.79.53//3.95), since God needs nothing (Seneca, *Ben.* 2.30.2; 4.9.1; 7.15.4). (5) Even the gift of gratitude is inadequate (Philo, *Leg.* 3.10; *Deus* 2.7), for no return could ever match the abundance of God's gifts. All of the same ideas are reflected in 1 Thess. 3:9, where Paul expresses his desire to offer God "thanks" (*eucharistia*) so as to "return" (*antapodounai*) the gift of the Thessalonians, while despairing that he cannot do so adequately.

In the opening of the letter, Paul said that he prays about the Thessalonians "unceasingly" (1:2), making special mention of their faith, love, and hope. Now he says that he **prays** about them **night and day**, while making two requests of God: **to see** the Thessalonians in the flesh (cf. 2:17) and **to perfect what is lacking in** their **faith**. Having introduced the subject of his prayers, he is now moved to offer a prayer for them on the spot (vv. 11–13).

Prayer for a Fresh Visit and for Strength (3:11–13)

3:11–13. The conjunction *de* marks a transition from Paul's remarks about his prayers for the Thessalonians into an act of prayer on their behalf. In form, 3:11–13 has been identified as a "wish-prayer" (Wiles 1974, 25–29), a prayer form in which the praying subject invokes God to bestow a blessing on the listener. First Thessalonians 3:11–13 is the first of five examples of this form in the Thessalonian letters (1 Thess. 3:11–13; 5:23–24; 2 Thess. 2:16–17; 3:5, 16). Similar prayers occur in the OT and other Jewish literature (Num. 6:24–26; 1 Kings 8:57–61; 2 Macc. 1:2–6) as well as elsewhere in Paul's letters (Rom. 15:5–6, 13, 33; 16:20a; cf. Phil. 4:19) and the NT (Heb. 13:20–21; cf. *Barn.* 21.5). It has been suggested that wish-prayers served a liturgical function (Jewett 1969; R. Collins 1984, 197), though there is no compelling evidence that these prayers served such a purpose for Paul's original recipients.

Charles Wanamaker (1990, 141) insightfully observes that the prayer presented here reflects a "profound change in prayer language," from the invocation of God alone in traditional Jewish prayers to the invocation of both **our very God and Father** and **our Lord Jesus**, where the title of "Lord" is now extended from Yahweh to Jesus. That Paul joins God and Jesus as a compound subject of a singular verb (*kateuthynai*, "direct") probably has theological significance. Paul closely associates the actors, though as other examples of this construction show, the two subjects are not necessarily conceived as being synonymous (e.g., "heaven and earth," Matt. 5:18; "the wind and the sea," Mark 4:41; "gold and silver," James 5:3).

In two parallel parts, Paul's prayer conveys two requests: one for himself and one for the Thessalonians. The two parts include elements common at the opening and closing of ancient letters: prayer for travels (cf. *BGU* 2:423.6–8) and a health wish on the recipient (*BGU* 2:623.3–4; P.Oxy. 3:528.3–6). As the first request, Paul asks that God might lead him safely back to the Thessalonians (**direct our way to you**). While Paul had earlier attributed his inability to return to the activity of Satan (2:18), his prayer here evinces his trust that God can overcome the obstacles and that his prayers can be instrumental in making that happen (cf. Philem. 22).

As his second request (3:12), Paul asks that God might increase the Thessalonians' love for both those within the community and those outside it (**make you abound and increase in love toward one another and toward all**). Here Paul may conceive of love as the embodiment of Christian living as a whole, reflecting his understanding of love as the greatest commandment (Rom. 13:8; Gal. 5:14; Matt. 22:39). While Paul has already expressed his gratitude to God for the Thessalonian believers' "labor of love" (1:3) and his joy over the good report of their love (3:6), even now he seeks for their love to increase (cf. 4:1, 10). In his letters Paul's overwhelming concern regarding Christian love is love toward one another as fellow Christians. Undoubtedly this is because Paul saw a trenchant divide between those in Christ and those in the world, where the virtue of love as inspired by Christ existed only among believers and could be exercised in its best form—reciprocally—only within the community of faith. Paul nonetheless adds that their love should increase also "toward all." This addition could indicate love toward other *believing communities*; yet Paul's apparent awareness of Jesus's teaching that love is the highest commandment and that Christians are to love their enemies (Matt. 5:43–47; Luke 10:25–37; cf. 1 Thess. 5:15; Rom. 12:16–18; 13:8–10) shows that Christian love toward unbelievers was indeed of concern to him. Moreover, Paul makes a similar statement in 1 Thess. 5:15 ("toward one another and toward all"; cf. Gal. 6:10, "good toward all"), where he prohibits retaliation against one's enemies. No one is a greater "enemy" than an outsider.

The final addition of **as also we toward you** (3:12c) is grammatically elliptical. Paul could mean "as also we (have) toward you." However, because of Paul's emphasis on his own example in this letter, it may be best to construe the clause "as also we [*had* or *showed*] toward you," thus emphasizing his love for them as an example of how to love.

Verse 13 explains *why* Paul is asking for their love to increase: by increasing in love, they **strengthen** their **hearts** (1QH^a XIII.9) so that they can stand **blameless in sanctification** before God **at the coming of our Lord Jesus with all his holy ones** (cf. 1 Cor. 1:8). In Jewish and early Christian literature, the title "holy ones" often refers to angels (*1 En.* 1.9; Zech. 14:5; Matt. 13:41; 25:31; Mark 8:38; 13:27; *Apoc. Pet.* 6) and often specifically to angels who are with either God (*1 En.* 1.9; Zech. 14:5) or Christ at God's/Christ's "coming" for judgment on the earth (Matt.

25:31; Mark 8:38; 2 Thess. 1:7; *Apoc. Pet.* 6). As in 2:19 ("before" the Lord Jesus "at his coming"), Paul connects the parousia of Jesus with judgment **before** God (cf. 1 Cor. 4:5). Paul's prayer thus serves an indirect hortatory purpose by connecting the state of the believers' hearts with their final fate.

The prayer in verses 11–13 is tightly integrated with what precedes but also anticipates themes that will be addressed in chapters 4–5 (Malherbe 2000, 211). The prayer makes mention again of the Thessalonians' love (1:3; 3:6, 12), the reciprocity of affection between the Thessalonians and Paul (3:6, 12), his constancy in prayer for them (1:2; 3:9), his desire to see them (2:17–18; 3:10), his apostolic example (1:6; 3:12), his desire to strengthen their faith (3:2, 13), the theme of suffering (1:6; 2:14; 3:3–4, 7), and the parousia of Christ (1:10; 2:19). Looking ahead, the prayer also anticipates further treatment of themes that appeared earlier, including the themes of love (3:12; 4:10), conduct toward outsiders (3:12; 4:12), sanctification (3:13; 4:3–4, 7; 5:23), and again, the parousia of Christ (3:13; 5:1–11, 23). Thus the prayer helpfully serves as both a conclusion to chapters 1–3 and an introduction to chapters 4–5.

Theological Issues

Living at a Distance

It is difficult to appreciate just how significant an inconvenience the problem of geographical distance was for Paul. Now it is possible to reach Thessalonica from Athens in just a matter of hours by car and in less than an hour by aircraft. By dialing a number, hammering out an email, or clicking out a text message, one can contact loved ones in other cities, states, or continents within a matter of seconds. Amid the recent COVID-19 pandemic, when much of the world has had to observe "social distancing," the spatial distance is still easily overcome remotely, thanks to the convenience of modern technology.

If we could imagine what life would be like without any of these conveniences, we would better understand the anxiety that Paul felt when he was suddenly separated from his beloved church during a perilous crisis and then blocked from returning, leaving him ignorant of their circumstances for many weeks. What is remarkable is that he continued to care. We can neglect to visit or forget to call friends and family even though contacting them is now easier than ever. The more mobile we have become, the more easily we have learned to let go of old friendships. It is a true testament to his love for the church that Paul fought for his relationship with the Thessalonians against immense logistical hindrances. They were not his summer buddies; they were his brothers and sisters in Christ.

Strengthening of Faith

First Thessalonians 2:17–3:13 reflects importantly on Paul's understanding of Christian "faith." For many people, faith is a matter of "belief." From this perspective, challenges to "faith" are intellectual in nature. They confront ideas that appear to contradict or undermine their beliefs, and as a result their "faith" is shaken or lost. They no longer "believe" the same things.

However, this does not capture the focus of Paul's concern. Although the Thessalonians may indeed have questioned whether Paul's gospel was "true" after all, afflicted as they were, in this text Paul's concern is not so much that arguments against the premises of Christianity would dissuade them from the faith. Rather, it was that their affliction would crush their living commitment. Paul's concern was practical. In seeking to "strengthen" the believers' faith (3:3), he sought to strengthen their faith*fulness*. As the final prayer in 3:11–13 shows, his desire was that they would grow in "sanctification," in readiness for the coming of Jesus and final judgment.

Rejoicing in Others' Welfare

Friends and families who live apart naturally wonder about each other's well-being. They wonder about each other's physical health, their external circumstances, their personal achievements. We are relieved and delighted to hear reports such as "She received a promotion," "He won an award," "She graduated from law school," "He received an inheritance," "She published a book," "He has lost 50 pounds," "She climbed out of debt," "The deal went through," or "He started a business." We celebrate these things with good reason, and Paul might have as well. However, in this letter Paul is shown to have measured the church's well-being primarily in terms of their *faith*. He had sent Timothy specifically to ascertain where their faith stood. Strikingly, when Timothy returned, reporting that their faith and love remained strong, Paul considered the report "good news." Yet he makes no mention of relief that their affliction has abated; indeed, it may have continued ("*these* afflictions," 3:3). So highly did Paul prioritize the faith of the Thessalonian believers that he found relief even when they were still being persecuted, just as long as their faith was strong.

1 Thessalonians 4:1–12

Exhortation, Part 1

Introductory Matters

Having prayed for his return to the Thessalonians, Paul commences the "final" portion of the letter (4:1). At this point a marked change of focus occurs: Paul's discussion moves from his relationship with the Thessalonians (chaps. 1–3) to their ethical responsibilities as believers (chaps. 4–5).

Which of these two parts constitutes the main body of the letter is open to question. If this is a "thankful" letter, then its body concludes with the prayer in 3:11–13 (Jewett 1986, 71–72). If it is a "paraenetic" letter, then chapters 4–5 constitute a continuation of the hortatory purposes evident in chapters 1–3 (Malherbe 1987, 74), as Paul now moves from appealing to his personal example to exhortation on specific ethical matters. The latter description more aptly describes Paul's purposes. The paraenetic terminology of "exhorting" and "instructing" abounds (*parakalein*, 4:1, 10; *parangelia*, 4:2; *parangellein*, 4:11). Paul continues to recall previous "instructions" (4:1), what he has "told them before" (4:6), how he "instructed them before" (4:11); he even reiterates things that he grants need not be addressed (4:9). Notably, the subjunctive and imperative moods now begin to appear (see introduction to 1 Thessalonians), as Paul's prolonged review of his relationship with the Thessalonians in chapters 1–3 has now prepared them to receive his advice.

First Thessalonians 4:1–12 is marked off as a discrete unit by an *inclusio* signaled by the word "walk" (*peripatein*). Three sections are contained within the unit. Verses 1–2 preface the whole of chapters 4–5 by introducing the general heading "how one should walk in a way pleasing to God" (v. 1), an idea that is re-encapsulated two verses later in the term "sanctification" (v. 3). Verses 3–8 cover the first area of ethical concern, that of sexual conduct. Finally, verses 9–12 offer instructions in the general area of "brotherly love," including also a component about "working with one's own hands." Like chapters 4–5 as a whole, 4:3–12 not only outlines what kind of conduct is pleasing to God but also implicitly defines the behavior that marks off the community of faith from the people of the world, thus further reinforcing the community's sense of identity.

Tracing the Train of Thought

Hortatory Introduction (4:1–2)

4:1–2. The opening formula *loipon oun, adelphoi* indicates a definite transition to a new section of the letter. The adverb *loipon* usually means "finally" (BDAG 602.3.b) and often occurs with this meaning at the conclusion of letters (2 Cor. 13:11; Phil. 4:8; P.Oxy. 1:119.13; but cf. Phil. 3:1). Oddly, in this case slightly more than half the letter remains (forty-three verses in chaps. 1–3 versus forty-six in chaps. 4–5). However, a clear move to hortatory material occurs here, and despite its length, the hortatory section that composes chapters 4–5 functions as a single unit, to which verses 1–2 serve as the introduction. Thus *loipon* could perhaps be rendered **as our final matter of concern**. As *oun* (**therefore**) shows, this section functions as a conclusion to what precedes (chaps. 1–3). Exactly what the conclusion is based on is not clear; perhaps it is best seen as a conclusion drawn from Paul's personal example (1:6; 2:1–12; cf. 2:14–15; 3:3, 7, 12). Thus, having offered paraenesis focused on his personal example in chapters 1–3, Paul now moves into exhortation in the form of precepts that didactically embody that example.

We ask and instruct you is one of several introductory paraenetic formulas that occur in 1 Thessalonians (see also 4:10; 5:12, 14). In this instance the words form part of a more extended formula characteristic of diplomatic letters (Bjerkelund 1967), or communiques from rulers to subjects. Shared elements include a verb of petition in the first-person plural (*erōtōmen* and *parakaloumen*), a vocative of address (*adelphoi*), a content clause introduced by *hina*, and a prepositional phrase indicating the authority by whom the petition is made (*en kyriō Iēsou*). A similar pattern occurs at other points in Paul's letters (Rom. 12:1–2; 15:30–32; 16:17; 1 Cor. 1:10; 4:16; 16:15–16; 2 Cor. 10:1–2; 1 Thess. 4:10b–12; 5:14).

Despite these formal similarities, however, Paul may have used the diplomatic formula for more paraenetic purposes (Malherbe 2000, 218). The connotations

---

1 Thessalonians 4:1–12 in the Rhetorical Flow

Letter opening (1:1–10)

Letter body (2:1–5:22)

  Paul's ministry in Thessalonica (2:1–12)

  Renewed thanksgiving (2:13–16)

  Paul's desire to visit again (2:17–3:13)

  ▶ Exhortation, part 1 (4:1–12)

    Hortatory introduction (4:1–2)

    Exhortation on sexual conduct (4:3–8)

    Exhortation on brotherly love (4:9–12)

of the appeal here may be influenced somewhat by the addition of *en kyriō Iēsou*. Yet, the force of this phrase is ambiguous. On the one hand, the phrase could indicate the *sphere* from which Paul speaks: he "asks and instructs" them as one *believer* speaking to other believers. While Paul normally uses *en christō* to communicate this idea, the *en christō* formula is noticeably absent from the Thessalonian letters, which could indicate that it only became common later. Alternatively, *en kyriō Iēsou* could identify the *authority by which* Paul speaks. In the next verse Paul refers in similar terms to the **instructions** he had given **through the Lord Jesus** (*dia tou kyriou Iēsou*), which perhaps indicates authority less ambiguously. However, the *parakl-* language in the letter has been oriented more around comfort than authority (it is unambiguously paraenetic in 3:2, 7; 4:18; 5:11), and in ancient sources the *parakl-* word group is sometimes explicitly contrasted with the language of "admonishment" (e.g., Stobaeus, *Flor.* 4.79.53 discusses the difference between exhorting/*paraklēsis* and admonishing/*nouthetein*). Perhaps a compromise interpretation is to see Paul exercising his "fatherly" role here (2:11), instructing his audience with authority but with a view toward encouraging more than enforcing compliance.

What Paul asks is that they **walk and live** in the way they **received** from Paul. Although the verb "received" often carries connotations of "tradition" (1 Cor. 11:23; 15:3; 2 Thess. 2:15), this is not the connotation intended here. Rather, the term refers to the way of life that Paul modeled and that the Thessalonians directly witnessed in him ("received") while he was among them. They know **how** to walk **in a way pleasing to God** because Paul himself acted in a manner "pleasing" to God (2:4).

Of course, they are already **walking** in this way. Although this might seem to make the hortatory section superfluous, Paul evidently reiterates his instructions for two reasons. First, he wants to strengthen the resocialization process in the church as they move from their pagan past further into their commitment to the true God. As the philosophers recognized, developing a radically new way of thinking and behaving requires reconditioning of the mind and reprograming of habits (Seneca, *Ep.* 94.48). This requires positive reinforcement (cf. Seneca, *Ep.* 25.4: "as indeed you are doing," trans. Gummere, LCL) and constant repetition of precepts foundational to the new way of life in order to reinforce what one knows or should already **know** (Seneca, *Ep.* 30.7, 15; 94.21; cf. 1 Thess. 2:1, 2, 5, 11; 3:3, 4; 4:2; 5:2) or to refresh one's memory when one has forgotten (Seneca, *Ep.* 94.21). Second, Paul reiterates his instructions because, despite the progress of these new believers, he sees room for further growth. Just as he expressed pleasure with the church's show of faith and love (3:6) and yet found room for progress in both (3:10, 12), so now he challenges them to **increase still more** in their general commitment to the way of "walking" that they previously saw embodied in Paul.

Paul's reference to his previous **instructions** (*parangeliai*) should be understood in connection with the philosophical concept of "precepts"—another possible rendering of the word (Malherbe [2000, 221] lists various references). Thus, whereas chapters 1–3 offered exhortation primarily by presenting Paul as a paradigm or "example" (*exemplum*), chapters 4–5 offer exhortation in the form of "precepts" (*praecepta*). The pairing of *exempla* and *praecepta* as complementary means of instruction was common in philosophical literature of the day (Seneca, *Ep.* 6.6; cf. Quintilian, *Inst.* 12.2.30). While Seneca believed that *exempla* were more effective than *praecepta*—since examples embodied doctrines in concrete form (see 1:6–8)—he also emphasized that *praecepta* were necessary and could function similarly (Seneca, *Ep.* 94.40; cf. Epictetus, *Diatr.* 4.1.169). In distinction from *doctrinae*, or the general principles of a particular philosophical system ("doctrines"), *praecepta* constituted concrete applications of those doctrinal principles (Seneca, *Ep.* 94.31; 95.12). Though some Stoic philosophers rejected the need for *praecepta* on the premise that *doctrinae* were sufficient to set one thinking correctly and therefore behaving correctly (Seneca, *Ep.* 94.5–12, 14–16; Epictetus, *Diatr.* 2.2.21–24; 2.11.18), others insisted that *praecepta* were valuable and indeed necessary (Seneca, *Ep.* 94.18–44; 95.34, 59–60), for *praecepta* divided the general principles of philosophy, or *doctrinae*, into specific applications, each pertinent to specific areas of obligation in the real world (Seneca, *Ep.* 94.21; 95.12). In the same way, Paul has introduced the general principle that Christians should live in a way that is "pleasing to God." Next, he pursues specific areas of application.

Exhortation on Sexual Conduct (4:3–8)

4:3–8. Paul now pursues the first topic of exhortation: appropriate sexual conduct. This section contains three parts: a general statement about the requirement of sanctification (v. 3a), instructions regarding a specific area of concern (vv. 3b–6a), and a warning about violating norms in this area (vv. 6b–8).

Paul begins by recharacterizing a life "pleasing" to God as a life defined by "sanctification": **for the will of God is your sanctification.** While Paul defines the "will of God" in various ways in his letters—in reference to God's salvific purpose in Christ (Gal. 1:4), God's choice of ministers (1 Cor. 1:1; 2 Cor. 1:1), and God's sovereignty over Paul's apostolic mission (Rom. 1:10; 15:32; 1 Cor. 16:12 NRSV note)—here he defines it as sanctification itself. For the Thessalonians, who had previously participated in the Greco-Roman cults, this would be a radically new expectation. While indeed philosophers commonly emphasized that God's will for people was "virtue" (Musonius Rufus, *Diatr.* 16), the Greco-Roman cults were rarely if at all concerned with morality. Rather, cultic worship centered around performing due observances in order to placate the gods or to sway them into bestowing some benefit, such as health, honor, or material gain. Paul reminds the Thessalonians of God's requirement in order to continue reorienting them into a new mode of worship.

Paul next unpacks sanctification with a series of infinitives, which selectively embody God's "will" and thus communicate indirect commands: *apechesthai* (**abstain**); *eidenai*, complemented by *ktasthai* (**learn how to gain mastery**); and two coordinate infinitives, *hyperbainein* and *pleonektein* (**cross into transgression** and take advantage). Paul's focus on actions implies that, in this context, he regards sanctification not as a state but as a process.

Although some scholars see a transition in 4:6 to either "greed" (see interpreters cited in R. Collins 1984, 317) or a more general focus on moral purity (Richard 1995, 201), the single issue actually treated in 4:3b–6a is that of sexual conduct. The first infinitive in 4:3 ("to abstain") enjoins abstinence from *porneia*. This term should be given its usual sense of **sexual immorality**, for contextual factors in no way render this meaning problematic (Malherbe [2000, 225] thinks that the meaning is simply "immorality"). This meaning accords well with the remainder of 4:3–6a. Indeed, the second injunction—expressed by *eidenai hekaston hymōn to heautou skeuos ktasthai*—also concerns the issue of sexual conduct. In the present context the term "vessel" (*skeuos*, 4:4) serves as a metaphor for the human body, if not for the (male) sexual organ specifically (see sidebar). Paul adjures the Thessalonians—the men, as 4:6 will show—to get their bodies under control, that is, to secure control over their sexual impulses. Thus, the ingressive force of the verb *ktasthai* implies the *acquisition* of mastery (**that each of you learn how to gain mastery over his own body**), as if control is being wrested back from the domination of some other agent. Paul may intend to characterize the **passion of lust** (*pathei epithymias*) as the offending agent. Personification of the "passions" (*pathē*), including "lust" (*epithymia/libido*) specifically, was common in the discourse of the Stoic philosophers. Paul personifies "sin" in this way in other places in his letters (see sidebar).

The final two infinitives (4:6) coordinate to express a single command, which again concerns sexual conduct (not business matters, as Holtz [1986, 161–62]

The Meaning of *Skeuos* (4:4)

The meaning of the term *skeuos* (4:4) is disputed here. The prevailing view traditionally—and still maintained by some interpreters (Best 1979, 161; R. Collins 1984, 313; Malherbe 2000, 227) and in some modern translations (NABRE 2011)—was that the term referred metaphorically to a "wife." On this interpretation, Paul is asking that the Thessalonians learn how to "acquire" a wife—the implication being that sexual activity is appropriate only within marriage and that marriage is able to serve as a check on impulses toward fornication (cf. 1 Cor. 7:1–7). However, most modern scholars as well as modern translations take the view that *skeuos* refers to the human "body" (Richard 1995, 198 is representative), if not specifically to the male sexual member (Donfried 1985, 342; J. Smith 2001; Weima 2014, 272). Among other considerations, the lexical evidence weighs overwhelmingly in favor of this meaning (e.g., *skeuos* as body in *T. Naph.* 8.6; 2 Cor. 4:7; *Barn.* 7.3; 21.8; *Herm. Mand.* 33.2 [5.1]; cf. 34.5 [5.2]). For proponents of each view, see R. Collins (1984, 311–12), and for their arguments, see J. Smith (2001) and Gupta (2019, 126–33).

thinks): **that no one cross into transgression and take advantage of his brother in the matter.** While the terminology is not specifically sexual, the specification "in the matter," using the definite article, is best understood as an anaphoric reference to the "matter" already discussed; moreover, "business affairs" is normally rendered with the plural "matters" (*pragmata*), not the singular (*pragma*). The continuity thus implies some relationship between "controlling one's body" (v. 4) and "not taking advantage of one's brother." The prohibited behavior could imply activity against the brother's will, for instance, if the perpetrator forced himself sexually upon some member of the brother's household—whether his wife, daughter, or slave—or if he defrauded him by advancing on the brother's betrothed. Alternatively, "taking advantage" could be Paul's characterization of the activity, while the believers themselves did not see things that way. In that regard, one can imagine a scenario in which a man in the community presumed upon another man's *consent* to engage in sexual activity with some member of his household (cf. Wanamaker 1990, 155). While more speculative, this construal arguably makes better sense of the language, which seems to connote a more

---

The Personification of Sin and the Passions

Paul describes slavery to sin personified in Rom. 6.

"Therefore, do not let sin exercise dominion in your mortal bodies, to make you obey their passions. No longer present your members to sin as instruments of wickedness, but present yourselves to God as those who have been brought from death to life, and present your members to God as instruments of righteousness. For sin will have no dominion over you, since you are not under law but under grace. . . . But thanks be to God that you, having once been slaves of sin, have become obedient from the heart to the form of teaching to which you were entrusted, and that you, having been set free from sin, have become slaves of righteousness." (Rom. 6:12–14, 17–18 NRSV)

Seneca describes slavery to the passions.

"Show me a man who is not a slave; one is a slave to lust [libido], another to greed [avaritiae], another to ambition [ambitio], and all men are slaves to fear [timor]." (Seneca, *Ep.* 47.17, trans. Gummere, LCL)

The Stoics often personified the passions.

"And anger is altogether unbalanced; it now rushes farther than it should, now halts sooner than it ought. For it indulges its own impulses, is capricious in judgement, refuses to listen to evidence, grants no opportunity for defence, maintains whatever position it has seized, and is never willing to surrender judgement even if it is wrong." (Seneca, *Ira* 1.17.7, trans. Basore, LCL)

subtle ("transgress and take advantage") and less flagrant kind of offense ("rape," "offend," "outrage" would describe a flagrant offense, for example).

One noticeable feature of this section is its abundance of traditional Jewish themes related to identity formation and sexual ethics as a defining norm. Israel's distinctness from the gentiles, or "nations," was central to its identity as defined by the Mosaic law (Lev. 18:3, 27). Canonical and extracanonical Jewish texts routinely characterize gentiles as ignorant of God (Ps. 79:6; Jer. 10:25; Jos. Asen. 6.7; 21.15) and attribute their sexual immorality to that ignorance (Wis. 14:22–27; Rom. 1:24–27); gentiles were thought to be particularly debauched in this matter (Jub. 20.3–6; 25.1; 39.6). Thus, in defining Jewish identity, sexual ethics was a major concern (Sir. 23:16–27; Philo, Decal. 131; Spec. 3.51; Jub. 20.3–6; 25.1; 39.6; Sib. Or. 3.591–600). For this reason, it has often been suggested that the background for 1 Thess. 4:3–8 is the holiness codes of the OT (Best 1979, 179), if not specifically the ethical tradition of the rabbis (R. Collins 1984, 315, 327–28). Indeed, (a) chief among Paul's concerns here is the distinctness of Christian identity, which he (b) defines against the foil of **the gentiles, who do not know God** (v. 5), (c) focusing on sexual ethics as a special point of difference (even though "sanctification" entails much more than this). Since the Thessalonians themselves were generally of gentile lineage (cf. 1:9), Paul's reference to "the gentiles" as a separate group illustrates that the characterization of the church as a kind of "third race"—more clearly described in the writings of the Apostolic Fathers (Diogn. 1; Pol. Phil. 10.2)—was already developing in Paul's day (cf. 1 Cor. 10:32).

Despite traditional Jewish polemics against gentile sexual practices, many gentiles shared the same sexual values as Jews (Horrell 2005, 155–63; C. Thomas 2010), as Paul would have known (see sidebar). Still, Paul's views remained distinctive in several ways. First, Paul differed from his gentile counterparts in that he located the *motivation* for sexual purity in a desire to "please" God, and the *means* of satisfying God's requirements as God's own Spirit (Malherbe 1983, 250–51). Second, Paul viewed the requirements of purity as having no relation to "sacred space" (C. Thomas 2010, 123). Gentile requirements for purity applied specifically in the context of sacred spaces (such as temples); these spaces could be considered contaminated if encroached on by the impure. For Paul, purity

---

Sexual Ethics in Musonius Rufus

"Men who are not wantons or immoral are bound to consider sexual intercourse justified only when it occurs in marriage and is indulged in for the purpose of begetting children.... So no one with any self-control would think of having relations with a courtesan or a free woman apart from marriage, no, nor even with his own slave." (Musonius Rufus, Diatr. 12, adapted from Lutz 1947, 56; cf. Stobaeus, Flor. 4.67.21)

was defined not by sacred space but by the state of the body itself. Finally, Paul would have affirmed that, though Christians may not live by distinctly different standards from pagans, they did "live up to, and beyond, the ethical standards that others share but do not follow" (Horrell 2005, 162).

Whether Paul raised the issue of sexual immorality because it applied to Christians generally or because of the specific situation in Thessalonica is a matter of debate (for an overview of the debate, see R. Collins 1984, 307–8). The appearance of similar hortatory material in multiple Pauline letters indicates that some early Christian paraenesis was probably generic (cf. 5:12–22; Rom. 12:9–18; Phil. 4:8–9). There is reason to believe, however, that paraenesis even when generic was partly tailored to the circumstances. In 1 Corinthians, for instance, Paul's inclusion of both fornicators and idolaters in the vice list of 5:11 makes good sense in a letter that clearly addresses both sexual immorality (5:1–13; 6:12–18) and idolatry (8:1–10:22) as areas of offense. A focus on sexual ethics also makes good sense within the religious context of Thessalonica. Some of the cults in Thessalonica either centered around sexual symbols and activities or professed a mythology that implicitly promoted these things.

Drawing attention to the centrality of the phallus and sensuality in the cult of Dionysus, Karl Donfried (1985) has proposed that Paul had such associations in mind when he referred to the *skeuos* in 4:4 (the male sexual member, as Donfried understands it). Noting the popularity of the Cabiri cult in Thessalonica, Robert Jewett (1986, 172) likewise identifies similarities between the ideology of the cult and attitudes common in millenarian movements, which tend to tout freedom from traditional mores, especially sexual ones. The topic of sexual immorality in 1 Thessalonians, then, may have been specific to the church's situation at least insofar as it resonated with their immediate environment. It seems improbable, however, that the topic was relevant to problems currently festering within the Thessalonian church. If male members of the Christian community were sleeping with the wives or relations of other members—whether without their knowledge or as a brazen act of insult—it is inconceivable that Paul would not have taken a more censorious approach, as he was quick to do elsewhere (e.g., 1 Cor. 5:1–13).

Having specified God's requirements for sanctification, Paul next spells out the motivation for fulfilling them (4:6b–8). Negatively, there are consequences for sin: **the Lord is vengeful in all these things** (v. 6b). The judgment of God is a traditional Jewish theme (Pss. 94:1; 99:8 [LXX: 93:1; 98:8]; Sir. 5:3); yet Paul may understand "the Lord" here to be Jesus (so in 4:1, 2), whom he elsewhere describes as the final judge (2 Cor. 5:10; cf. Phil. 1:6, 10; 2 Thess. 2:1–12; 2 Tim. 4:1) and whom he describes specifically in 2 Thess. 1:8 as an avenger. As elsewhere in the Thessalonian letters, judgment is here understood not to be immediate but eschatological (1 Thess. 1:10; 3:13; 5:3, 23; 2 Thess. 1:7–10; 2:1–12). Paul also declares that living in **impurity** amounts to rejecting the power that God gives in order to enable this very thing (1 Thess. 4:8). As Paul in his letters more frequently refers to the "Spirit" without further description, the name "Holy Spirit" here is shown to be "thematic" (drawing attention to a particular theme about the Spirit) and lays special emphasis on the role of the Spirit as sanctifier.

Positively, believers should pursue sanctification because it is essential to their calling: God's purpose for believers is not a life of **impurity** but a life lived **in a state of sanctification** (v. 7). While Paul now describes sanctification as a state (cf. v. 3), the present tense of the participle (**is giving his Holy Spirit**, 4:8) implies that sanctification is nevertheless a durative process and must be maintained (cf. the present tense "is delivering" in 1:10; "is calling" in 2:12; 5:24).

Paul's insistence that his message is not of his own invention (**rejects not a man but the God** who gives his Holy Spirit) repeats a theme in the letter (cf. 2:2, 4, 13). It does not suit the context to view this claim as a defense of Paul's apostolic authority, for his *apostolic* authority would not have mattered to any "ignorant" gentiles whose sexual norms he opposed (which is the topic of discussion). Given the traditional Jewish stance that he espouses, he also cannot have imagined pushback from Jewish opponents on the points relevant to the topic. Stated in this form, Paul's remark may allude to a logion of Jesus (Matt. 10:40; Mark 9:37; Luke 10:16; John 13:20; cf. 12:44; *Did.* 4.1; Ignatius, *Eph.* 6.1; *Trall.* 3.1), which Luke's Gospel preserves in a form very close to that found here: "whoever rejects me . . . rejects the one who sent me" (Luke 10:16 NRSV). In this regard, Paul presents himself as God's ambassador. Yet Paul attaches his message to God, not to emphasize the authority of the messenger but rather to emphasize the authority of the message, which his audience might have doubted only because of its novelty and the stringency of its demands. Paul might with good reason have suspected that his instructions regarding a powerful impulse like the sex drive would be questioned by those accustomed to a more permissive view. It might be easy to ignore or downplay his instructions as nonessential. This is harder to do when the instructions come down from none other than God.

Exhortation on Brotherly Love (4:9–12)

4:9–12. The introductory formula *peri de* (**now concerning**) and a distinct change of topic marks the beginning of a new paragraph, the boundaries of which are clearly indicated by an *inclusio* (**you have no need**, v. 9; **you might have need of no one**, v. 12). The paragraph continues to elaborate on the theme of "walking" in a way that is "pleasing to God" (4:1), thus extending the hortatory section that began in verse 1. A concern with community boundaries also remains in view.

Paul's basic rhetorical strategy here mirrors his approach in 4:1–2. Regarding **brotherly love**, the Thessalonians are already **doing this very thing** ("as also you are walking," v. 1), and yet Paul asks them to **increase** in it more ("we ask you to increase more," v. 1). In reaffirming his previous instructions, Paul now abandons the expressions "as you know" and "as you are doing," instead employing the rhetorical device of "paralepsis" (cf. 5:1), in which he explicitly states what he initially admits does not need to be said (**You have no need for us to write to you**). He has no need to write to them because they are **God-taught** (4:9). He

Philo and the Person Taught by God

"But, while the divine judgement was still waiting, Moses was carrying out the exercises of virtue with an admirable trainer, the reason within him, under whose discipline he laboured to fit himself for life in its highest forms, the theoretical and the practical." (Philo, *Mos.* 1.474–8, trans. Colson and Whitaker, LCL)

"These lessons he received when he and God were alone together, like pupil and master, and while the instruments of the miracles, the hand and the staff, with which he was equipped for his mission were both in his own possession." (Philo, *Mos.* 1.80, trans. Colson and Whitaker, LCL)

does not specify in what way this is true. The Cynic philosophers claimed to be "self-taught" (*autodidaktoi*), having acquired wisdom from practice as opposed to study. The Epicureans claimed that they were "untaught" (*adidaktoi*), since they relied on innate understanding rather than conventional education (Malherbe 2000, 244–45). The shared lexical basis of Paul's expression (*theodidaktoi*) may suggest antagonistic resonances. Although the term itself seems to be a Pauline coinage, the concept may have its background in Hellenistic Judaism. As Calvin Roetzel (1986, 327–28) has shown, Philo of Alexandria characterizes the biblical patriarchs as having needed no human teacher because they received wisdom, knowledge, and virtue directly from God. If Paul has a similar idea in mind here, his meaning is that the Thessalonians have learned *love* directly from God, who has loved them.

The precise meaning of the term "brotherly love" (*philadelphia*, 4:9) is vague here, but its general meaning can be inferred from the context. In non-Christian literature, *philadelphia* commonly meant love between blood brothers (and/or sisters). Consistent with his use of the term *adelphoi* (brothers), Paul uses the term *philadelphia* to describe relationships between believers. The brotherly love practiced by the Thessalonians appears to have consisted in either hospitality or the provision of financial support, or perhaps a mixture of the two. Indeed, the practice of brotherly love **toward all the brothers in all of Macedonia** naturally suggests travel (4:10). Paul's churches were in constant contact with each other, most of all through the visits of leaders or the sending of delegates, and there would be a need for hospitality as these moved from location to location.

The topic of brotherly love frames verses 9–12 as a whole. In this regard, Paul uses the coordinating conjunction "and" (*kai*) to connect his remark about brotherly love in 4:9–10 with what follows in verse 11, linking the infinitive "increase" (in brotherly love) with the four infinitives that follow. "Increase" is directly coordinate with the second infinitive only; the third, fourth, and fifth infinitives complement the second. Thus Paul asks the church (1) to increase more in brotherly love **and**

(2) **to make it your ambition to live quietly and to mind your own affairs and to work with your own hands** (4:11). The general instructions for pursuing this ambition resonate with common sentiments about engagement in public affairs found in contemporary philosophical discussions. "Make it your ambition to live quietly" is an oxymoron in that it echoes the values of the honor-seeking culture ("being ambitious") while also recommending retreat from the limelight ("living quietly"). Dismissing the honor game that so defined their culture (Lucian, *Nigr.* 3–5; see Newman 2008 on Seneca), many philosophers recommended withdrawal from society to pursue philosophy (Seneca, *Ep.* 14.14; 19; 36; 56.11–12; Diogenes Laërtius, *Vit.* 10.119) and to devote oneself to writing, quiet contemplation, and private study within the walls of one's home. Other philosophers idealized manual labor as fitting for philosophical contemplation and chose it voluntarily (Musonius Rufus, *Diatr.* 11), despite common disdain for manual labor among elites (Cicero, *Off.* 1.150–51). For other people, withdrawal from the public sphere was practiced more out of expedience than ideals. Private associations (for which Paul's little communities could be mistaken) had a rocky history with the Roman government, and various associations had been banned out of suspicion or because they were viewed as nuisances to public life (Rulmu 2010). Therefore, it was in the best interest of associations to present themselves as nonthreatening to the Roman government and as nondisruptive to society by keeping themselves occupied with work and minding their own affairs.

Paul's reasons for broaching these issues are unclear. His instructions may reflect generic paraenesis, which he includes here only because of their general relevance to Christians everywhere. Ronald Hock (1980, 43), for instance, interprets Paul's instructions against the background of Hellenistic moral discourse. Noting that Paul addresses the Thessalonians as members of the lower classes, Hock (1980, 43) views Paul's instructions as analogous to the recommendations of the philosopher Dio Chrysostom, who advocated a lifestyle of manual labor to the urban poor because it provided a sufficient means of self-support while also being a seemlier means of livelihood in the eyes of society than other alternatives (cf. Malherbe 2014: 372–73). In the same way, proposes Hock, Paul advocated manual labor as an honorable means of livelihood and hard work as crucial to maintaining a respectable image in the eyes of outsiders. Thus Paul addresses the topic of work (and idleness) only because it was "always of pressing importance among Christian converts" (Hock 1980, 43).

Paul's choice to discuss manual work in this particular letter, however, cannot have been arbitrary since he does not discuss this topic outside the Thessalonian letters (also 2 Thess 3:11–12). Moreover, there are indicators here that the issue may have been of current concern to the Thessalonians. First, the special relevance of 4:9–12 to the Thessalonian church is indicated by the formula that introduces the paragraph: "now concerning" (*peri de*). In letters, this formula often served to introduce a response to an inquiry raised by the addressees in a prior letter (Faw 1952). Even when no written correspondence was involved, the formula served to introduce topics of which both parties already had knowledge, likely from a previous discussion (Mitchell 1989). Additionally, Paul's instructions here depict the audience as members of a particular socioeconomic class: that of manual laborers. Paul's undifferentiated advice to "work with the hands" assumes that this description appropriately matches the church more or less as a whole, though this description would not be equally accurate of all his churches (notably the Corinthian church). Finally, if the topic of work is integrally connected with that of brotherly love—as the syntax and framing of the paragraph seem to indicate—then the specific circumstances of the Thessalonian church likely occasioned not only the discussion of brotherly love but also the content of the paragraph as a whole (see also 5:14).

Some thesis needs to be offered, then, as to what prompted these instructions. This would need to account for the connection between brotherly love and work, as well as explain not only why Paul *urged* them to work, but also why he urged upon them a style of life that, if he is describing their natural socioeconomic location, they had little choice but to pursue.

Reconstructions of the situation can be divided into two categories. Until the end of the twentieth century, most interpreters viewed the Thessalonians' behavior as motivated by their *eschatology*. Paul urged them to "work" because some had ceased from doing so (or had at least deprioritized work), and had done so either in expectation of Christ's imminent return (Marshall 1983, 219) or because they believed that the day of the Lord had already come (Beale 2003, 251).

Since the final part of the twentieth century, many scholars have highlighted possible *sociological* explanations for Paul's remarks. According to John Barclay (1992, 53; 1993), Paul urged the Thessalonians to "live quietly" and mind their "own affairs" because they were engaging in a harsh and off-putting form of evangelism in response to social opposition (cf. De Vos 1999, 161–64). Other scholars, emphasizing the pervasiveness of the empire's patron-client culture, have proposed that Paul's injunction to "work" addresses those who had ceased working because they had either presumed upon the support of the church's wealthier members (Russell 1988) or were preoccupied with their client duties (Winter 1994, 41–60). A strength of the patron-client explanation is that it makes possible a direct connection between the issue of work and that of brotherly love: brotherly love is exercised when believers support those who are not self-sufficient; conversely, brotherly love is not exercised when the supported party takes advantage of the other's generosity and chooses not to be self-sufficient in the expectation that someone else's work will provide their means. In other words, 4:9–12 concerns the ethics of both giving *and* receiving.

The patron-client explanation appears to fit both the social and the literary contexts, but it makes less sense of the fact that Paul describes brotherly love as being practiced toward those outside Thessalonica and not just locally (the patron-client relationship *typically* functioned locally). Two alternative readings are possible that would explain this consideration. The topos of the "false prophet" was common in both the NT (Matt. 7:15; Mark 13:22; Luke 6:26; Acts 13:6; 2 Pet. 2:1–22; 1 John 4:1;

Rev. 16:13; 19:20; 20:10) and the writings of the Apostolic Fathers (*Herm. Mand.* 43.7–8, 12 [11.1]; *Did.* 11.1–12). The *Didache* devotes fairly extensive discussion to the rights of prophets with regard to hospitality and financial support (11.1–12; 13.1–7) and explores these issues explicitly in reference to false prophets (11.1–12). The *Didache* (along with *Shepherd of Hermas*) describes false prophets in terms that echo several elements of Paul's instructions here. Of special importance is the common connection between false prophets and the demand for material support. The apparent implication in 1 Thess. 4:10 that brotherly love involves travel ("in all of Macedonia") resonates with the depiction of false prophets as itinerants (*Did.* 11.1–12). Consistent with Jesus's teaching about supporting ministers (Matt. 10:10//Luke 10:4–8), the *Didache* (13.1–7) emphasizes that prophets are worthy of support but decries false prophets who presume upon hospitality, demand an extended stay (11.4–5; 13.1), and request meals (11.9) and money (11.12) while claiming to speak "in the Spirit." Such people, says the *Didache*, should be cast out (11.5). Whether Paul discerned false prophets in the Thessalonian church may be debatable, but his concerns with hospitality and work as seen here reflect the same kind of concerns that surrounded such figures. This paradigm would make sense of the topic of brotherly love and of Paul's related instructions about living quietly, minding one's affairs, and working. In short, Paul's instructions would concern the giving and receiving of hospitality: the community should continue offering hospitality, but they should not take advantage of others' kindness and should be wary of those who might do so.

A second possibility is that brotherly love concerns the reciprocal exchange of resources between basically equal, subsistence-level Christians, who balanced on the edge between need and financial sufficiency (Schellenberg 2018). Though nearly all lacked a surplus of resources, they supported one other, extending brotherly love as each had need. On this view, Paul's command to work would imply that each was obligated to contribute so as not to burden the community through one's own laziness (Schellenberg is not clear to what extent this practice applied outside of Thessalonica, though in theory it could have).

Paul's instructions conclude with a purpose clause that explains why the audience should behave as he advises (4:12). The clause is compound, and each of its two parts correlates with a specific behavior (or behaviors) from the previous verse (see table). The first part, **in order that you might walk presentably toward outsiders**, correlates specifically with the commands to "live quietly" and mind one's "own affairs." The second part, **and that you might have need of no one**, explains the command to "work" with one's own hands. In sum, Paul's instructions in 4:11–12 have two concerns in view. His first concern is the perception of outsiders: good order in the community not only prevents negative attention but also attracts outsiders into the community. His second concern is to promote an ethos of reciprocal love within the community: while some provide material support to others, recipients should not presume upon it and should do what they can to mitigate the need for it.

Table 1. The Parallel Relations in 1 Thess. 4:11–12

"to make it your ambition to live quietly and to mind your own affairs" (v. 11a, b)	"in order that you might walk presentably toward outsiders" (v. 12a)
"and to work with your own hands" (v. 11c)	"in order that you might have need of no one" (v. 12b)

Theological Issues

Ethics Define the Community

Noticeably lacking in this letter—at least on the surface—is extended attention to "theology." Rather, moving from a lengthy recounting of his history with the Thessalonians, Paul comes "finally" (4:1) to ethics. While his foregrounding of ethics over theology in this letter does not undermine the importance of the latter, it does demonstrate that he considered a particular way of life essential for defining what a believer is. For those in Christ, "sanctification" is not optional: it is "the will of God" (4:3). It is not (or not only) the person who thinks in a certain way but the person who lives in a certain way that counts as a believer. What's more, not to follow God's will counts as active "rejection" of his Holy Spirit. The implication is that the Spirit's work is *natural* in believers; therefore, when one does not demonstrate conduct pleasing to God, then the Spirit is not at work in them, or worse, is not in them.

Ethics That Define the Community

Many modern Christians may be surprised to find what Paul focuses on as defining behaviors of believers. Sexual restrictions as acknowledged by many Christians today, particularly in North America among other places, are probably more permissive than they have been throughout the history of Christianity, and yet Paul identifies sexual purity as a key behavior separating believers from "the gentiles, who do not know God." Furthermore, while probably not many people today consider hospitality to be an important expression of their faith, Paul views it as an expression of love between believers ("brothers") and finds occasion in this short letter to address it. Finally, withdrawal from the public sphere to "mind one's own affairs" runs squarely counter to what many (esp. American) believers see as a Christian duty to bring to realization a Christian political culture.

Paul's instructions were surely shaped by both the cultural and the church's immediate context, but if we are inclined to adopt contrary views or practices today, it deserves serious reflection on what grounds we lean that way and how Paul might respond.

1 Thessalonians 4:13–5:11

Exhortation, Part 2

Introductory Matters

First Thessalonians 4:13–5:11 is the first section in the letter that involves any sustained theological discussion. The unit as a whole is thoroughly eschatological, having as its focus the parousia of Jesus. Still, overt paraenetic purposes continue to be evident (esp. 4:13, 18; 5:11). The unit contains two subsections, which share significant verbal ties: sleeping (*koimān*, 4:13, 14, 15; *katheudein*, 5:6, 7 [2×], 10), believing (4:14; 5:8), the mediation of Jesus (4:14; 5:9), being "with" Jesus (4:17; 5:10), contrast between believers and "the rest" (4:13; 5:5), and a final exhortation to "encourage" one another (4:18; 5:11). In the first subsection (4:13–18), Paul assures the church that they should not grieve over deceased members, since the dead will meet Christ at his return along with the living. After previewing the parousia event (4:13–18), Paul then extends the discussion into the question of the parousia's timing (5:1–11). Although this section has the final fate of believers in view, the focus of the section turns out to be the stark differences that exist between believers and nonbelievers.

Apocalyptic theology. Both 1 Thess. 4:13–18 and 5:1–11 are replete with language and themes that occur commonly in Jewish apocalyptic literature like *1 Enoch*, *4 Ezra*, and *2 Baruch*: the blowing of a final trumpet (4:16), the sudden destruction of the wicked (5:3), fleeing from God's wrath (5:3), the revelation of the Messiah from heaven (4:16), the death of the Messiah (4:14), the resurrection of the Messiah and of the righteous (4:14, 16–17), the question whether the living will be more blessed than the dead (4:15), the assumption of the living into heaven (4:17), the return of the Messiah into heaven (4:14), life together "with" the Messiah (4:17; 5:10), and an emphasis on consolation (4:18; 5:11). These parallels show that Paul shared many of the beliefs common in the apocalyptic thinking of his day. However, 1 Thess. 4:13–5:11 also reflects elements that are uniquely Christian. Aside from the critical point that Paul identifies the Messiah as Jesus, Paul insists—against many contemporary apocalyptic works—that those who are living when the Messiah returns will in no way be more blessed than those who have passed away. Quite the contrary, the dead will rise to meet Christ first, and then the living "will be snatched up." Consistent with one of the main functions of apocalyptic literature, Paul's purpose is not primarily to make a theological argument but to console his audience, who here are grieved over the deaths of their own.

Group boundaries. Paul's strategy of consolation relies heavily on a differentiation between believers and unbelievers. Believers should not grieve like "the rest," for they have hope in the resurrection and in the attainment of salvation through Jesus Christ. The church's distinctiveness, however, concerns not only their final destination but also their very nature as Christ-people. Throughout the section, Paul develops an extensive antithesis between believers ("sons of light," "sons of day," etc.) and unbelievers (they belong to "darkness" and the "night").

The lordship of Jesus and the Roman Empire. While opposition to empire—and the Roman Empire in particular—is in no way at the fore in these verses, subversive resonances may lie beneath the surface. James Harrison (2002, 79–92; 2011, 52–63) has made extensive efforts to demonstrate that this passage specifically critiques Roman imperial propaganda. Harrison observes, for instance, that the term "savior" (cf. 5:8–9) was "an official title for sovereigns in the Hellenistic ruler cult and in the Roman imperial cultus" and that the personified virtue of "Hope" (cf. 4:13) appears on a Roman coin minted by the emperor in 41 CE, implying that hope comes from Rome. Harrison also argues that Paul's description of Jesus as "Lord" (5:2, 9) constituted a challenge to the rule of the emperor, who was also described as "lord" (2011, 56–63), and as a challenge to the professed divinity of the emperors both living and dead (see 1:10). Harrison observes, furthermore, that Roman texts sometimes describe the "arrival" of the emperor as his *parousia* (4:15; cf. 5:2) and an official "meeting" with an emperor to welcome him into a city as an *apantēsis* (4:17), so that Jesus's return, no less than his status as lord, could be viewed as a threat to the emperor. Finally, Harrison takes the cry of "peace and security" made by the unidentified speakers in 5:3 as imperial propaganda touting the news that Rome had ushered in a Golden Age of prosperity.

Public Domain

Figure 7. A Roman coin featuring Julius Caesar described as *theos* (top) and Octavian described as *sebastos* (bottom)

Despite such resonances, Peter Oakes (2005) has criticized attempts to read Paul's language as directly oppositional to Roman ideology. Oakes observes that while

1 Thess. 4:15–17 and 5:3 do "conflict" with Roman ideology, Paul is not "writing polemic against Rome" (301) in the sense that he is reacting to conflict stemming specifically from Rome. Rather, Paul is "re-drawing the map of the universe" (301), with the return of Jesus radically altering its power structure. Since the Roman Empire "provided the main perceived structure of world order around the Mediterranean," any movement "that challenged the status quo of the social structure would, to some extent, be challenging Rome" (309). Oakes proposes that, while Paul's eschatology would have equal implications for, say, the empire in ancient China, this would not necessarily mean that Paul's writing "consciously" related to China and its power structures (315). In other words, while 1 Thess. 4:13–5:11 may not attack the Roman Empire specifically, according to Oakes, the text does radically subvert "empire."

Tracing the Train of Thought

The General Resurrection of Believers at the Parousia (4:13–18)

Three features at the opening of verse 13 indicate a distinct transition to a new unit: the developmental conjunction "now" (*de*), the vocative "brothers" (*adelphoi*), and the metacomment "we do not want you to be ignorant." The new topic concerns those who are "asleep," that is, the deceased.

The metacomment formula used to introduce this section is rare in Paul's letters (also in 1 Cor. 10:1; 12:1). In distinction from the informative "I want you to know" (1 Cor. 11:3; Col. 2:1) and the somewhat sarcastic "Do you not know?" (Rom. 6:16; 10× in 1 Corinthians), "I do not want you to be ignorant" connotes an urgency either to prevent or to reverse the consequences of some critical misunderstanding. The formula need not indicate that Paul failed to cover this ground previously. Indeed, several facts of the situation seem evident. First, Paul had previously taught them about both the resurrection of Christ and the resurrection of believers. Second, he had presented the resurrection as a physical event. Third, he had told them that the general resurrection would occur at the parousia. Fourth, he had indicated that the resurrection and parousia could very well occur within their respective lifetimes. Fifth, some of the Thessalonians had died in the interval between their conversion and Timothy's recent visit (while martyrdom may be suspected as the cause, too little evidence exists to determine this with certainty; cf. Gupta 2019, 63). Sixth, the living are grieving over the deceased. Seventh, they are grieving over them because they are either uncertain or unaware of what their fate will be.

What is not evident is why the Thessalonians had developed doubts about the fate of the deceased. Several possibilities can be identified. (1) They had become *theologically* convinced that the deceased would not experience the resurrection. (2) They had developed *existential* doubts about the resurrection of the deceased. (3) Paul *had not taught* them about the fate of the deceased. (4) Paul's teaching about the resurrection *had been misunderstood*. The first option would probably require the existence of "false teachers," for which evidence is very weak in this letter. The third option is possible, particularly since Paul's stay with the Thessalonians was brief and his departure occurred prematurely; the same points can be said in favor of the fourth option. Perhaps the best explanation is to see the community's rising doubts in the face of persecution and loss (option 2) as overcoming, suppressing, or distorting the truths they had been taught. As he has done throughout the letter, Paul now "reminds" them of his prior teachings (4:2, 6, 11).

The discussion about the deceased contains four parts: an introduction of the topic (v. 13), a "creedal" statement (v. 14), grounding of the creedal statement by means of a "word of the Lord" (vv. 15–17), and a concluding exhortation (v. 18).

4:13. Paul does not want the Thessalonians **to be ignorant about those who are sleeping**. While Paul's discussion of the deceased will be of a "theological" nature, he frames his response in terms of consolation. His depiction of the deceased as "sleeping" is itself consolatory. "Sleep" was widely used as a euphemism for death in Greco-Roman literature (as early as Homer, *Il.* 1.476). Many Jewish texts of the Second Temple period depict death followed by resurrection in terms of waking from sleep (Malherbe 2000, 263; citing Dan. 12:2; 2 Macc. 12:44–45; *1 En.* 92.3; 2 Esd. [*4 Ezra*] 7:31–32). Nonetheless, it is interesting and perhaps significant that Paul depicts only believers in this way (KJV: 1 Cor. 11:30; 15:6, 18, 51), never nonbelievers. The latter are never sleeping but rather "perishing" (1 Cor. 1:18; 2 Cor. 2:15; 4:3; 2 Thess. 2:10; cf. Rom. 14:15; 1 Cor. 8:11).

The words **lest you grieve as also the rest, who do not have hope** raise several difficulties. First, Paul's description of "the rest" as people "who do not have hope" could be understood either restrictively (i.e., "the rest who have no hope," describing a smaller group within "the rest") or nonrestrictively ("the rest, who have no hope," identifying all "the rest" as all nonbelievers). The latter is more likely correct. Indeed, the former would imply that the Thessalonians and the "rest" together comprise those who have no hope. Paul's point, however, is not that the Thessalonians have no hope and therefore grieve, but that they grieve despite having hope, and that this is inconsistent.

This conclusion appears to pose a further problem, however, for not all nonbelievers viewed death as the end. Many Jews (other than Christ-followers) believed in either a bodily resurrection (2 Macc. 7:14, 20; *2 Bar.* 30.1; 50.2–51.9) or immortality of the soul (Wis. 2:22; 4 Macc. 16:13; Philo, *Abr.* 258; Josephus, *Ant.* 18.18). Among pagans, belief in annihilation was not uncommon, but neither was belief in an afterlife. Elite sources suggest that most people believed in an afterlife as depicted in traditional mythology (Plato, *Resp.* 599A; Augustine, *Civ.* 6.6; Lucian, *Philopseudes*; *De luctu*). According to Seneca, the view that the soul is immortal is the "general opinion of mankind" (*Ep.* 117.6). Epitaphs (Hope 2009, 111–15) and burial rituals (Hope 2009, 102; Lucian, *De luctu*) sometimes point to hope beyond the grave. Adherents of some of the mystery religions believed in an afterlife in some form (Nigdelis 2006, 15). Several philosophical groups believed that the soul was immortal (Plato, *Resp.* 620A–D; *Phaed.* 80D–E), or at least that it could survive after death (Diogenes Laërtius, *Vit.* 7.156–57), and imagined its postmortem existence being spent on a mythical "blessed island" (Cicero, *Tusc.* 1.40.98). Moreover, philosophy could allay the fear of death itself (Lucretius, *Rer. nat.* 3.830–1094; Seneca, *Ep.* 75.17). For many, death is natural rather than evil (Marcus Aurelius, *Med.* 2.12; 9.3; 12.21), and if natural, why "hope" beyond it?

There is yet a further difficulty. Depending on the function of the comparative clause in 4:13 ("as also the rest"), Paul could be prohibiting either grieving in a certain manner ("Do not grieve in the *manner* of the rest") or prohibiting grief categorically ("Do not grieve, as also the rest do"). If Paul indeed describes the "rest" (i.e., nonbelievers) as people without hope, while many not following Christ did indeed believe in an afterlife, even a blessed one, then Paul's prohibition against grief might seem to be a matter of degree. Several points, however, weigh in favor of the categorical meaning. First, the conjunction *kathōs* (just as) less frequently indicates a comparison in degree than a comparison in kind (BDAG 493). Second, Paul regards "hope" (*elpis*) as related specifically to the final redemption of believers, not just to an afterlife of any kind. Third, 1 Thess. 4:13–5:11 as a whole maintains a sharp contrast between believers and nonbelievers (Barclay 2016), who are characterized respectively by "day" and "night" (5:4, 5), "light" and "darkness" (5:5), "watchfulness" and "sleep" (5:6), and "soberness" and "drunkenness" (5:7–8). "The rest" (4:13) appear again in 5:6, where they correlate with night, darkness, sleep, and drunkenness. The two categories, then, may be generalizing and "massively stereotyped" (Barclay 2016, 224), but the distinction elaborated between believers and nonbelievers serves to strengthen the sharp boundary between the community and the world that Paul has emphasized throughout the letter and will continue to emphasize in 5:1–11. Paul here reaffirms the differences: while nonbelievers might grieve, believers should not. In sum, Paul makes a comparison in *kind* ("that *you* might not grieve, as *the rest* do"), and he defines "the rest" *nonrestrictively* ("as the rest do, who have no hope"). Paul's statement is surely rhetorically exaggerated (like the differences between the two groups themselves), but this is nonetheless how he formulates the expectation.

A comparison with the Stoic philosophers highlights a key distinctive of Paul's framework for consolation. On the one hand, some definite similarities exist. The Stoics listed "grief" (*lypē*) as one of the four cardinal "passions" (see 3:1–5). Since the passions resulted from ignorance, the Stoics advised that the passions should be completely eradicated. Likewise, Paul depicts grief as a result of ignorance ("I do not want you to be ignorant, lest you grieve . . .") and advises that grief be not mitigated but eliminated. A key difference, however, is the element of hope. For the Stoics grief could be eliminated simply by reevaluating the perceived cause. One ought not to grieve at death because death is "no evil"; rather, it is "indifferent" (Seneca, *Ep.* 75.17). Paul's solution is not to *reevaluate* death as indifferent but to *balance* the evil of death against the weightier "hope" of the resurrection.

4:14. The next verse explains why believers should not grieve. It is because (**for**) grief belies what Christians "believe." The word "believe" sets off a statement that many scholars understand to reflect a pre-Pauline creed (R. Collins 1984, 54–57, 158). If the statement reflects creedal material, however, it is unlikely that the creed appeared in precisely this form, for the syntax is asymmetrical (it begins as a conditional statement and concludes as a comparison). The difficulty is alleviated if "we believe" reflects an aside: **if (as we believe) Jesus died and rose**. If the same logic is at work here as in 1 Cor. 15:12–28, then the statement implies a cause-effect relationship between the death and resurrection of Jesus and the gathering of believers with him at the parousia: *since* Jesus was raised, believers also will be raised (cf. *1 En.* 51.1–4).

The word order of the second half of the statement is rendered into English only with difficulty, and the placement of **through Jesus** (*dia tou Iēsou*) is ambiguous in the Greek text. Some take *dia tou Iēsou* to modify **those who previously fell asleep**—presumably meaning that some "fell asleep through Christ," or rather "fell asleep *as Christ-people*." Paul, however, would normally have used *en* (in) to express this idea, not *dia* (through). Instead, Paul means that Jesus will be the *instrument* through which God gathers those who are asleep (cf. 1 Cor. 15:21): **so also will God,** *through* **Jesus, lead with him** those who previously fell asleep. Use of the word "lead" in place of "raise" creates an allusion to the prophetic idea of the "gathering" of God's people (Isa. 11:12; 43:5; LXX Jer. 38:10; etc.), though "lead with him" clearly implies a general "resurrection," as verses 16 ("will rise") and 17 ("snatched up into the clouds" to be "with" Jesus) make evident.

4:15–17. Paul has explained that believers should not grieve if they believe they will be raised. Now he states why they should believe they will be raised: it is confirmed by the very **word of the Lord**. Paul proceeds to report the word, although a couple of points remain uncertain. First, the nature of the "word of the Lord" is subject to question (Pahl 2009). Nothing in verses 15b–17 approximates a Gospel saying closely enough to confirm it as a statement from the historical Jesus, although the word could be rooted in an agraphon (a saying not known from our written accounts of Jesus). If this word derives only loosely from the historical Jesus, then its material could reflect a midrashic expansion of apocalyptic teaching of the kind found in Matt. 24, perhaps inspired by texts like Dan. 7:13 and 12:2–3. Alternatively, the "word" could have derived from a reputed Christian prophet. Indeed, the phrasing "word of the Lord" recalls an

OT formula used for the transmission of God's message to a prophet: "the word of the LORD came to . . ." (cf. Hosea 1:1; etc.). The prophet might even have been Paul, for Paul describes himself as a recipient of revelations (2 Cor. 12:1, 4; Gal. 1:12; 2:2; Eph. 3:3) and visions of the heavenly abode (2 Cor. 12:1–4), he imparts "mysteries" (Rom. 11:25–26; 1 Cor. 15:51–52), and in this letter he has already described his message as "a word of God" (2:13; cf. 4:8).

The second uncertainty concerns the boundaries of this "word" in the text. The content of verse 15b appears to be elaborated in verses 16–17. In this regard, verse 15b could represent a summary of the "word," which is then expanded in verses 16–17 in the "word" itself; or verse 15b could represent the "word" and verses 16–17 reflect Paul's elaboration; or the "word of the Lord" may span all of verses 15b–17. This issue cannot be resolved apart from a decision about the "word's" original source. Unfortunately, as noted above, that question is difficult to answer.

Extensive similarities exist between 1 Thess. 4:15–17 and 1 Cor. 15:51–52, and a common tradition may lie behind them (if Paul himself is not the source). Here Paul's concern is the relationship between the general resurrection and the parousia. Verse 15b captures the main point: **We who are alive, who remain at the coming of the Lord, will surely not precede those who fell sleep.** Paul amplifies this point in verses 16–17 with a more detailed account: (1) a command will be given; (2) the Lord will descend; (3) dead believers will rise; (4) living believers will rise; (5) together the two groups will meet Christ in the air; (6) all of them will be with the Lord always.

The **command** is given through **the voice of an archangel**, accompanied by the blasting of **the trumpet of God** (4:16). The identity of the archangel is not specified. While the concept of angelic hierarchy is foreign to the OT (except in Dan. 10:13), archangels appear frequently in Second Temple literature. Michael is named among the archangels in *1 Enoch* (20.1–7; 40.9–10) and is found in the company of Gabriel and Raphael in the Dead Sea Scrolls (1QM IX.15). It may be telling (regardless of the dating) that Michael is the one to blow the trumpet before the judgment in the *Life of Adam and Eve* (*Apoc. Mos.* 22.1–3). The trumpet was commonly used in the OT to signal battle. In apocalyptic literature it came to signify the arrival of the Messiah (*Apoc. Ab.* 31.1), final destruction (Rev. 11:15; *Sib. Or.* 4.173–82; 7.115; 2 Esd. [*4 Ezra*] 6:23), or final judgment (*Sib. Or.* 8.239).

Here as elsewhere, Paul depicts Jesus as currently residing in **heaven** (Rom. 8:34; 10:6; Eph. 1:20; Col. 3:1), whence he **will descend** at the parousia (cf. Phil. 3:20; 1 Thess. 1:10; 2 Thess. 1:7). Parallels occur in several Jewish apocalyptic texts. These texts predict a time when the Messiah will be "revealed" (2 Esd. [*4 Ezra*] 7:28; *2 Bar.* 29.3; 39.1–8; *1 En.* 38.2; 48.6; 52.9; 62.7); in some cases they clarify that before his arrival, he lived in the presence of God in heaven (*1 En.* 48.6; 62.7; cf. 2 Thess. 1:7).

The parousia, Paul suggests, coincides with the general resurrection. Uniquely among early apocalyptic writings, Paul identifies two *stages* of the resurrection:

(1) **the dead who are in Christ will rise first** and (2) **then we who are alive, who remain** (4:16–17). Paul makes no distinction in order elsewhere in his letters (cf. 1 Cor. 15:23). His explicit distinction between groups here would be gratuitous unless there had been some question on the point, for he indicates that both groups will experience the same outcome. His earlier use of the emphatic negative ("will surely not precede") to deny that the living will precede the dead suggests that the main point at issue was an uncertainty about the deceased. As to why this question arose, parallels in Jewish apocalyptic texts may prove illuminating. Some texts affirm that only those who are living when the messiah comes to set up his kingdom will be blessed to participate (Dan. 12:12–13; 2 Esd. [*4 Ezra*] 13:24; *Pss. Sol.* 17.44). If the Thessalonians did not derive their conclusions from the apocalyptic tradition directly, they could have arrived at a similar conclusion by their own route: they expected the return of Jesus, and some of their number had died before it occurred. How would these experience the parousia?

Paul's spectacular claims in verse 17 (**will be snatched up together with them in the clouds for a meeting with the Lord in the air**) have inspired the theological imagination of interpreters for centuries. "Snatched" (*harpazein*) implies that the subjects participate passively in an action that is externally caused; verse 14 shows that the agent is God: "*God will*, through Jesus, lead with him those who sleep." Since the latter half of the nineteenth century, the term *harpazein* has often been thought to denote a "rapture" (from the Latin equivalent *raptus*, "snatched") in which God snatches believers from the earth to spare them from a great tribulation doomed to fall upon the earth and unbelieving humanity, after which Jesus will return (again), together with his own, and establish his messianic kingdom on earth.

There is no evidence in the text that "snatching" implies deliverance from a coming tribulation. In other apocalyptic works, the righteous live through the tribulation, even though they are finally saved (*1 En.* 1.1–8; 10.17; 2 Esd. [*4 Ezra*]

"The Rapture" and Dispensationalism

The doctrine of "the rapture" has a special place in the theological system of Christian dispensationalism. Popularized in North America by John Nelson Darby during the mid- and late nineteenth century, dispensationalism became enshrined as a fundamental evangelical doctrine through the study notes of the *Scofield Reference Bible* (1909) and was championed by institutions such as Moody Bible Institute and Dallas Theological Seminary through the twentieth century. As developed by Darby, the doctrine predicted a two-stage return of Christ: the first, when Christ raptures his own before the tribulation, and the second, following the tribulation, when he establishes his messianic kingdom on earth. First Thessalonians 4:17 was a linchpin text for the rapture doctrine.

"Assumption" into Heaven

The concept of "assumption," "translation," or "taking up" as God's way of bringing the righteous, especially unique individuals, into his company at death was commonplace in apocalyptic literature. The assumption of Enoch is described in Gen. 5:24 LXX and more overtly in *1 Enoch* (70.1–71.17), the assumption of Baruch in *2 Baruch* (46.7), the assumption of Ezra in *4 Ezra* (= 2 Esd. 14:9), and the assumption of Moses in Philo's *Life of Moses* (2.291). Similar examples occur elsewhere in both Jewish and early Christian writings. According to some texts, at death the soul is summoned to heaven and receives its judgment there (*T. Ab.* 1.7; 7.7; 17.3; *1 En.* 22.9–14; *LAB* 23.13; cf. 33.3). Paul uses the term *harpazein* in 2 Cor. 12:2, 4 to describe his journey to the third heaven. In Greco-Roman literature, ascent of the deceased into heaven is described in terms of apotheosis: the soul, or rather the "divine" portion of the person, escapes the body and is "translated" into the heavenly region of the universe in the form of a comet. This is said to have been the fate of Julius Caesar (Vergil, *Aen.* 1.290; Suetonius, *Jul.* 88; Ovid, *Metam.* 15.745–870). In Lucian's satirical history *A True Story* (*Vera historia*), a certain Endymion is said to have been "raptured" (*anarpastheiē*) to the moon.

5:1–13; 6:13–25; 7:27; 9:3–12; 13:48; *2 Bar.* 25.1–4; 29.2; 1QM I.11–12; 15.1; Add. Esth. 11:2–12 LXX [in add. A of NRSV]), or are shielded during the time of tribulation (2 Esd. [*4 Ezra*] 13:48; *2 Bar.* 29.2; *Sib. Or.* 3.702–7). The notion of a snatching, or "rapture," into heaven, however, had strong precedent in Second Temple Judaism; though modern scholars typically prefer the label "translation" or "assumption" (see sidebar). Like other Jewish writers, Paul here affirms that believers will be translated or assumed *bodily* into heaven.

Indeed, the remainder of 4:17 describes those who are resurrected as being gathered **for a meeting with the Lord in the air**. Paul's reticence here leaves open the question of what happens next; he concludes simply with **and in this way we will be with the Lord always**. The word "meeting" (*apantēsis*) has often been understood as a technical term for the welcoming of a dignitary or triumphant leader by its citizens outside the city gates, who then conduct the individual back into the city with pomp. The same Greek term occurs in this sense, untranslated, in Cicero's letters (Cicero, *Att.* 8.16.2; 16.11.6; cf. the Latin term *curia* in Seneca, *Ben.* 5.15.5; *prosequi* in Suetonius, *Aug.* 57; the cognate term *hypantēsis* in Josephus, *Ant.* 11.327, 329; cf. *TDNT* 1:380–81). If this pattern is superimposed onto 1 Thess. 4:17, the situation as Paul describes it would be that, after resurrected believers meet the Lord in the air, they then conduct him *back* to earth, where presumably he sets up his messianic kingdom. This interpretation, however, is improbable on several counts.

First, though scholars continue to reiterate the claim that *apantēsis* was a "technical term" for a royal meeting of this kind, Michael Cosby (1994) has ably shown that it was not. Second, in no place in his letters does Paul describe a future messianic kingdom on earth, not even in other texts that address the parousia and final resurrection (1 Cor. 15:23–28, 51–57; Phil. 3:20–21). Third, the sequence "meeting with the Lord in the air" and "in this way we will be with the Lord always" most naturally implies that "with the Lord always" will occur "in the air," since nothing is said to occur in between these two events. Fourth, the meeting is said to happen so as to "be with the Lord," which is not the purpose of typical royal "meetings." Fifth, Paul describes the resurrection of believers in verse 14 as being parallel to the resurrection of Jesus. Hence, just as Jesus was raised into heaven, *so also* God will lead believers with him into heaven. Sixth, what is said here does not accord with the "royal meeting" pattern, since believers do not *take themselves* out to meet the Lord but are rather "snatched up" by God (Cosby 1994; Malherbe 2000, 277). Seventh, apocalyptic literature commonly affirms (a) that the righteous will be assumed into heaven and that they will spend their existence there with the Messiah (for the idea that the righteous are assumed into heaven, see sidebar above), (b) that the Messiah will return to heaven (*1 En.* 51.4; 2 Esd. [*4 Ezra*] 7:29–32), and (c) that the righteous will spend life together "with" him in heaven (2 Esd. [*4 Ezra*] 14:9; *1 En.* 39.6–7; 62.14; 71.16).

4:18. Paul's conclusion to this section shows that he does not discuss the resurrection and parousia as a doctrinal exercise. Rather, he has framed the unit with paraenetic concerns in view. At the outset he states a desire to set his listeners straight "lest they *grieve*," and he concludes by exhorting them to "*comfort*" one another. Apart from affirming the resurrection of the deceased at the time of the parousia, Paul does not set out to address the state of the individual between death and resurrection, nor does he have any reason to address the nature of the resurrection body (as in 1 Cor. 15:42–47; Phil. 3:20–21). His concern is to offer encouragement as a counter to grief: **therefore** = having been assured of the resurrection of the deceased along with the living. Just as he had been an encouragement to the Thessalonians while he was among them (2:12), and just as he seeks to comfort them further now, he also asks the Thessalonians to **comfort one another**.

Abraham Malherbe (1987) has found similarities between Paul's paraenetic approach in this passage and nurturing approaches practiced in the philosophical schools. For the ancient philosophers, philosophy was a way of life: taking on the lifestyle that it advocated required a reorientation of thinking, reprogramming of habits, and—due to the difficulty of assimilating to a demanding new lifestyle— encouragement when one felt that the demands were too difficult to manage. In this regard, Paul's exhortation to repeat **these words** to each other may suggest something like a mantra (cf. Seneca's conclusion to *Ep.* 78: "Refresh yourself with such thoughts as these") to be repeated not only by their teacher but also to one another as a reminder of what they believe and to inculcate a mentality that, though it is not shared by others, reflects the essence of their own hope.

---

1 Thess. 4:13–18 and Paul's Later Letters

Gerd Lüdemann (1980) has proposed that the Thessalonians' apparent ignorance on the question of the deceased owed to the fact that Paul himself had not yet considered the prospect that Christians—including himself (*"we* who are alive")—might die prior to the parousia; and that Paul therefore had not previously instructed the Thessalonians on the question of the deceased. According to Lüdemann, it was the death of believers in Thessalonica that first prompted Paul to consider the prospect of dying believers, and it was out of this situation that he developed the idea of a two-stage resurrection/ascension (the dead first, followed by the living). Furthermore, based on Paul's lack of attention to the notion of a transformed resurrection body, as found in such texts as 1 Cor. 15:42–57 and Phil. 3:21, Lüdemann concludes that Paul had not yet developed this idea either.

While it seems reasonable to believe that Paul may have developed his thinking as he went along in his ministry, it would be a serious overinterpretation of the evidence to draw hard conclusions about stages in Paul's theological development based on a meager description of the parousia and resurrection that does not have "doctrine" primarily in view. Paul addresses the immediate concern: they grieve for the deceased. The Thessalonians should be comforted in knowing that the deceased will experience the parousia just as those still living will experience it. Having offered them this comfort, Paul's purpose has been accomplished.

The Day of the Lord (5:1–11)

In 5:1 a *peri de* formula (cf. 4:9) indicates that the topic now introduced is one with which the Thessalonians are familiar: "the times and the seasons." It is possible, as many scholars have suggested, that the Thessalonians had inquired about the topic by letter, asking Paul about the timing of the parousia specifically, and that Paul here gives them an answer: because the parousia could happen at any time, they must be ready at every time. As at 4:9, however, the *peri de* formula need not indicate that the Thessalonians had inquired about the topic, much less by letter. Thematically, 5:1–11 relates closely with 4:13–18 and serves a similar paraenetic purpose. This section continues to impress upon the listeners a strong sense of community boundaries and a keen sense of identity, which Paul reinforces through a series of emphatic contrasts: between outsiders / "the rest" (*hoi loipoi*) and "you" (emphatic *hymeis*), between people of night and people of day, between children of darkness and children of light, and between those who sleep and those who watch. Finally, Paul asserts that the Thessalonians should draw comfort from knowing that they are destined for salvation, while outsiders (their persecutors) are destined for wrath, and that in this way the Thessalonian believers will be vindicated against their persecutors (Still 1999, 194–97). As in 4:18, the final word is an exhortation to "comfort" one another.

These emphases reveal that this section does not serve to answer a question distinct from that in 4:13–18 but to elaborate further the contrast between Christians and "the rest," which was first introduced in 4:13 (Barclay 2016, 222–28). Like 4:13–18 this section also continues to reflect tension between indicative and imperative in the lives of believers: the Thessalonians are naturally different from the rest, but they must also act *in accordance with* their identity.

As a whole, 5:1–11 contains extensive echoes of the apocalyptic material found in Matt. 24//Luke 21, probably suggesting use of a common apocalyptic tradition: "times and seasons" (cf. "day and hour," Matt. 24:36), the coming of a thief (Matt. 24:42–44//Luke 12:39), unexpected destruction (Matt. 24:39//Luke 21:34–35), labor pains (Luke 21:23), and watchfulness (Matt. 24:42–43) and preparedness (24:45–51). However, Paul adds his own creative touch, evinced most clearly in his varied use of the metaphors of day and night, light and darkness, and wakefulness and sleep.

This section has five discernible parts: an introduction of the topic (v. 1), a pronouncement about the suddenness of the parousia (vv. 2–3), a contrast between believers and unbelievers (vv. 4–7), a contrast between the fates of believers and unbelievers (vv. 8–10), and a concluding exhortation (v. 11).

5:1. Despite the thematic connection between 5:1–11 and 4:13–18, the *peri de* formula in 5:1 (**now concerning**), together with the vocative *adelphoi* (**brothers and sisters**), marks the introduction of a new subsection, in which Paul addresses **the times and the seasons** (*tōn chronōn kai tōn kairōn*). *Chronos* and *kairos* occur as a pair several times in the LXX (Dan. 2:21; 7:12; Wis. 8:8; cf. Neh. 13:31; Wis. 7:18). While the two nouns are subtly different in meaning, the pair generally functions as a simple collocation of synonyms (like "day and age" in English). The coordination of synonyms is especially common in Paul's letters, and several examples occur in the Thessalonian letters themselves ("in a holy and righteous and blameless manner," 1 Thess. 2:10; "distress and tribulation," 3:7; "abound and increase," 3:12; "signs and wonders," 2 Thess. 2:9; "labor and toil," 1 Thess. 2:9; 2 Thess. 3:8).

Paul does **not have need to write** to the Thessalonians on this topic (cf. 4:9). Undoubtedly this is because he already addressed the topic during his founding visit. There is, then, no compelling reason to believe that he is answering a separate query from the Thessalonians about "the timing of the parousia." Rather, as he has done so often in the letter, he says again what he "does not have need" to say (4:9) and reviews what the Thessalonians already "know" so as to continue to imbue them with a new and distinctively Christian way of thinking and—inseparable from this—of living.

5:2–3. A contrast between the audience and outsiders is now implicitly reinforced through the use of the intensive *autoi* (**you *yourselves* know**, i.e., while others do *not* know), a contrast that will continue to be elaborated throughout this section. The believers' knowledge concerns the **day of the Lord**. The OT describes a "day of the LORD" on which Yahweh will pour out judgment on the

105

earth (Isa. 2:12; Joel 1:15; Amos 5:18–20; etc.). Apocalyptic literature adapted the day of the Lord idea by depicting the Day as the time of eschatological judgment, when the righteous are rewarded with eternal life and the unrighteous with damnation (*1 En.* 58.3; 62.1–63.12). This eschatological meaning carried over into early Christian theology (1 Cor. 5:5; Rom. 2:5; also "the Day," 1 Thess. 5:4; 2 Thess. 1:10), though within Christian theology the day also coincided with the parousia of Jesus (1 Cor. 1:8; 4:5).

Paul has no need to write to them on the subject because (**for**) they are already as well informed as they can be. They know **accurately** that the day of the Lord **will come just like a thief in the night** (5:2; Matt. 24:42–44//Luke 12:39; 2 Pet. 3:10; Rev. 3:3; 16:15). Thus Paul is content to leave the timing of the day quite indefinite: it may come at any moment. "Accurately" is an ironic overstatement, for no one knows the appointed time. They know all that they need to know: that its coming will be sudden and unexpected.

The Thessalonians should not be deceived. Destruction will fall on the unwary. Ironically, it will fall specifically on the people who are most assured that they are living in prosperity and who declare, **"Peace and security."** The speakers are identified only by a generic "they," indicated by the verb's personal ending (*legōsin*). The continuous aspect conveyed by the verb's present-tense form shows that the reference is not to a certain climactic event in the future but to the characteristic attitude of an age, or indeed possibly of any age. It cannot be determined whether the slogan itself was current or whether the formulation was Paul's own. The words themselves evoke multiple resonances. Conceptually, they are redolent of the messages of prosperity characteristic of false prophets in the OT, who were accused of preaching "'peace,' when there is no peace" (Jer. 6:14; Ezek. 13:10). Linguistically, the words resonate both with imperial propaganda and the language of Epicurean philosophy. Imperial propaganda of the day declared that Roman rule had inaugurated a "Golden Age" (Vergil, *Aen.* 6.792–93). The term "peace" encapsulates the Roman construct of the *Pax Romana*, the "Roman peace," said to have been established by the emperor Augustus (described in Tacitus, *Hist.* 4.74; Vergil, *Aen.* 6.851–53). The specific language of peace and security (*pax* and *securitas*) occurs as a description of Roman rule in various numismatic, monumental, inscriptional, and literary sources (Weima 2012; though White 2013 observes that the terms never occur in the coordinated form cited in 1 Thess. 5:3, and the language of *securitas* does not appear in Roman ideology until

Public Domain

Figure 8. A Roman coin featuring Emperor Claudius and Roman "Peace" (*Pax*)

later, during the reign of Nero). Alternatively, Paul could intend to evoke the ideals of Epicurean philosophy, which promised peace and security of mind if one followed Epicurean principles.

Despite these parallels, there is no precedent in ancient sources for the precise slogan "peace and security," and resonances in 5:3 are likely multilayered. Viewed in one way, the text points to actual false prophets in the Thessalonians' environment and attributes to them a message similar to that of the false prophets of the OT. Viewed in another way, the text adapts the prophecies found in Isaiah and Ezekiel in order to challenge Roman propaganda (Tellbe 2001, 125). And viewed in yet another way, the text adapts Epicurean language in order to challenge contemporary false prophets (Malherbe 2014, 368).

In whatever way the slogan is construed, Paul's point is that the church should not be lulled into a false sense of security, rooted in some source other than the gospel of God. When people locate peace and security elsewhere, **sudden destruction is coming upon them** (5:3). This destruction is eschatological, for it concerns the "day" of Christ's return (5:4), when people are requited either with "salvation" or with "wrath" (see 5:9).

The verb's present tense (*ephistatai*, 5:3) is subject to various interpretations; it suggests perhaps the imminence of destruction (it is near), perhaps the initiated movement of destruction (the ax has begun to fall), or perhaps the subjects' unavoidable destiny (such are now destined to be destroyed). The cry "peace and security" is not a "sign" of coming destruction but rather a cause of it. Their cry makes their assessment of things official and exposes their ignorance and blindness (4:4–7). Having announced their view, they will now receive the consequences.

Although the destruction is eschatological, the act of crying peace and security is not here confined to the climactic end of the age; people are "*saying* 'peace and security'" all the time. It is their judgment that happens at the end. Paul does not specify what "destruction" entails for the unrighteous, either here or elsewhere in his letters. Apocalyptic literature typically predicts a period of postmortem punishment, sometimes indefinite or eternal (*1 En.* 22.11; 2 Esd. [*4 Ezra*] 7:79–80; *LAB* 44.10; *Apoc. Ab.* 24.6–8; 31.1–4; *T. Ab.* A 11.11; 4 Macc. 9:9; 10:11; 12:12; 18:5) and sometimes lasting long enough at least for the wicked to witness the vindication of the righteous (*1 En.* 27.3; 108.11–15; 2 Esd. [*4 Ezra*] 7:83; *2 Bar.* 30.4; 51.1–6) or for the righteous to witness the punishment of the wicked (*1 En.* 108.11–15; 2 Esd. [*4 Ezra*] 7:88–101). But in some texts "destruction" could be interpreted as gradual if not immediate annihilation (*1 En.* 38.5–6; 45.6; 48.10; *2 Bar.* 30.4; 51.1–6; cf. *Pss. Sol.* 14.9; 15.10, 12; Wis. 2:1–5). Since Paul does not elaborate here, the reference to "destruction" ultimately remains ambiguous (see also 2 Thess. 1:9).

The phrase **like the travail that comes upon a woman with child** makes a comparison between the "suddenness" of inevitable destruction at the end of the age and the sudden and unavoidable onset of labor when gestation reaches full term (5:3). Because destruction is inevitable and because it strikes quickly and without warning, the unrighteous **will surely not escape**. Apocalyptic literature that depicts the destruction of the wicked on judgment day often promises that the righteous will be preserved (see references at 4:17) or will "escape" (*1 En.* 10.17–22). This is also the implication here.

5:4–7. The conjunction *de* together with the emphatic pronoun *hymeis* creates a strong contrast between believers and the ignorant people destined to suffer destruction (v. 3): **But on the other hand** *you*, **brothers and sisters, are not** (cf. "you *yourselves* know," v. 2), a contrast repeated in **such that the Day overtakes** *you* **like a thief** (and later, "not like the rest," v. 6). The contrast introduces a new section, which draws on a rich abundance of overlapping metaphors to amplify the "night-and-day" difference between believers and nonbelievers. The constituent elements of the metaphors are used inconsistently throughout the section. A "day" is both the time when final judgment occurs (vv. 2, 4b) and a domain in which the righteous live (v. 5b). "Night" is both the time when a thief comes, at the end (v. 2), and a domain in which the unrighteous live (v. 5c). The "night" on which the thief comes is the "day" of the Lord. Believers are "not in darkness" (v. 4a), yet they are to stay on night watch (v. 6b). In 4:13, 14, and 15 those who "sleep" are believers, yet in 5:6a, 6b, and 7a they are unbelievers, and while sleep in 4:13–15 indicates a literal state of death, in 5:6–8 it signifies insensitivity to the Day.

Despite the mixing of metaphors, these figures map impressively onto each other conceptually and reduce to two basic sets. Each set consists of two pairs. Each pair in turn consists of a negative metaphor complemented by a positive metaphor, which together describe believers. The first set addresses what people *know*: believers (1) are not in darkness / are in the light and (2) should not sleep / but be awake. The other set addresses what people *do*: believers (1) are not of night / are of the day and (2) should not be drunk / should be sober.

Besides the conceptual coherence of the metaphors, verses 4–7 are structured according to a remarkable symmetrical pattern. A first round of metaphors (vv. 4a, 5a, 5b–c) is paralleled by a second (vv. 6a, 6b, 6c). These parts in turn antithetically parallel a final round of metaphors in verses 7–8 (vv. 7a–b, 7b–8a).

First, Paul describes the church as **not in darkness** (v. 4a) but as **sons of light** (v. 5a). Although the metaphor of darkness can correlate with behavior (Eph. 5:8–11), here it primarily highlights understanding. Those in darkness are ignorant of God, ignorant of the truth, and live accordingly. In the OT, light is associated with God or his word (Ps. 119:105) and darkness with alienation from God (Job 22:9–11; Ps. 27:1) or ignorance of God (Job 22:9–11; Ps. 82:5; Prov. 2:13). An antithesis between light and darkness is especially prevalent in sectarian theology. Writings from Qumran frequently employ the pair "sons of light" and "sons of darkness" to describe the righteous and the wicked respectively (1QM I.1–7; 1QS I.9–10). The same writings often have an epistemological emphasis: God gives understanding (1QS IX.21; XVIII.27), insight (1QS XIX.28), and secrets through the Holy Spirit (1QS XX.12). In places these texts explicitly connect knowledge of the truth with light, and ignorance of the truth with darkness (1QS III.17–26).

The light/darkness metaphor is also common elsewhere in the NT, especially in the Johannine literature. In 1 John, "God is light" (1 John 1:5); in the Gospel of John, Jesus is "the light of the world" (John 8:12; 9:5), and those in him will "not walk in darkness" (John 8:12). The parable of the dishonest manager specifically refers to the "sons of light" (Luke 16:8). In Paul's letters darkness is a common metaphor for ignorance (Rom. 1:21; 2:19; 2 Cor. 4:6; Eph. 4:18; cf. 2 Cor. 6:14; Eph. 6:12; 5:8–11; Phil. 2:15; Col. 1:13). Likewise, the Greco-Roman moral philosophers employed the metaphor of darkness to describe ignorance of the truth (Seneca, *Ep.* 110.7; 122.4; cf. *Nat.* 1.pref.1); closely related is the metaphor of blindness (*Ep.* 119.8; 120.18; 122.4).

Next, Paul describes the Thessalonians as **sons of day** (5:5b) and declares that they **do not belong to the night** (v. 5c). Although the metaphors of night and day correlate conceptually with the metaphors of darkness and light respectively, they shift the focus from epistemology to ethics. The ethical emphasis of the metaphor is evident in its occurrence in Romans: "the *night* is far gone, the *day* is near. Let us then lay aside the *works of darkness* and put on the armor of light; let us *live honorably as in the day, not in reveling and drunkenness, not in debauchery and licentiousness, not in quarreling and jealousy*" (13:12–13 NRSV). Here in 1 Thess. 5 the ethical emphasis is further elucidated by the symmetrical parallel between verses 5b (of day) and 5c (not of night) on the one hand, and verse 6c (sober) on the other.

Verse 6 introduces a transition into the final two pairs of metaphors. These are introduced as a conclusion (**therefore**) to verses 4–5 and correlate with the pairs in verses 4a and 5a (darkness = **let us not sleep like the rest**, but **let us be watchful**) and verses 5b and 5c (night = **let us be sober**), respectively. That is, "not sleep" but "be watchful" (v. 6b) correlates with the idea of mental awareness signified by the darkness (not sleep) and light (be watchful) pair (v. 4a and 4b). Those who are asleep are ignorant of the truth and unaware that the Day is imminent. Those who are awake are knowledgeable about its coming and thus remain mentally alert. The same two pairs of metaphors map onto each other in Rom. 13:11–13, where Paul moves from epistemology to the corresponding ethical behaviors: "It is now the moment for you to *wake from sleep*. . . . *The night is far gone, the day is near*. Let us *then* lay aside the works of *darkness* and put on the armor of *light*" (Rom. 13:11–12 NRSV). Like the darkness/light pair, the sleep/wakefulness pair was also common in the Greco-Roman philosophical tradition, where the metaphor was used to contrast ignorance with intellectual enlightenment (Seneca, *Ep.* 53.7–8).

While "be sober" (v. 6) could evoke echoes of local cultic activity (Donfried 1985, 342), this metaphor is probably selected because of its conceptual parallel with the night/day metaphor (vv. 5b, 5c): both metaphors highlight the necessity of ethical preparedness. Like the other metaphors, that of soberness is paralleled in the Greco-Roman philosophical tradition, where soberness equates with life lived according to reason (Malherbe 2000, 305, listing Philo,

Ebr. 166; and Diogenes Laërtius, *Vit.* 10.132; among others) or a life lived according to virtue.

Verse 7 maintains the section's parallel structure. Now Paul grounds his assertions about not being in darkness (vv. 4a, 5a) and not sleeping (vv. 6a–b) on the one hand, and about not being of the night (vv. 5b–c) but being sober (v. 6c) on the other, by contrasting believers with those who sleep (v. 7a) and get drunk (v. 7b): **For those who sleep sleep at night, and those who get drunk are drunk at night.** Here again the metaphors correlate respectively with epistemology (sleeping) and ethics (drunkenness). The ignorant sleep, while believers stay on watch. Some English translations render this portion in such a way that people are "*getting* drunk at night" (NASB, NIV, NRSV). This rendering, however, disregards the difference between *methyskō* (get drunk) and *methyō* (be drunk) and directly contradicts what has just now been said about what takes place at night: *sleep*, and one cannot drink while sleeping. The alternation of vocabulary then is significant: the people who "get drunk" (*methyskō*) do not "*get* drunk" at night but "*are* drunk" (*methyō*) at night, when evidently they are, as "ignorant" people, "sleeping." *Methyō*, in other words, is focused not on the behavior but on the state: they *are* drunk/ignorant/asleep.

5:8–10. Paul continues to assert a sharp contrast between believers and nonbelievers—those who are awake and those who sleep, those who are alert and those who repose in "peace and security"—by using the contrastive conjunction *de* and the emphatic pronoun *hēmeis*: **But we on the other hand** (cf. v. 4, *hymeis de*). Having used the second-person plural throughout most of vv. 1–7 (cf. v. 5c), Paul now shifts to the inclusive first-person plural. The change also coincides with a move from "indicative" to "imperative," marking a change of emphasis from identity (who believers are) to ethics (what they should do): **Since we belong to the day, let us be sober** (5:8). Paul often moves to the inclusive first person in his letters when engaging in exhortation (Rom. 13:12, 13; 14:13, 19; 1 Cor. 5:8; 9:25; 2 Cor. 7:1; Gal. 5:26; 6:9, 10; Phil. 3:15; 1 Thess. 4:7; cf. 3:3, 4). In that light, the shift to the first person here serves to highlight Paul's inclusion of himself as one to whom the same demands apply. Subtly, this strategy supports the mimetic theme of the letter: Paul desires to see the Thessalonians become as he is (see 1:5).

Having urged soberness upon the Thessalonians, Paul next shifts to another metaphorical domain, that of warfare: **having put on the breastplate of faith and love and the helmet that is the hope of salvation** (5:8). Conceivably the two metaphors are meant to relate systemically; that is, if the participle has a temporal relationship with the verb ("let us be sober, *after putting on* the breastplate . . ."), soberness could be viewed as conduct appropriate to the soldier prepared for battle. More likely, however, the participle relates to the verb circumstantially: donning the armor of faith, love, and hope creates the circumstances under which soberness becomes possible. Put differently, a transformation of character (having "put on" the breastplate) enables a transformation of behavior (being "sober"). Paul commonly uses the language of "putting on" to convey such transformation

Table 2. The First-Person Plural and Exhortation in 1 Thess. 5:8–10

first-person plural	imperative/subjunctive	ethics
second-person plural	indicative	identity

(Rom. 13:12, 14; Eph. 4:24; Col. 2:11; 3:9–10, 12). Faith, love, and hope, then, represent something like "Christian virtues": when someone has them (has put them on), they are brought to expression in particular acts of "sober" behavior. In that respect the metaphors of soberness and warfare are not systemically related; rather, they map onto each other as two different ways of describing Christian behavior.

Paul borrows the armor imagery from Isaiah (59:17; cf. Wis. 5:18–20), but in a Hellenistic adaptation he places the armor not on Yahweh but on Christ-believers, who wage war, as it were, on behalf of the Christian virtues of faith, love, and hope. In Greco-Roman moral philosophy, the language of warfare often describes the inner human struggle against vice. Most often the emphasis was defensive. The armor of virtue (4 Macc. 13:16) or the impregnable fortress of philosophy (Seneca, *Ep.* 53.12) makes the soldier impervious to vice's attacks. The soldier stands alert and poised to defend himself (Seneca, *Ep.* 59.7–8). Here also, Paul describes only defensive gear: a breastplate and a helmet. One need not assign significance to the pairing of faith and love with a "breastplate" and hope with a "helmet." Paul's selection of equipment is determined by the text of Isaiah, and the three virtues of faith, love, and hope are traditional (see 1:3), probably summing up Christian virtue as a whole.

Paul indicates that the object of hope lies in the future: "salvation." Salvation is not yet an accomplished fact. However, Paul offers grounds for hoping for salvation, in the knowledge that God has already destined them to attain it: **For God did not position us for wrath but for the acquisition of salvation** (5:9; cf. 1:4). By keeping this hope before them, they will stay mindful and stand ready for the imminent Day. Why Paul denies their destiny as objects of wrath is uncertain. Although the remark could be intended to allay any lingering anxiety about God's displeasure toward them, it could also serve to extend the antithesis between believers and unbelievers that has characterized 4:13–5:11 as a whole: "sudden destruction" is coming upon those who cry "peace and security" (v. 3) on the one hand, since they are ignorant that the day of the Lord is imminent, while believers on the other hand will *not* suffer this fate. It perhaps merits reflection that, if God's act of "positioning" applies just as much to nonbelievers as to believers, then Paul's language could imply double predestination. Though Paul never affirms election to damnation (but compare his *consideration* of the possibility in Rom. 9:22–24), there was strong precedent for such a theology in the writings at Qumran (1QH^a VII.21; 1QS III–IV).

Despite the shared use of martial imagery here and in Greco-Roman moral philosophy, Paul's addition of the words **through our Lord Jesus Christ, who** died for us introduces a critical difference between the Christian soldier and the philosopher (5:9–10). The philosopher claimed to attain perfection (embodied in virtue) through faculties innate to his human nature; though "reason" was a divine thing, it was not bestowed from without but was available within by virtue of birth (Seneca, *Ep.* 41.1–2; 73.16; 80.4–5). By contrast, while Paul enjoins the Christian soldier to suit up for battle, God is the one who has destined the believer for salvation, and it is through Christ's death that salvation is ultimately achieved. It is not said how Christ's death achieves this end, though Paul's later letters explicitly connect his death with the forgiveness of sins (1 Cor. 15:3; on "for us," see also Rom. 5:6, 8; 2 Cor. 5:15, 21; Gal. 2:20; 3:13), and 1 Pet. 2:24–25 links this idea with Isa. 53:4.

As Paul draws this section to a close, he reverts to the language of 4:13–18: Christ died for us **so that whether we are awake or asleep we might live together with him** (5:11). The words "awake" and "asleep" echo 4:13, 14, 15 ("those who sleep"; cf. KJV). Now, however, those who are "awake" and "asleep" no longer represent, respectively, those who are mindful and those who are ignorant (as in 5:6–7). Instead, they represent believers who are still alive and believers who are dead (as in 4:13–18). Paul's affirmation that both the living and the dead will ultimately "live together with him [the Lord]," moreover, echoes 4:17, where it is said that after both groups have been raised to meet the Lord in the air, they "will be *with the Lord always*."

The language of "being *with* the Lord" is significant in respect to Paul's wider theological framework. Central to Paul's later letters is a conception of salvation as unity with Christ, or "participation" with Christ (Gorman 2009). By contrast, neither the participation formula "in Christ" (*en Christō*) nor compound verbs that express active participation with him ("crucified with Christ," etc.) appear anywhere in the Thessalonian correspondence. Yet here the expression "might live with him" (*syn autō zēsōmen*), despite separating the preposition from the verb (cf. Rom. 6:8, *syzaō* = *syn* + *zaō*), undoubtedly adumbrates this theology. Verse 10 therefore brings together two important soteriological ideas: Christ's death and believers' life with him. *Because* Christ died "for" believers (v. 10), believers can be "with" him (v. 11).

5:11. Verse 11 ties 4:13–5:10 together as a whole. Mirroring 4:18, this verse again urges the church to **comfort one another**, based on (**therefore**) the hope of being "with Christ" at the parousia on the one hand and on the prospect of their enemies' judgment on the other hand. Mention of "comfort" also closes the circle by resolving the "grief" to which Paul refers in the opening verse of the unit (4:13). Now Paul adds a parallel command to **build up** (*oikodomeite*) **one another.** The verb *oikodomein* appears frequently in 1 Corinthians in reference to strengthening the faith of others (8:1, 10; 10:23) or strengthening the unity of the church body through the exercise of spiritual gifts (14:4 [2×], 17; the noun *oikodomē* in 14:3, 5, 12, 26). Here the verb takes its connotations from the word "comfort."

Finally, Paul grants that what he asks the church to do, they **also are doing** (cf. 4:1, 9). The fact that they are doing it does not make his exhortations superfluous. Rather, Paul recognizes that the Thessalonians stand in need of constant positive reinforcement, particularly at so early a stage in their faith and particularly in this present moment of distress.

Theological Issues

Grief and the Resurrection

Alongside certain streams of Jewish theology, early Christian theology was unique in its ancient context in affirming the hope of a bodily resurrection. Christ-believers had a hope beyond death that others did not have. Yet Paul's suggestion that, because of the resurrection, Christians should not grieve will surely strike many people as insensitive, even coldhearted. To fully appreciate his meaning, however, his remarks need to be understood relative to his wider theological framework. In principle, Paul's eschatology involves a presently irreconcilable tension between "already" and "not yet": what God has done in Christ and what he will do in the future. While the power of "life" is at work in making creation new, creation is still vulnerable to the corrupting activity of "death." In that respect, Paul did not affirm (as the Stoic philosophers did) that death is "indifferent." Death remains an evil; the resurrection would not be good news otherwise. Paul's prohibition of grief, then, was not absolute but rather involved a degree of rhetorical imbalance, wherein he inclines decidedly on the side of resurrection, the "already" over the "not yet." In other words, death is *not "no evil"* but rather is *an evil that is overcome.* Christians should "not grieve," then, not because death is not tragic, but because they have set their sights on the future, measuring "now" by comparing it with what "will be." As resurrection will triumph over death, so hope shall triumph over grief.

The Delayed Parousia

It is evident from this passage that early Christians (many of them at least) likely did not see the return of Christ and the ascent of believers to meet him as a remote event. Both the disappointment of the Thessalonians at the passing of some of their own and Paul's inclusion of himself and his generation as being possibly among those "who are alive, who remain at the coming of Christ," reveal that they expected the end to occur, not unlikely, within their lifetimes. As time drew on, and the first generation of believers passed away completely, one must suspect that the delay of Christ's return became increasingly disconcerting and that for some it was ultimately crushing. At some point the church had to come to terms with the delay. By now it has been not merely one generation but two millennia since the first Easter, and an indefinite delay is generally taken for granted. And yet, Paul's answer to the Thessalonian church is just as applicable today as it was then: since the parousia could happen at any time, believers should be ready at every time. A sense of *urgency* is perhaps more difficult to maintain now, after so great a passage of time: we shall probably die as so many others have before us. However, as Paul assures the Thessalonian church, the parousia will be of no less benefit to the dead than to the living.

Apart from this, Paul's discussion of preparedness is not just conditioned by the possibility of an *imminent* end. Rather, it is also conditioned by the partly "realized" nature of his eschatology. The future new age reaches back into the present. Believers have a new identity *now*. Indeed, 1 Thess. 5:1–11 is just as concerned with the difference between believers and nonbelievers in the present as it is with the final event itself. Believers should live as sons and daughters of light and of day, not just in case the end comes today, but because that is what they are.

1 Thessalonians 5:12–22

Final Exhortations

Introductory Matters

The main concerns that occasioned the letter have been exhausted. Now a succinct collection of exhortations draws the body of the letter to a close (5:12–22).

Tracing the Train of Thought

The formula that opens 5:12 echoes the wording of 4:1, minus the word "finally" (**we ask you, brothers and sisters**). Whereas the transition in 4:1 indicated a move to the second and "final" unit of the letter *body*, Paul now winds down to the letter's conclusion.

The relevance of the final hortatory section to the Thessalonians' situation is difficult to determine. While exhortations were not a common element of the letter closing in Hellenistic letters (Klauck 2006, 41), exhortations commonly occur at the closing of the body in Paul's letters (Rom. 16:17; 1 Cor. 16:13–18; 2 Cor. 13:11; cf. Eph. 5:1–6:17; Col. 4:2–6) as well as in other early Christian letters (1 John 4:1–21; 2 John 8–9; 3 John 11). Moreover, the considerable overlap between the paraenetic material here and

1 Thessalonians 5:12–22 in the Rhetorical Flow
Letter opening (1:1–10)
Letter body (2:1–5:22)
Paul's ministry in Thessalonica (2:1–12)
Renewed thanksgiving (2:13–16)
Paul's desire to visit again (2:17–3:13)
Exhortation, part 1 (4:1–12)
Exhortation, part 2 (4:13–5:11)
▶ Final exhortations (5:12–22)
First round of exhortations (5:12–15)
Second round of exhortations (5:16–22)

that found in Rom. 12:9–18—which in both cases contain multiple apparent echoes of the teachings of Jesus (1 Thess. 5:15, 16, 17)—suggests that a generic body of traditional Christian paraenesis had already formed, the substance of which was probably considered pertinent to Christians at basically any place and time. Finally, together with the largely generic nature of this material, the placement of this material in the "hortatory closing" suggests that Paul is not introducing any new "issues" of special relevance to the church, at least not any issues substantial enough to merit attention in the letter's body. Paul, however, has probably shaped this material in light of the Thessalonians' circumstances, since this material echoes themes addressed elsewhere in the letter (joy, prayer, thanksgiving), and some subjects (nonretaliation; the disorderly, fainthearted, and weak) conceivably relate to issues we know the church was facing (persecution and other challenges).

The hortatory section consists of two rounds of exhortations (vv. 12–15, 16–22). Both of these concern the members' orientation toward others within the community of faith (although in 5:15 the community's orientation toward outsiders is also in view). The first round consists of instructions concerning the community's conduct. The second round concerns members' spiritual practices and inner dispositions.

First Round of Exhortations (5:12–15)

5:12–15. The first round of exhortations consists of three sets of instructions (vv. 12–13, 14, 15). The three sets exhibit a notable measure of structural symmetry: each begins with either an indirect (we ask you) or direct command formula (we urge you; or see to it) followed by a command (to acknowledge . . . and to regard; or admonish . . . encourage . . . help; or see . . . that no one repays) and then a summary command (be at peace; or be patient; or always pursue the good) and finally ends by naming the group to whom the required behavior should be directed (among yourselves; or toward all such people; or toward one another and toward all people).

1. The first set of instructions (vv. 12–13) concerns the relationship of the community to **those who labor among you and are set over you and admonish**

Table 3. The Structural Symmetry of 1 Thess. 5:12–15

	Introductory formula	Command or request	Summary command	Target of behavior
5:12–13	"we ask you"	"to acknowledge . . . and to regard"	"be at peace"	"among yourselves"
5:14	"we urge you"	"admonish . . . encourage . . . help"	"be patient"	"toward all such people"
5:15	"see to it"	"that no one repays"	"always pursue the good"	"toward one another and toward all people"

you. It is not clear to whom Paul makes reference. A single article (*tous*) governs all three participles (*kopiōntas, proistamenous, . . . nouthetountas*), showing that the same group is responsible for all three actions. Abraham Malherbe (1987, 88–90) has argued that Paul is referring to *all* believers and their obligations toward *one another*. However, this seems unlikely on several counts (see below). More likely, the individuals to whom Paul refers are "leaders" of sorts, although interpreters debate whether they held well-defined "offices" or were officially appointed for leadership. Here Paul assigns no label to their positions (e.g., "bishop," 1 Tim. 3:1–7; "deacons," 3:8–13; "elders," 5:17–19; "elders and bishops," Titus 1:5–7), and he describes their activities without reference to any specialized duties (e.g., teaching, administering the Eucharist, baptizing, delegating responsibilities).

Whether these individuals functioned as leaders—and if so, in what capacity—depends largely on the semantic nuances of each of the three participles. While the verb "labor" (*kopiān*) could refer to work carried out with the "hands" to earn one's livelihood (2:9; cf. 1 Cor. 4:12; 2 Thess. 3:8), Paul often uses this verb to refer to his or others' labor carried out as ministers of the gospel (Rom. 16:6, 12; 1 Cor. 15:10; 16:16; Gal. 4:11; Phil. 2:16; Col. 1:29; the noun *kopos* in 1 Cor. 15:58; 1 Thess. 1:3). The second participle, "set over," is more critical. The verb *proistanai* usually denotes some kind of authority over others—whether as a leader, administrator, or manager—as evidenced by both the NT and other Greek literature (e.g., 1 Tim. 3:4, 5, 12; 5:17; Titus 3:8, 14; see LSJ 1482–83, meaning B.II). While the verb could also loosely connote the activities of a "patron," in the sense of a person to whom charge has been given, authority would naturally grow out of such a position (Meeks 1983, 82). Moreover, the phrase **in the Lord** limits the sphere of their charge to the corporate life of the church, which would surely entail oversight of corporate activities if not also enforcement of proper behavior and even extensive reach into the spiritual lives of individual members, making patron duties per se less relevant. The third participle ("admonish") connotes authority insofar as the person responsible puts themselves in a position as judge and critic of another. Paul viewed admonishment as part of his role as "father" of the Corinthian church (1 Cor. 4:14–15). Some kind of leverage over others would normally be implied in the act of admonishing (see the distinction between "exhortation" [*paraklēsis*] and "rebuke" [*nouthetein*] in Stobaeus, *Flor.* 4.79.53), though Paul also presents admonishment as a duty of every believer (Rom. 15:14; 1 Thess. 5:14; Col. 3:16); indeed, he does so here just two verses later (5:14).

Also crucial to the question of leadership are the infinitives that specify what Paul is "asking": he is asking the community to **acknowledge** those who labor and to **regard them highly** (5:12). While resonances of submission are not inherent to the semantics of these verbs (*eidenai, hēgeisthai*), asymmetrical connotations are surely implied. The church is not just to "acknowledge" or "regard" these people in the sense of "looking" at them or acknowledging their existence. They are to look at them in a special way. The addition of the qualifying adverb *hyperekperissou* with the second infinitive specifies the need for a high, or comparatively higher, *estimation* of them.

In deciding the nature of these leaders' roles, a comparison with 1 Cor. 16:15–18 is also instructive, since this text has several features in common with 1 Thess. 5:12–13 (see table). Both texts occur within their respective letters' final hortatory sections (cf. 1 Cor. 16:13–14; 1 Thess. 5:16–22), both begin with a formula of petition, both include a request to acknowledge certain individuals within the community in a special way, and both ground the request in the work that these individuals do (**on account of their work**). What is explicitly added in 1 Corinthians is that the church should "be subject" (*hypotassēsthe*) to these individuals (16:16). Even if the community's submission was not institutionally enforced, the verb nonetheless conveys obligation. A uniformity in the status structure of Paul's many communities ought not to be *presumed*, but based on the analogies between 1 Thess. 5:12–13 and 1 Cor. 16:15–18, it would not be unwarranted to suppose that a hierarchical arrangement of some kind was involved.

The evidence, then, favors the view that the Thessalonian church did have some sort of leadership in place and that there was some degree of asymmetry in the organizational structure. On the other hand, it cannot be confidently determined whether leadership positions existed by appointment, whether they were designated by official titles, or whether they came with a precise job description.

The inclusion of this section in the letter could suggest that the community was feeling discontentment with its current leadership (Weima 2014, 389–90). Masson (1957, 79), following Dibelius (1937, 58), maintained that Paul addressed the letter to the church's leaders and that these leaders were personally at odds with the congregation. Although verses 12–13 quite evidently address the church as a whole, Masson takes verses 14–15 as specifically addressing its leaders ("admonish," etc.) and the preceding two verses as an order for the congregation to obey them (vv. 12–13). However, if discontentment was present in the church, it must have been slight. Paul does not censure the church, nor does he demand subordination. Moreover, the phrasing suggests that Paul's main request was *not* that they "*regard their leaders highly*"; if that had been his purpose, such phrasing alone would have been sufficient. Rather, the phrasing *assumes* that

Table 4. Paul's Appeals in 1 Thess. 5:12–13 and 1 Cor. 16:15–18

1 Thess. 5:12–13	1 Cor. 16:15–18
"now we ask [*erōtōmen*] you, brothers and sisters" (5:12)	"now I urge [*parakalō*] you, brothers and sisters" (16:15)
"acknowledge [*eidenai*]" (5:12), "regard [*hēgeisthai*]" (5:13)	"recognize [*epiginōskete*]" (16:18)
"because of their work" (5:12)	"be subject *to such people and with everyone who works and labors* together with them" (16:16)

the Thessalonian believers regard their leaders highly; it *asks* that they regard them highly **in *love*.** The addition of this phrase implies that, even if a power differential was present, Paul does not directly address maintenance of the power differential but rather the *attitude* with which the related entities should regard each other. That is, respect for their leaders should be based not on fear but on voluntary consent inspired by an attitude of love toward them. Paul's remark echoes discussions of the dynamics between leaders and their subjects widely discussed in ancient sources. It was commonly said that people "hate" those whom they "fear" (1 John 4:18; Seneca, *Ben.* 4.19.1; *Ep.* 47.18–19; cf. *Ira* 1.20.4; *Clem.* 1.12.4; 2.2.2; Cicero, *Amic.* 15.53; Plutarch, *Superst.* 170E; Augustine, *Civ.* 6.9 on Varro). Seneca remarked that "love and fear cannot be mingled" and on this basis advised masters to demand from their slaves not fear but respect, for "respect means love" (*Ep.* 47.18–19). Similarly, Paul asks that the Thessalonians regard their overseers not with fear but with love.

The command **be at peace among yourselves** is not independent of what precedes (5:13). Rather, it refers specifically to the parties just mentioned. In this regard, "yourselves" encompasses the whole community, though the command especially has in view relationships between the leaders and the rest (and perhaps also relationships as affected by potentially divergent attitudes *about* the leadership).

2. Verse 14 introduces a second set of instructions. The opening formula **and we urge you, brothers and sisters,** like other formulas of this kind ("now we ask and urge you, brothers and sisters," 4:1; "but we urge you, brothers and sisters," 4:10; "now I ask you, brothers and sisters," 1 Cor. 16:15), often serves to introduce a new topic or major structural unit in a letter. Here, however, the formula runs parallel to the one that introduced verse 12 ("now we ask you, brothers and sisters") and thus introduces a set of parallel instructions: **admonish the unruly, encourage the fainthearted, help the weak.**

There is no indication that Paul has specific referents in mind, and the vague nature of the descriptions makes it difficult to determine where the deficiencies lie. Theoretically, the descriptions could indicate, respectively, social ("unruly"), emotional ("fainthearted"), and moral deficiencies ("weak"). James Frame (1912, 197–98) proposed that each of the commands correlates with some group described earlier in the letter: the unruly are "idlers" (4:11–12), the fainthearted are those who grieve over the dead (4:13–18) or fear for their salvation (5:1–11), and the weak are those tempted to impurity (4:3–8). This proposal is intriguing, and even if the three commands serve as a selective summary of possible deficiencies, the examples may have been inspired by the issues at hand.

"Admonishing" appeared as one of the duties that describe the leaders in 5:12. It is now made a duty of all believers: they are to admonish the *ataktoi* (5:14). The meaning of this substantive adjective—here translated "unruly"—is uncertain due to a lack of developed context. In its root sense the term denotes the quality of being "out of order," or being "disorderly." In military contexts, this quality could describe any failure to maintain proper order, from abandoning one's post to falling out of formation to disobeying a commander's orders.

Nonetheless, many interpreters have taken the term here as a reference to "idlers," basing their evidence primarily on two other passages in the Thessalonian letters. (1) The term *ataktoi* appears in 2 Thess. 3:6–13, where it clearly refers to those who are not working. Joining 2 Thess. 3:6–13 with (2) Paul's command in 1 Thess. 4:11 to "work with one's hands," it is then conjectured that the *ataktoi* who were not working when Paul wrote 2 Thessalonians were also not working when he wrote 1 Thessalonians. Other interpreters, however, counter that there is no warrant for importing the situation reflected in 2 Thess. 3:6–13 into the situation reflected here (though often this objection is based on the belief that 2 Thessalonians is pseudonymous), and they instead maintain that the term keeps its root sense of "disorderliness." If the culprits' disorderliness concerned their conduct in public, it could have involved public disturbances in the form of censorious public evangelism (Barclay 1993) or disruption of civic meetings (De Vos 1999, 161–62) in response to opposition from local outsiders. Alternatively, disorderliness could have been internal, involving rebellion against either Paul (Jewett 1986, 106; Gupta 2019, 267–68) or institutional leadership in general (Gaventa 1998, 82), or a rejection of the church's traditional body of instruction, its "community rule" (Donfried 2002, 231).

Whatever the situation, granting that "disorderliness" or "unruliness" is in view, it is still possible to suppose that the unruly *ataktoi* were also lazy or willfully unemployed (Wanamaker 1990, 196–97; Malherbe 1987, 92; De Vos 1999, 161–62). Given Paul's renewed attention to the *ataktoi* in 2 Thessalonians (which we shall assume is authentic), it seems best to assume that there was some continuity to the situation and that, with idleness being in view there, it is also in view here. If such was the case, then the activities of the *ataktoi* (in addition to being "disorderly") were *taking the place* of working.

Next, Paul instructs the church to "encourage the fainthearted." The language of "encouraging" occurred earlier in the letter. Just as "admonishing" appeared as an activity of church leaders in 5:12 and as an activity of all believers in 5:14, similarly "encouraging" was named as an activity of Paul in 2:12 and is named as an obligation of all believers here. The word "encourage" (*paramythousthai*) is milder than "admonish" and arguably better adapted to the condition of the recipients: they are "fainthearted." Assuming that Paul's words reflect sensitivity to the Thessalonians' situation, he might envisage the fainthearted as those who are disheartened by their affliction (1:6; 2:14; 3:3–4), mournful over the deceased (4:13–18), or vulnerable in their faith (2:17–3:10); though he would not have wanted to exclude other forms of faintheartedness. As Ernest Best (1979, 230) astutely remarks, "A thousand and one other things might have reduced them to this condition."

Finally, Paul instructs the church to "help the weak." The meaning of this is somewhat clarified by the context. While the reference could be to the physically

Psychagogic Practice in Schools of Philosophy

Abraham Malherbe (1987, 81–88) proposes that 1 Thess. 5:14 should be understood in relation to the psychagogic practices of the philosophical schools. Psychagogic theory stressed that philosophers should "give close attention to the psychological condition of those they intended to help" and "adapt their exhortation accordingly." Such exhortation, philosophers believed, "should always be timely, preferably in private and thus individualized, and conducted patiently, without expecting immediate success" (88). For instance, Paul here urges the harshest approach for the disorderly ("admonish") but a gentler approach for the fainthearted ("encourage") and the weak ("help"; 90–94). In turn, Malherbe continues, the recipients of exhortation were "urged to receive admonition willingly, with love, affection, honor, and gratitude to those who wish to help them and not to be irritated and lash back at them" (88). Malherbe proposes that it is with this in mind that Paul reminds the community to "be patient" with one another.

weak or economically disadvantaged, against this possibility is that the other two groups mentioned are described in terms of deficiencies of *conduct* ("disorderly," "fainthearted"). Moreover, if the meaning of "weak" were physical or economic, Paul's final command to **be patient toward all such people** would feel strangely out of place, as it seems implicitly to anticipate the rise of irritation toward these people (5:14). As in the first two cases, it is better to take this remark as a request for believers to be patient as they help one another (or "the weak") along in the *faith*. The language of "weakness," especially in philosophical literature, frequently indicates moral failure: weakness consisted in a lapse in the reasoning faculty, which then gives rise to vice (see comments on 3:3). Paul himself often uses this language similarly (Rom. 4:19; 5:6; 8:26; 1 Cor. 8:7, 9, 10; 9:22). Since moral weakness could be expected in his young converts, he asks the community to strengthen those who are struggling in this regard.

3. With his final set of instructions (5:15), Paul advises appropriate responses to injury. **See to it that no one repay evil for evil** expresses a rule that is nowhere seen in quite this form in antecedent literature. The rule may have been an early Christian aphorism (Wanamaker 1990, 198), as the construction "see to it" is anomalous in Paul's letters and the pronoun "someone" lends the rule indefinite application. The idea that vengeance belongs to God (Deut. 32:35) and ought not to be taken into one's own hands (Ps. 7:4–5; Prov. 17:13) finds representation in the OT. A rule of nonretaliation is explicitly stated in Qumran documents, though the rule there applies only to conduct between members of the group (1QS X.17). In the Greco-Roman moral tradition from as early as Socrates, it was an axiom that it was "better to be wronged than to wrong" (Plato, *Gorg.* 469C; Aristotle, *Eth. Nic.* 5.11.7–8; Musonius Rufus, *Diatr.* 3; Seneca, *Ep.* 95.52; so also 1 Cor. 6:7). The

aphorism as stated in 1 Thess. 5:15, however, is more extreme than conventional moralities on at least two points. First, Paul's axiom requires not only a negative response (do not retaliate) but also a positive one (**but always pursue the good**). Second, it applies not only to the treatment of members within the community but also to people universally (**both toward one another and toward all people**). The sentiment closely reflects the teachings of Jesus on love of enemies (Matt. 5:44//Luke 6:28). For the Thessalonians, the rule must have struck close to heart, for they had been persecuted "at the hands of their own countrymen" (2:14). In this regard, it is perhaps not by accident that the expression "*pursue* the good" (*to agathon diōkein*) employs a verb that commonly meant "persecute." Paul, then, may have intended double entendre: the Thessalonians are to "pursue" good toward those who "pursued" them with evil.

Second Round of Exhortations (5:16–22)

5:16–22. The second round of exhortations consists of eight imperative statements (plus a parenthetical remark), each putting the verb last. The first three imperatives address believers' dispositions. Thereafter the syntactical structure changes from *adverb/adverbial phrase + verb* to *direct object + verb*, while the topic shifts to prophecy, a topic that will occupy the remainder of the section. Thus the unit breaks down into two main segments: (1) a set of three imperatives that concern dispositions (vv. 16, 17, 18) and (2) a set of five imperatives that concern the exercise of prophecy (vv. 19, 20, 21 [2×], 22).

1. *First segment.* The three imperatives in the first segment (5:16–18) reprise themes that appeared earlier: **always rejoice** (1:6; 2:19, 20; 3:9), **constantly pray** (1:2–5; 2:13; 3:9–10, 11–13; 5:23, 25), **in everything give thanks** (1:2–10; 2:13–16; 3:9). While Paul enjoins the same activities upon believers in other letters (to rejoice constantly, Phil. 4:4; to pray unceasingly, Rom. 12:12; Phil. 4:6; Col. 4:2; to give thanks always, 1 Cor. 1:4; Eph. 5:20; Phil. 1:3; 2 Thess. 1:3; Philem. 4), the repetition of these themes in 1 Thessalonians may suggest that his paraenesis is selective. In this regard it may be illuminating to reflect on the relevance of these exhortations within the context of the Thessalonians' present social situation. The theme of *rejoicing* is often connected with suffering in Paul's letters (1 Thess. 1:6; 2 Cor. 6:10; 7:4–5; 8:2; Col. 1:24; cf. 2 Cor. 12:10). The command to "rejoice always," even in suffering, may trace to the teachings of Jesus, who considered those who suffered "blessed" and enjoined them to "rejoice" since their "reward is great in heaven" (Matt. 5:10–12//Luke 6:22–23; cf. John 16:20–22; 1 Pet. 4:13). Next, a constant impulse to *pray* would be essential for the Thessalonians in maintaining their faith, difficult as their conversion had proved to be (to pray "constantly" implies iterative rather than continuous prayer, though it suggests a frequency that goes quite beyond fixed routine). Parallels, again, in the teaching of Jesus suggest that the command to pray constantly could also be related to suffering. In Luke 18, Jesus illustrates his teaching that the disciples "ought always to pray" (18:1) with the parable of the unjust judge, concluding that God will "grant justice to

Table 5. The Parallel Structure of 1 Thess. 5:12–13; 5:14; and 5:16–18

5:12–13	5:14	5:16–18
"we ask you to acknowledge … and to regard" (5:12, 13)	"Admonish the unruly, encourage the fainthearted, help the weak" (5:14)	"Rejoice … pray … give thanks" (5:16, 17, 18)
"Be at peace among yourselves" (5:13)	"Be patient toward all such people" (5:14)	"for this is the will of God for you" (5:18)

his chosen ones who cry to him day and night" (18:7 NRSV). Finally, *gratitude* toward God may not have been the Thessalonians' most natural instinct under their circumstances, but Paul's commending of this activity implies that they possess some good thing that far transcends the afflictions they presently suffer.

Following this triad of commands, Paul adds the words **for this is the will of God for you.** While this statement could qualify only the command to give thanks, a structural parallel between verses 12–13, 14, and 16–18 suggests that it qualifies all three of the commands in 5:16–18. Indeed, in each instance two or more commands are followed by a summary command, or in the case of 5:18, a summary remark (see table).

Paul used a similar expression in 4:3, where he identified the will of God as the Thessalonians' "sanctification." Something must have provoked Paul to highlight the nature of God's will. Conceivably, he perceived that the Thessalonians doubted whether God's will for them was in fact for good. In the same regard, Paul's assurance in 5:9 that God did not destine them "for wrath" may suggest that their experiences had led them to question God's benevolence. Paul had taught that they were "destined for" affliction (3:3), and now they had experienced the onslaught of this affliction for themselves (3:4), an experience that must have been unpleasant for them. The possibility that they doubted God's benevolence fits neatly with the Thessalonians' ethnic (gentile) profile. Greco-Roman sources are insistent that most people believed that God / the gods could be propitiated with vows and sacrifices but were nonetheless petty, vindictive, and cruel (Plutarch, *Superst.* 170D–E), both in this life and in the next, and that torment awaited humans in the underworld (*Superst.* 166F– 167A). To top all this, ill fortune fell upon people by a decree of Providence / God's will (*Superst.* 168A–B, F), and it fell upon them because they supposedly deserved it (*Superst.* 168B–C). Thus, according to many sources, people feared and detested God (albeit secretly), hating their lot but seeing no way to escape his punishments (Plutarch, *Superst.* 165D–E, 166D, 170E; Lucretius, *Rer. nat.* 3.830–1094; Cicero, *Nat. d.* 1.45, 56, 117; Augustine, *Civ.* 6.9 on Varro). While this summary surely overgeneralizes popular perspectives on the gods (as noted in Cicero, *Nat. d.* 1.86; *Tusc.* 1.10, 48), it must have some basis in reality for it to have merited repeating (see sidebar).

The Gods in Popular Piety

"You see what kind of thoughts the superstitious have about the gods; they assume that the gods are rash, faithless, fickle, vengeful, cruel, and easily offended; and, as a result, the superstitious man is bound to hate and fear the gods. Why not, since he thinks that the worst of ills are due to them, and will be due to them in the future?" (Plutarch, *Superst.* 170D–E, trans. Babbitt, LCL)

"For he [the superstitious person] puts the responsibility for his lot upon no man nor upon Fortune nor upon occasion nor upon himself, but lays the responsibility for everything upon God, and says that from that source a heaven-sent stream of mischief has come upon him with full force; and he imagines that it is not because he is unlucky, but because he is hateful to the gods, that he is being punished by the gods, and that the penalty he pays and all that he is undergoing are deserved because of his own conduct." (Plutarch, *Superst.* 168A–B, trans. Babbitt, LCL)

Paul assures the Thessalonians that, in contrast with the will of *that* god—the god of superstition—the will of God for them **in Christ Jesus** is good (5:18). Knowing this God, they have every reason to rejoice, to give thanks, and to pray for their own and for others' well-being.

2. *Second segment.* The second segment within 5:12–22 contains five imperative statements. Although "prophecy" is mentioned just once, all five imperatives should be seen in reference to it. Admittedly, the command **Do not quench the Spirit** (v. 19) could refer generally to the exercise of spiritual gifts, which Paul attributes to the Spirit elsewhere (1 Cor. 12:4–11). However, prophecy is one of the gifts that the Spirit inspires (1 Cor. 12:10), prophecy is the only gift specifically mentioned here (**Do not despise prophecy**, v. 20), and verses 21–22 make coherent sense in connection with it (see below).

First Thessalonians is the first extant Christian source to discuss Christian prophecy, though its great importance in early Christianity is evident, especially from Paul's letters (Rom. 12:6; 1 Cor. 12:10, 28–29; 14:6, 22, 29–33), Acts (11:27–28; 13:1; 15:32; 21:10), and the book of Revelation (1:3; 22:19). These texts show that prophecy primarily consisted of "revelation" from God, including revelation of both heavenly mysteries (reflecting Jewish apocalyptic) and future events (reflecting a contemporary understanding of OT prophecy). Prophecy could be abused, however, as is evinced in the NT's frequent denunciation of "false prophets" (see 5:3). Thus Paul complements his commands not to prohibit prophecy with conditions that place limitations on it: **but test all things, cling to what is good, abstain from every type of evil** (5:21–22). While the details are bare, these commands apparently dovetail with Paul's remarks about prophecy in 1 Corinthians 12–14: the task of "testing" belongs to those with the gift of "discernment of spirits"

(1 Cor. 12:10; cf. 14:29), and the "good" or "bad" resulting from a prophecy—for instance, whether or not the church is edified (1 Cor. 14:3, 4 [2×], 5, 12, 17, 26)—determines whether its message should be received as legitimate.

Paul's evenhanded advice here resembles the instructions that he gives about the gifts of tongues and prophecy in 1 Cor. 14. Yet in 1 Thessalonians the situation seems to be reversed. The Corinthians had let the gifts pour forth in excess; thus, while not wishing to "hinder" speaking in tongues (1 Cor. 14:39), Paul nevertheless put constraints on their deployment (14:27–28) and countered the Corinthians' overemphasis on tongues by actively promoting prophecy (although he put constraints on prophecy as well, 14:29–33), since prophecy "edified" the whole body. Here, however, the problem is not one of excess but of deficiency: the Thessalonians appear to have inordinately suppressed spiritual gifts, or prophecy specifically.

Paul's choice to devote relatively more space to prophecy than to the behaviors enjoined in verses 16–18 points to the special relevance of this topic to the Thessalonians. Indeed, the juxtaposition of negative (vv. 19, 20) with positive (vv. 21, 22) commands here suggests that Paul is trying to balance a high estimation of prophecy and spiritual gifts with an emergent skepticism about them among the Thessalonians. Modern interpreters have offered various explanations for Paul's tack. It was once believed that he sought to counter a skepticism that had arisen in the church in reaction to an emphasis on spiritual gifts by gnostic opponents (Schmithals 1972, 172–75). While the presence of gnostics in Paul's milieu has now been called into question (Yamauchi 1973; 1983), it does seem that Paul was reacting either to a dismissing of prophecy or to doubts among the Thessalonians about prophecy itself. Perhaps they rejected all Christian prophets out of a fear of *false* prophets (Malherbe 2000, 335), or were reacting against their pagan past, now associating prophecy with either the ecstatic prophets of the Dionysus cult (Donfried 1985, 342) or with the many "pretender" figures that could be found deceiving the masses in cities all over the empire (see esp. Lucian, *Alexander the False Prophet*). Other scholars have proposed a link between this passage and the preceding discussion about the church's leaders (vv. 12–13), arguing that resistance to spiritual gifts stemmed from the leaders themselves, whose position was being undermined by those who preferred a less institutional and more charismatic form of governance (Jewett 1986, 103, 175). Whatever the case may have been, interpreters agree that these verses are directed at a lack of prophetic enthusiasm rather than an excess of it and that Paul aims to restore a proper balance between free expression and restrictive discernment.

Theological Issues

Believers in Relation to Each Other

Strip away two thousand years of church institutional growth—no confirmation classes, Sunday school, or counseling centers; no lectionaries, orders of service, or hymnals; no discipleship curricula and no podcasts; and no seasoned leaders to look to—and one is a bit closer to understanding what it was like to be a new believer in first-century Thessalonica. Add to this the fact that it was not Jewish monotheism or the stories of the Jewish Scriptures that had shaped you from childhood, but paganism and its various mythologies. Add finally that there is only one small local church to speak of, your own, and it was established just yesterday. As a believer in that church, just finding your footing, you would have none of the resources available that believers in the church today take for granted.

With this in mind, Paul's instructions in 5:12–15 take on somewhat different significance. In the first place, without the availability of other kinds of resources, one had to rely on the guidance of the believing community. Moreover, because believers were so few and all equally young in the faith, the church could not afford for anyone to sit on the sidelines. Apart from the church's emergent leadership, who played some role in "admonishing" the others in the church, all believers had a vital part to play in each other's development. As each other's only resources, they had a bilateral obligation to help each other uphold behavioral expectations and theological principles that differed from the ones they had held for so long. The faith of each believer was not just a private matter. They were truly each other's business.

Believers in Relation to Nonbelievers

Sharp group boundaries often create a dynamic of escalating tensions. A perception of difference creates enmity; feelings of enmity produce acts of injustice; and acts of injustice provoke retaliation; retaliation comes, enmity increases, and the process repeats itself with greater intensity. While the ingredients of such a conflict were all in place for the Thessalonian church, Paul refused to allow the church to follow that path; he encouraged them, even while still maintaining a strong sense of group separateness, not to retaliate.

A principle of nonretaliation is not so controversial in theory. Most people would probably uphold such a principle as a worthy ideal, to be pursued often. Many would even profess that it should be practiced sometimes toward enemies. Endorsing such a principle as an abstract ideal, however, is much easier to do than actually practicing it. Paul asked the Thessalonians not to retaliate against injustice when they had just experienced it—and likely were still experiencing it. For the Thessalonians, this injustice took the form of severe social ostracism, with both emotional and economic consequences, as well as physical abuse and possibly death (see the introduction to 1 Thessalonians, above). In many places in the world, executions and even pogroms have been, and in some places continue to be, carried out for religious (and anti-religious) and other reasons. Anyone who has experienced much lesser evils will be aware of how difficult it is to maintain a commitment to non-retaliation when injury has been suffered. It is easy for those who profess non-retaliation even upon enemies, when injustice falls, to claim exemption from the principle due to special circumstances or to repress their professed ideal beneath surges of outrage. In the inward battle of feelings, the common triumph of "justice" over love demonstrates just how radical is the message to love one's enemies—not just those with whom one disagrees, but real enemies: those who cheat you out of your earnings, who turn everyone against you, who emotionally or physically abuse you and do so without remorse, and sometimes with relish. When one is able to love *that* kind of enemy, one is closer to doing what Paul is advocating.

Believers' Inner Attitudes

For the Thessalonians, Paul's instructions to "always rejoice, constantly pray, and in everything give thanks" were not just platitudes; they were not just the happy lyrics of a children's nursery song. Although they must have struck an unusual note for the Thessalonians, these instructions were challenges that penetrated to the heart of what made the gospel good news. The church could rejoice, pray, and give thanks, not because they prospered, but despite the fact that they did not. There was a future good that surpassed the present bad.

1 Thessalonians 5:23–28

Letter Closing

Introductory Matters

Having spoken a final word of exhortation, Paul comes to the letter's closing. This consists of a wish-prayer (vv. 23–24), a prayer request (v. 25), a greeting (v. 26), a request for the letter to be read (v. 27), and a benediction (v. 28). These elements are often found in various forms at the conclusion of Hellenistic letters (Klauck 2006). Paul's own modifications naturally reflect the distinctive aspects of traditional Christian practice and theology. Abraham Malherbe (2000) observes, for instance, that a prayer for health often occurred at the beginning or the end of Hellenistic letters (343); yet Paul's prayer is striking by comparison in that, among other differences, he focuses on spiritual rather than physical well-being.

Tracing the Train of Thought

Second Wish-Prayer (5:23–24)

5:23–24. Verses 23–24 comprise the second of two "wish-prayers" in 1 Thessalonians. The first (3:11–13) concluded the first main unit of the letter's body (2:1–3:10). The second now concludes the second and final unit of the body (4:1–5:22) and provides a transition into the letter-closing proper. The two wish-prayers share several elements: God as the grammatical subject, God's agency in believers' sanctification, an expressed desire that the recipients' heart or spirit/soul/body be blameless, and the importance of believers being found in this condition at Jesus's parousia. The prayer serves as a fitting conclusion to the letter's body as it reprises several themes that appeared earlier, including the themes of peace, sanctification, God's calling, and the parousia.

The themes of peace, sanctification, and God's calling emphasize what God *has done* and *is doing* in the lives of the Thessalonians. Paul refers to God as the **very God of peace**. As the context indicates, the connotations of the word "peace" here are soteriological and eschatological. The emphasis of Paul's expression is either on God's activity in *making* peace with humanity through Jesus Christ or on the *result* of God's activity as experienced by humanity.

Paul's request involves two verbs, both of which have God as their agent. First, Paul asks: May the very God of peace **sanctify you to the point of completion** (5:23). This is now the fifth time that Paul has referred to sanctification in the letter (3:13; 4:3, 4, 7;

> **1 Thessalonians 5:23–28 in the Rhetorical Flow**
>
> **Letter opening (1:1–10)**
>
> **Letter body (2:1–5:22)**
>
> Paul's ministry in Thessalonica (2:1–12)
>
> Renewed thanksgiving (2:13–16)
>
> Paul's desire to visit again (2:17–3:13)
>
> Exhortation, part 1 (4:1–12)
>
> Exhortation, part 2 (4:13–5:11)
>
> Final exhortations (5:12–22)
>
> ▶**Letter closing (5:23–28)**
>
> Second wish-prayer (5:23–24)
>
> Prayer (5:25)
>
> Greeting (5:26)
>
> Final instruction (5:27)
>
> Benediction (5:28)

5:23). In three of these instances, Paul provides some further elaboration. In 4:3 sanctification is identified as "the will of God." In 4:7 it is declared to be the purpose of God's calling. In 4:8 we learn that sanctification is enabled by the Holy Spirit, which God "is giving" the Thessalonian believers for this purpose. The connection that Paul makes across the letter between God's will/calling on the one hand and sanctification on the other implies that sanctification is integral to salvation itself.

Paul's second request is formulated with a passive verb construction, although God functions as the implied agent: **May your spirit and soul and body be kept perfectly whole** (5:23). Whereas the first request asks that the Thessalonians might be sanctified, the second asks that, once sanctified, they might be *preserved* in this state. It would be an overinterpretation of Paul's language to find significance in his verbal differentiation between "spirit," "soul," and "body." Various anthropological terms occur in Paul's letters ("spirit," "soul," "body," "mind," "heart," "flesh"), in various combinations ("soul" and "spirit," 1 Cor. 15:45 KJV; "flesh" and "spirit," 1 Cor. 5:5; Col. 2:5; "body" and "spirit," Rom. 8:10; 1 Cor. 5:3; 7:34; "mind" and "flesh," Rom. 7:25), and without technical consistency (Jewett 1971, 175–83, although Jewett himself [1986, 107–8] finds significance in the distinction here). This particular combination occurs nowhere else in the Pauline corpus. Rather than naming the "parts" of a person in a technical sense,

129

these terms imprecisely express various aspects of personhood (Dunn 1998, 78), which together communicate the idea of human wholeness.

This focus on God's activity leads Paul to refer to God as **the one who is call-ing you**. The present tense of the participle (*kalōn*) should not be overlooked: it highlights that God not only takes the initiative when he *calls* believers to salvation but that he now *continues* calling them. While the continuous nature of the call implies a need for human perseverance, Paul's focus is not on human response to the call but on God's *effective* call. This is shown by Paul's immediate affirmation that God **is faithful** and **will also bring to pass** what he requires (5:24). Thus Paul highlights the incompleteness of salvation and reiterates a theme that appears at several other points in the letter: God "is calling you" (also in 2:12), "is delivering us" (1:10), and "is giving his Holy Spirit" (4:8); God destined the Thessalonians "not for wrath" but for "the *acquisition* of salvation" (5:9). In all cases God is the acting subject (but Jesus acts in 1:10). Moreover, even Paul's earlier reference to "election" (1:4), which is closely connected with the theme of calling, focuses not so much on the completed act as on the *proof* of election evinced by the Spirit's *ongoing* work in them (1:5!).

The *purpose* of God's activity is to make the Thessalonians' sanctification com-plete before **the parousia of our Lord Jesus Christ** (5:23). The parousia has been a major theme in the letter (1:10; 2:19; 3:13; 4:15). Here and in three other instances, the parousia is connected contextually with the final judgment (1:10; 2:19; 3:13); both here and in two other instances, God's present activity is linked contextually with believers' fate at the judgment (1:10; 3:13). These twin themes—God's work in the Thessalonians and their final fate at the parousia—work together to play an important role in Paul's paraenetic strategy. Paul urges his audience onward through their affliction by drawing attention to what God is currently doing and by pointing them to where they are ultimately going. By emphasizing God's pres-ent work in them, Paul with all good intentions puts significant pressure on his audience: to quit now would be to act counter to what God is presently doing in them (cf. 4:7–8). What God is doing will bring them safely to the goal for which they are destined, a hope on the other side of their affliction: life "with" Jesus.

Prayer (5:25)

5:25. With the vocative *adelphoi* (**brothers and sisters**), Paul transitions to the letter's closing proper. This consists of three imperative statements followed by a benediction.

First, Paul asks for prayer: **Pray also for us** (v. 25). Paul gives no indication why he needs prayer, though in other letters such requests concern either his own safety (Rom. 15:30–32; 2 Cor. 1:10–11; Phil. 1:19; Philem. 22) or the success of his ministry (Eph. 6:18–20; Col. 4:3; 2 Thess. 3:1). In Col. 4:3 and Eph. 6:19 Paul asks his audience to pray "also," just as he does here: in Col. 4:3 this means, "Just as you pray for yourselves"; in Eph. 6:18–19 it means, "just as you pray for the other saints." Here it indicates reciprocity: the Thessalonians should pray for him, just as he prays for them (i.e., as he "always" prays for them, 1:2; or as he has just prayed for them, 5:23–24).

Greeting (5:26)

5:26. Second, Paul sends greetings (**Greet all the brothers and sisters with a holy kiss**), as he generally does in closing his letters. Final greetings in Paul's letters come in several forms, all of them conventional in ancient letters (Klauck 2006, 13): from author to the addressee (1 Cor. 16:21; Col. 4:18; 2 Thess. 3:17), from author to a third party (Rom. 16:3–15), or from a third party to the addressee (Rom. 16:16, 21, 23; 1 Cor. 16:19, 20; 2 Cor. 13:12; Phil. 4:21; Col. 4:10–14; Philem. 23; cf. 2 Tim. 4:21; Titus 3:15). Since long-distance travel was arduous and consumed more time and resources than most people had, third-party greetings were a useful way of maintaining relationships. Yet Paul sends no greetings from third parties in Corinth. This datum supports the view that Paul was not long departed from Thessalonica. If he had arrived in Corinth only recently, he might not yet have known anyone, or at least the Thessalonians would not have been acquainted with them, and greetings from named individuals would have been pointless.

Among the kinds of greetings normally conveyed through letters, Paul's request to "greet all the brothers and sisters with a holy kiss" seems to align with the author-to-third-party type, but this interpretation depends on the identity of the brothers and sisters. The exhortation to greet "one another" with a holy kiss is repeated in three other Pauline letters (Rom. 16:16; 1 Cor. 16:20; 2 Cor. 13:12). The word "holy" shows that the kiss had religious significance. Claims that the holy kiss was a liturgical directive (Bruce 1982, 133–34) are merely speculative, although this interpretation can be found as far back as the church fathers. The gesture seems to have been distinctive to the early church. It functioned as a symbol of fellowship among the body of believers and apparently became a widespread practice in the early church (1 Pet. 5:14; Justin Martyr, *1 Apol.* 65.2).

The gesture, however, is described differently here: Paul requests, not that they "greet *one another*" with a holy kiss, but that they so greet "*all the brothers and sisters.*" This third-person designation may suggest that the letter was addressed to a smaller group within the church—for instance, the leadership (Dibelius 1937, 58; Masson 1957, 79)—and that Paul is now asking them to greet the church's other members. Alternatively, Paul could be asking that (1) greetings be passed on to any believers who happen to be absent when the letter is first read or that (2) they pass on greetings to the other Christians around Macedonia (Malherbe 2000, 341), perhaps as leaders and representatives passed between the churches. While uncertain, the identity of the "brothers and sisters" may be somewhat elucidated by reference to them again in verse 27 (see below).

Final Instruction (5:27)

5:27. Paul's final command feels surprisingly severe: **I adjure you in the name of the Lord that this letter should be read to all the brothers and sisters.** Here is the third of only three examples in 1 Thessalonians of the first-person singular (also 2:18; 3:5). The explanation for this could lie in the process of composition itself. In closing many of his letters, Paul indicates that the final greeting is written with his own hand (1 Cor. 16:21; Gal. 6:11; Col. 4:18; 2 Thess. 3:17; Philem. 19). The probable implication in these instances is that the letters themselves, as Paul's Letter to the Romans explicitly notes (16:22), were written through an amanuensis. Use of an amanuensis was a common practice even for highly literate people (Klauck 2006, 55), in which cases the sender signed off on the work in closing. Many extant papyri plainly illustrate this practice by a change in handwriting (Klauck 2006, 16). Here nothing plainly suggests a transfer of the pen. Paul does not add his own greeting (1 Cor. 16:21; Col. 4:18; 2 Thess. 3:17), identify himself by name (1 Cor. 16:21; Col. 4:18; 2 Thess. 3:17; Philem. 19), or draw attention to his handwriting (Gal. 6:11; 2 Thess. 3:17), and no amanuensis is named (Rom. 16:22). Nonetheless, some explanation for the first-person singular is needed, and if signing off in his own handwriting was indeed his common practice (as 2 Thess. 3:17 suggests), this could explain the change. Paul would not have needed to announce the change in hand (even if he did in other letters) since the handwriting itself would have made that change clear.

"Adjure" (*enorkizo*), strengthened by an oath "in the name of the Lord," feels somewhat threatening. The reason for Paul's forcefulness is not clear. The theory that Paul demanded reading of the letter as a part of church "liturgy" (implying repeated reading) has little in its favor and is undermined by the fact that Paul elects to use an aoristic infinitive ("for the letter to be read") rather than a present-continuous ("for the letter to be read again and again," "to be read routinely"). Paul seems to have suspected that the letter might not be made available for common viewing and hearing.

A critical factor in determining why he makes his request is the question of the identity of "all the brothers and sisters" (as also in v. 26), whom he evidently does not anticipate being among the letter's initial readers. As to their identity, several possibilities exist. (1) If the brothers are identified as others within the Thessalonian church, then (a) Paul may foresee the letter being retained by the leadership or by some faction, who either failed to share the letter out of negligence or intentionally withheld it out of factiousness; or (b) he may be anticipating that some of the church's members will be absent at the gathering when the letter is first read. Two other possibilities are also plausible. (2) If multiple house churches existed in Thessalonica (for the possibility of multiple Roman churches, see Rom. 16:5, 10, 11, 14, 15; for the possibility of multiple Corinthian churches, note Rom. 16:23), Paul could be requesting that the letter be shared with each of them. Or (3) Paul may be asking the church in Thessalonica to share the letter with other churches around the region (note Paul's request in Col. 4:16 for the churches in Laodicea and Colossae to exchange letters).

Some version of the first option seems most likely. The initial recipients must have represented a smaller portion of the local church. Paul cannot have expected the person who was first handed the letter to wait for all the church to gather around before he broke the seal. It is probably telling, moreover, that Paul refers to the "brothers and sisters" without any qualification. From the perspective even of the initial recipient(s), the words "all the brothers and sisters," without further qualification, would refer more obviously to the rest of the church locally than to people from churches elsewhere. Finally, the absence of some members of the church during the first gathering to read the letter seems a likely possibility. As members of the artisan class, most of the church's members would have been short on leisure and in some cases may have had no choice but to work seven days a week, sunup to sundown (Hock 1980, 31–37).

Benediction (5:28)

5:28. As was his custom, Paul ends the letter with a benediction: **The grace of our Lord Jesus Christ be with you**. This basic formula concludes every letter in the Pauline corpus, although no two instances are identical (cf. Rom. 16:20; 1 Cor. 16:23; 2 Cor. 13:13; Gal. 6:18; Eph. 6:24; Phil. 4:23; Col. 4:18; 1 Thess. 5:28; 2 Thess. 3:18; 1 Tim. 6:21; 2 Tim. 4:22; Titus 3:15; Philem. 25). With mention of the Lord's "grace," the letter ends as it began: Paul greeted the Thessalonians by wishing grace upon them in the first verse of the letter ("Grace to you and peace"), and he wishes them farewell by wishing grace upon them in the final verse of the letter ("Grace be with you"). Grace brackets the letter, showing that, even though it is not mentioned once in the letter's body, grace is vital to Paul's gospel message and never far from view.

2 Thessalonians

Introduction to 2 Thessalonians

History knows of only two letters from Paul to the church in Thessalonica. In contrast with the first of these letters (1 Thessalonians), doubts have been raised about the authenticity of the second (2 Thessalonians). If the letter is authentic, the circumstances that led to its composition are somewhat more obscure than they are for the earlier letter. Indeed, while the circumstances leading to the composition of 1 Thessalonians can be reconstructed fairly confidently based on internal indicators in the letter and on the narrative of Acts, the letter we know as 2 Thessalonians provides only general clues about the circumstances of writing and cannot be correlated specifically with what Acts records. What one decides about the issues of authorship and the letter's background and purpose, however, has significant bearing on how the letter is read and understood, both historically and theologically. The following introduction covers these issues and sets the stage for the commentary in the chapters that follow.

The Letter as a Literary Composition

Reception History

Compared to other letters in the Pauline corpus, 2 Thessalonians has been somewhat of a "Cinderella." Nonetheless, from the earliest centuries of church history until today, this letter has been cited, commented on, and written about to an extent worthy of a canonical text. Nijay Gupta's (2019) recent critical introduction to the Thessalonian letters has helpfully summarized the reception of 2 Thessalonians throughout history, from the early Christian and patristic period (270–75) to the Reformation (275–78) and the modern era (278–84), covering in the last portion the main critical issues that have been treated in modern scholarship. An older review of modern scholarship can be found in Trilling (1987).

Text History

Direct evidence for the existence of 2 Thessalonians comes no later than it does for 1 Thessalonians. A probable allusion to the letter occurs in Polycarp (Pol. *Phil.* 11.4//2 Thess. 3:15), a definite allusion is found in Justin Martyr (*Dial.* 110), and the letter is cited abundantly in the writings of Irenaeus, Tertullian, and other second-century writers. The Muratorian Canon (controversially dated ca. 200 CE) lists 2 Thessalonians among the canonical letters of Paul. In contrast to 1 Thessalonians, however, 2 Thessalonians is not found in the earliest extant collection of Paul's letters ($\mathfrak{P}^{46}$, ca. 200 CE). That manuscript, however, has not survived intact, and 18 of its 104 original leaves are missing, which can reasonably be assumed to have contained 2 Thessalonians and Philemon. Second Thessalonians appears in several other complete or fragmentary third- and fourth-century manuscripts, including $\mathfrak{P}^{30}$ (3rd cent. CE), $\mathfrak{P}^{92}$ (3rd or 4th cent.), Codex $\aleph$ (4th cent.), and Codex B (4th cent.) as wells as other important manuscripts from the fifth and sixth centuries: Codices A (5th cent.), D [06] (6th cent.), and I (5th cent.). Though many textual variants occur in the manuscripts (for a summary, see Gupta 2019, 186–88), few if any of these significantly affect the text's meaning (but see discussion of "firstfruit" at 2 Thess. 2:13).

Minor text-critical issues notwithstanding, the letter as we have it is undoubtedly virtually identical to the original. Walter Schmithals (1964) proposed that the letter we know as 2 Thessalonians consists of two originally separate letters, one composed of 1:1–12 + 3:6–16 and the other of 2:13–14 + 2:1–12 + 2:15–3:5 + 3:17–18. The manuscript evidence, however, lends no support to this view. Moreover, after a close examination of the evidence, Schmithals's theory turns out to be internally improbable (Best 1979, 45–50) and ultimately too ingenious to be provable. Not surprisingly, no other modern scholar has adopted his view. Interpolation theories—such as Munro's (1983, 82–93) theory that 2 Thess. 2:15; 3:4; and 3:6–15 were added between 90 and 140 CE—have also been universally rejected.

Authorship and Audience

For centuries, 2 Thessalonians was regarded without question as an authentic letter of Paul. The letter's prescript explicitly identifies him as the sender, along with his companions Silvanus and Timothy (1:1). While the assumption of authenticity remained unchallenged until the end of the eighteenth century, from that point confidence in the traditional view began to crumble. In 1798 J. E. C. Schmidt published an article on the two Thessalonian letters in which he argued, based on ostensible differences in eschatology between the two letters, that the letter known as 2 Thessalonians was pseudonymous and written by a post-Pauline forger. While Schmidt's argument won few advocates, a century later Wilhelm Wrede (1903) revived the issue, arguing for the pseudonymity of 2 Thessalonians based on its apparent literary relationship with 1 Thessalonians. It was not until Trilling's 1972 monograph (carried further in his 1980 commentary), however, that the tide of opinion began to turn. Marshaling an array of linguistic, theological, literary, and historical arguments, Trilling succeeded in convincing a sizeable portion of critical scholars to embrace his position (R. Collins 1988; Krentz 1992; 2009; Menken 1994; Richard 1995; Furnish 2007; Redalié 2011; Boring 2015; Crüsemann 2018; Niklas 2019; among many others). Those who take this position generally believe that the letter is the product of a forger from the post-Pauline era, writing in the late first or early second century (cf. Trilling 1980, 27–28; Gaventa 1998, 94; Furnish 2007, 139).

While statements to the effect that "most critical scholars think" or "a vast majority of critical scholars think" are not uncommon (and actually occur on both sides), the split of opinion on the question of the letter's authorship is difficult to evaluate. Many formidable names, speaking with equal conviction, can be marshaled on either side (the following scholars view the letter as authentic: Jewett 1986, 17–18; Wanamaker 1990, 17–23; Murphy-O'Connor 1996, 111; Dunn 1998, 13n39; Malherbe 2000, 349–75; Johnson 2001, 55–90; Foster 2012, 169–70; Wright 2013, 56–62; Campbell 2014; Longenecker and Still 2014, 80–82; and many others, including, tentatively, Barclay 1992, 72). What is almost universally ignored is that not everyone takes a firm position on either side. A 2012 survey indicated that as many as one-third of the scholars surveyed remain agnostic on the question of the letter's authorship (Foster 2012, 171). If this uncertainty is even marginally representative of the wider scholarly community, a well-executed survey would likely indicate that those neither for nor against could claim a true majority.

Still, with so many interpreters doubting the letter's authenticity, the arguments for pseudonymity should be given serious consideration. A full overview of the evidence adduced for each argument cannot be given here. Below we note only the main lines of argument.

1. The existence of extensive structural, verbal, and thematic similarities between 1 and 2 Thessalonians indicates that the author of the latter depended on the former.
2. The two letters exhibit incompatible theological differences, particularly in the area of eschatology (cf. 1 Thess. 4:13–5:11; 2 Thess. 2:1–12).
3. Many theological motifs prominent in Paul's later letters are missing from 2 Thessalonians (e.g., the law, flesh, sin, slavery, justification), and some that are present in 2 Thessalonians are non-Pauline (e.g., emphasis on God's wrath).
4. Second Thessalonians exudes a much "cooler" tone toward the audience, betraying a lack of a real personal relationship.
5. The letter uses un-Pauline vocabulary or uses Pauline vocabulary differently than Paul uses it.
6. The syntax and style of the two letters are different.
7. Internal indicators suggest that the letter was written after Paul's lifetime.
8. The letter is too insistent that it was written by Paul to be trusted (3:17; cf. 2:2).

Not all the evidence carries equal weight, and much of it is weak on its own. The case for pseudonymity therefore depends on the weight of the evidence considered cumulatively. Nonetheless, counterarguments can be made to each point, and readers are then left to decide whether the arguments, even considered cumulatively, mount a strong enough case to overturn the unanimous traditional view that the letter is authentically Pauline. Below is a brief evaluation of the arguments for pseudonymity in light of counter considerations.

Arguments 2, 3, 4, 5, and 6

Arguments 2 through 6 are predicated on perceived differences between 2 Thessalonians and the undisputed letters, especially 1 Thessalonians, in the areas of theology, tone, vocabulary, and style. Such arguments, however, have been indirectly undermined by several trends in critical scholarship over the last thirty to forty years.

a. The rise of rhetorical criticism of the NT through the 1980s and 1990s created an awareness of the way in which the "rhetorical situation" shapes both what Paul says (theology, vocabulary) and how he says it (tone, style). Differences in the situation, therefore, make differences in theology, tone, and so on to be, not just a possibility, but a rhetorical probability, since not every situation calls for discussion of the same topics or elicits the same mood.

b. Concurrent with the rise of rhetorical criticism was a change in the way scholarship viewed "Pauline theology." Previous scholarship tended to treat his theology as an essentially static entity, complete from the moment he turned to Christ and essentially unchanging over the course of his ministry (with Galatians and Romans serving as the touchstones of "authentic" Pauline theology). But scholarship from the 1980s onward (particularly as driven by the initiative of the Society of Biblical Literature's Pauline Theology Consultation/Group) has come increasingly to regard his theology as a dynamic entity, which developed as the unfolding of his ministry prompted ongoing reflection and which took different shapes as he faced varied new contingencies.

c. Apart from the subjectivity of interpreters' "impressions" of stylistic differences between authentic and allegedly inauthentic letters of Paul, even the theoretically "scientific" approach of "stylometrics" (which utilizes computer technology to determine stylistic differences based on selected quantitative criteria) has yielded inconsistent, often contradictory, and therefore inconclusive results.

d. Scholars have increasingly emphasized that Greco-Roman antiquity defined "author" more loosely than we do today. Not only the agent who penned or dictated a letter but also those who collaborated with others or even authorized others to write in his or her name could be considered legitimate "authors." The potential use of scribes, the involvement of coauthors, or the delegation of writing to coworkers tremendously frustrates attempts to establish the inauthenticity (or the authenticity) of Paul's letters based on stylistic evidence.

By themselves, these trends in no way prove that Paul wrote 2 Thessalonians. Differences between 2 Thessalonians and Paul's other letters could indeed exist because Paul was not (in any sense) the letter's author. But in light of these considerations, it is evident that they could also exist even if he did write the letter.

Argument 7

Second Thessalonians contains numerous alleged anachronisms, clues showing that the author wrote after Paul's lifetime. Potential indicators of a later date include the following: references to forged Pauline letters (2:2; 3:17), a cryptic reference to Nero (2:3–4), the presumed intensity of persecution (1:4, 6), frequent appeal to Paul's authority (2:15), the issuing of commands (3:4, 6, 10, 12, 14–15), references to "tradition" (2:15; 3:6), mention of false teachers (2:2–3, 10–11), and the prevalence of apocalyptic themes (1:6–12; 2:1–12).

Whether these are actually anachronisms is debatable. Indeed, forged letters within the lifetime of the alleged authors were not uncommon (see comments on 3:17). A host of historical figures before Nero fit the description of the "man" discussed in 2 Thess. 2:3–4 (see comments there). There is solid evidence of the persecution of Christians during the period of Paul's ministry (see comments on 1 Thess. 2:13–14). Similar appeals to Paul's authority or teaching occur in his undisputed letters (1 Thess. 2:13; 4:1, 2; cf. Rom. 16:17). Paul also refers to false teachers in several other letters (Rom. 16:17–18; 2 Cor. 11:13; Gal. 1:7). And apocalyptic theology and literary works not only preceded the late first century CE but existed before the first century BCE (e.g., parts of *1 Enoch*). In short, there is no reason to conclude that these examples are anachronisms unless one has already decided on other grounds that 2 Thessalonians is pseudonymous.

Argument 8

Two statements in the letter could be interpreted as implying the existence of forged Pauline letters: "not to be quickly shaken in mind or alarmed, either by spirit or by word *or by letter, as though from us* . . ." (2 Thess. 2:2 NRSV); and "I, Paul, write this greeting with my own hand. *This is the mark in every letter of mine; it is the way I write*" (3:17 NRSV). From one point of view, these remarks betray the intentions of a pseudepigrapher: by reaffirming his truthfulness (while lying), he tries to win the trust of his audience, knowing that most people would not believe that someone could be so disingenuous as to discredit pseudonymity while committing it. Insidious as that may sound, this is indeed a possible interpretation; yet it is only compelling if one has decided in advance that the author is lying, for the remarks read exactly as one would expect if a spurious letter in Paul's name was in fact circulating.

Argument 1

The argument from the literary similarities between 1 and 2 Thessalonians has been saved for last because it is by far the most compelling argument for the letter's pseudonymity (detailed synopses can be found in Richard 1995, 21; Friesen 2010, 198–99; Krentz 2009, 456–61; Klauck 2006, 396–97; *ABD* 6:518; among other places). (1) In the first place, the two letters share an abundance of distinct *literary forms* (thanksgivings, exhortations, wish-prayers, reported prayers, prayer requests, appeals, transitional formulas), some of which are not found in Paul's other letters. (2) In several cases these units share uncommon, almost *verbatim content* to the extent of at least four, and in one case as many as twelve or thirteen, more or less consecutive words (1 Thess. 2:9//2 Thess. 3:8). (3) Overall, the two letters also share a remarkable *structural symmetry*, including among its features—anomalously in Paul's letters—two thanksgiving sections. This symmetry makes possible a synoptic outline in which the various structural elements of 1 and 2 Thessalonians parallel one another from beginning to end. Together with the many verbal parallels that the two letters share, these structural similarities have led many scholars to conclude that a pseudonymous author has used 1 Thessalonians as a model to compose a convincing Pauline imitation (e.g., Richard 1995, 361–63). The adjacent table offers a synopsis illustrating the apparent structural parallels and nine of the most significant verbal parallels, numbered (in brackets) according to the sequence in which the examples appear in 1 Thessalonians.

Table 6. Synopsis of Structural Parallels between 1 and 2 Thessalonians

1 Thessalonians	2 Thessalonians
Prescript (1:1)	Prescript (1:1–2)
Thanksgiving (1:2–10) including [1] "brothers and sisters, beloved by God . . . your election . . . our gospel" (1:4–5)	**Thanksgiving (1:3–12)** concluding with a reported prayer
Paul's ministry in Thessalonica (2:1–12) including [2] "from you the word of the Lord rang out" (2:8) and [3] "our labor and toil. Working night and day so as not to burden any of you" (2:9)	**Signs preceding the parousia (2:1–12)** beginning with [8] "now we ask you, brothers and sisters" (2:1) and including [4] "so that you are not . . . shaken" (2:2)
Thanksgiving (2:13–16)	**Thanksgiving (2:13–14)** including [1] "brothers and sisters beloved by the Lord . . . God chose you . . . our gospel" (2:13–14) and [7] "[God] also called you . . . for the acquisition of the glory of our Lord Jesus Christ" (2:14)

1 Thessalonians	2 Thessalonians
Timothy's visit (2:17–3:10) including [4] "so that you are not shaken" (3:2–3) and [5] "when we were with you, we were saying to you that . . ." (3:4) and concluding with a reported prayer	**Exhortation (2:15)**
Wish-prayer (3:11–13) including [6*][1] "Now, may our God and Father himself and our Lord Jesus . . . strengthen your hearts" (3:11, 13)	**Wish-prayer (2:16–17)** including [6*][1] "Now may our Lord Jesus Christ himself and God our Father . . . encourage your hearts and strengthen them in every good deed and word" (2:16–17)
Exhortation (4:1–5:11) beginning with "finally" (4:1) and including [7] "that God did not position us . . . but for the acquisition of salvation through our Lord Jesus Christ" (5:9)	**Exhortation (3:1–5)** beginning with "finally" and a prayer request (3:1–2), including [2] "in order that the word of the Lord might race" (3:1), and concluding with a wish-prayer
Concluding exhortations (5:12–24) beginning with [8] "now we ask you, brothers and sisters" (5:12), including [9] "Now may the God of peace himself . . ." (5:23), and concluding with a wish-prayer	**Concluding exhortation (3:6–13)** including [3] "in labor and toil working night and day so as not to burden any of you" (3:8) and [5] "when we were with you, we were teaching this to you, that . . ." (3:10)
Letter closing (5:25–28) beginning with a prayer request	**Letter closing (3:14–18)** including [9] "Now may the Lord of peace himself give you peace through everything and in every way" (3:16)

[1] Asterisk indicates that the structural parallel also includes verbal similarities.

Table 7. Other Verbal Similarities between 1 and 2 Thessalonians

	1 Thessalonians	2 Thessalonians
faith and love	1:2–3	1:3–4
"pray for us"	5:25	3:1
"you yourselves know"	2:1	3:7
"strengthen"; "comfort"	3:2	2:16–17
"who do not know God"	4:5	1:8

Additional verbal similarities include the following:

1 Thessalonians	2 Thessalonians
2:12	1:5
3:11–13	2:16–17

1 Thessalonians	2 Thessalonians
3:11–13	3:5
4:1; 5:1	3:4
5:23–24	3:16
5:24	3:4

Other parallels are too common in Paul's letters to be significant (e.g., 1 Thess. 5:28//2 Thess. 3:18).

The two letters also share additional thematic similarities:

Theme	1 Thessalonians	2 Thessalonians
previous teaching	4:2, 6, 11	2:5; 3:6, 10
the parousia of Jesus	1:7, 10; 2:19; 3:13; 4:15; 5:23	1:10; 2:1, 8

The parallels are perhaps not as exact as they can be made to appear. A more detailed comparison shows that the mirror-structure is only skeletal, and artificial even then. It is true that in both letters a second thanksgiving section introduces the second major unit of the letter's body, but the remaining sections of the letter do not generally mirror each other internally. For instance, based on the content there would be no reason to align 1 Thess. 2:17–3:10 and 2 Thess. 2:15 if both had not come between a thanksgiving (1 Thess. 2:13–16; 2 Thess. 2:13–14) and a wish-prayer (1 Thess. 3:11–13; 2 Thess. 2:16–17). Moreover, in no instance where the two letters share formulas or verbal content do the parallels occur *within* the ostensibly parallel structural sections. The apparent exception involving the wish-prayers in 1 Thess. 3:11–13 and 2 Thess. 2:16–17 (indicated by the *) turns out to be contrived, since the two prayers do not come at the same structural points in their respective letters: in 1 Thessalonians the wish-prayer provides the conclusion to the letter's second main unit (3:11–13 as conclusion to 2:1–3:10); in 2 Thess. 2:16–17 the similar wish-prayer does not serve a concluding function but comes shortly after the second thanksgiving (2:13–14) and prior to the closing paragraph of the section (3:1–5). Likewise, the two wish-prayers that occur at the end of their respective letters (1 Thess. 5:23–24; 2 Thess. 3:5) come only approximately at the same location. That is, although both 1 Thessalonians and 2 Thessalonians include wish-prayers *near* the end of the letter, in 1 Thessalonians the prayer occurs at the end of the concluding exhortations (5:23–24) and therefore in the letter *closing* (5:12–28), while in 2 Thessalonians it occurs at the end of the letter *body* (3:5).

The only other instance of ostensibly identical structure occurs in the use of *to loipon* to introduce new sections in both 1 Thess. 4:1 and 2 Thess. 3:1. This transitional expression, however, also occurs at structurally different points in the two letters: in 1 Thessalonians the transition introduces the second of two major units of the letter (4:1–5:22) where a clear juncture in the letter's main sections occurs (cf. 2:1–3:13); in 2 Thessalonians it comes, not at a point of major disjunction, but in the middle of a unit (2:13–3:5).

Finally, eight of the nine verbal parallels noted above occur in structurally nonparallel sections, and eight of the nine also occur in a completely different sequence in the two letters. Following the sequence of 1 Thessalonians, the nine verbal parallels identified in the table correlate as follows:

1 Thessalonians	2 Thessalonians
1	3
2	6
3	7
4	2
5	8
6	5
7	4
8	1
9	9

What has not commonly received attention in examinations of the synopsis, moreover, is the differing applications and contextual differences evident between instances of shared verbiage. For instance, the wish-prayers in both 1 Thess. 5:23–24 and 2 Thess. 3:5 have in common the words "direct," "hearts," and "love," but the language is applied in a consistently different manner: "direct *our way* to you" versus "direct *your hearts* to the love of God"; "increase *your love toward one another*" versus "direct your hearts to the *love of God*"; and "strengthen *your hearts so that they are blameless* at the parousia" versus "direct *your hearts to the love of God.*" Furthermore, while the coordination of "love" and "endurance" in 2 Thess. 3:5 recalls the use of the same terms in 1 Thess. 1:3—where Paul refers to "the work of faith," "labor of *love*," and "hope of *endurance*"—in 2 Thess. 3:5 it is not the *Thessalonians'* love and endurance, but *God's* love (subjective genitive) and *Christ's* endurance (subjective genitive) that Paul has in mind. Finally, while both 1 Thess. 3:2 and 2 Thess. 2:16–17 coordinate the terms "strengthen" and "comfort," in the first letter these verbs appear in narrative about the activities of Timothy, whereas in 2 Thessalonians these are divine activities expressed in a wish-prayer.

Despite these differences, the similarities between the two letters admittedly remain conspicuous. In the eyes of many readers, the similarities are too coincidental to allow for the conclusion that the first letter was not in some way involved in the composition of the second. Pseudonymity is a plausible explanation for this literary relationship. The differences between the two letters may only suggest that, if the author of 2 Thessalonians did use 1 Thessalonians as a model, he did not use it slavishly, but rather scrounged bits of verbal content, borrowed a rough outline of its structure, and assembled this material into a newly integrated whole.

A defense of Pauline authorship would need to provide an alternate explanation for this apparent literary relationship, an explanation at least as equally plausible as a theory of pseudonymity. Several explanations have been proposed:

1. There is in fact no literary relationship between the two letters, and similarities are not as great as they are made out to be (Malherbe 2000, 356–61).
2. Paul wrote the two letters to the Thessalonians at the same time but addressed them to different readerships:
   a. One was sent to the entire church and one to a Jewish faction within it (Harnack 1910).
   b. One was sent to the church in Thessalonica and one to the church in Berea (Goguel 1925, 4:327–37).
   c. One was sent to the church leadership in Thessalonica and one to the entire congregation (Dibelius 1937, 58).
3. Paul wrote the second letter so soon after the first that his mind was flooded with memories of what he had written before (Dobschütz 1909, 46–47).
4. A coauthor took the lead and used 1 Thessalonians as a resource.

The final option should be given serious consideration. Paul names Silvanus and Timothy as cosenders, and in that role either one of them might have taken the lead in writing. To account for the close literary similarities between the two letters, it would then need to be supposed that Paul granted a certain degree of independence to the writer, who then consulted 1 Thessalonians as a resource for manufacturing something close to Paul's theological framework, natural personality, and epistolary style. Presumably, the final composition would have received Paul's approval, if not also his own input, contributions, and recommendations for revision. A composition of this kind would remain in a true sense a composition of "Paul," by ancient standards of authorship (e.g., Cicero, *Att.* 3.1.5). One might feel that this is a rather strained way of holding on to Pauline authorship, but arguments other than those based on the literary similarities between the two letters are arguably question-begging and contribute nothing to the strength of the view for pseudonymity. What is being balanced, then, is only the (easily overstated) literary argument against the unanimous and very ancient view that Paul was the letter's author.

An extreme version of a coauthorship theory would see Paul's coauthor(s) as having worked completely independently. In this regard, Karl Donfried (2002, 53–56) has proposed that Timothy was actually the letter's author. While the letter, then, was "non-Pauline in the technical sense" (53), Timothy indeed wrote "on behalf of the apostolic group" (55). A major obstacle to this view is the explicit use of the first-person singular in reference to Paul in 3:17, where the author draws attention, in the name of "Paul," to the personal uniqueness of his handwriting.

At this point Donfried (55–56) can only suggest that Timothy so completely identified himself with Paul that he believed such a scheme to be legitimate (e.g., "Could not Timothy . . . ?" and "Is it not possible that . . . ?"). Donfried's suggestion with regard to 3:17, however, reflects an unnecessary adaptation of a theory that is otherwise satisfying. If Timothy indeed took the lead in writing the letter, at the very least Paul could have signed off on it.

In my view, some version of option 4 is most likely correct, although the point of the first thesis has serious validity as well. Paul neither penned nor dictated the letter. At least one of the letter's cosenders was involved in the letter's composition, such that he took responsibility for its general structure and much of its phrasing. There is no need, however, to assume that Paul's role was reduced to that of a reviewer. Both the priority of his name in the list of senders in 1:1 and the inclusion of references to Paul in the first-person (2:5; 3:17) and to no other individual in the letter suggest that he was the "executive" author as far as the general content was concerned and that at points he probably directly contributed in the process, most of all in 3:17. The predominant use of the first-person *plural*, then, most likely serves to highlight the *inclusion* of others in the collective will that is behind the letter but not necessarily to indicate their authorial voice. For this reason, the present commentary will simplify the authorial identity by referring to the author, and writer, of the letter as Paul.

The Date, Provenance, and Occasion of the Letter

While it is generally assumed that 2 Thessalonians was written after 1 Thessalonians, traditionally this assumption owes only to the fact that 1 Thessalonians is longer (the modern canon arranges Paul's letters to churches in order of decreasing length). Most modern scholars conclude on critical grounds that the canonical order matches the order in which the Thessalonian letters were actually written, although a few argue for the priority of 2 Thessalonians (Grotius 1679, 2.2.948; West 1914; Weiss 1959; Manson 1962; Gregson 1966; Wanamaker 1990, 37–45).

Scholars share a rare agreement that the interval separating the two letters was very short. That Silvanus and Timothy are still present with Paul (2 Thess. 1:1) as he writes the second letter suggests that he wrote while still residing in Corinth, during his second missionary journey (Acts 18:1–17). In the first place, Silas/Silvanus does not appear as a companion of Paul after his time in Corinth came to an end, according to the final chapters of Acts. Moreover, if Acts accurately limits Paul's time in Corinth to eighteen months (18:11) and Paul's first letter to the Thessalonians was written in the early months of that visit, then his second letter to the church must have been written, at most, within twelve to sixteen months after the first. The minimum interval between the first letter and the second can be fixed at five or six weeks, for sufficient time is needed for the first letter to make its way to Thessalonica, for the Thessalonians' reaction to become evident, and for a report of their reaction to return to Paul. Therefore, assuming that the standard date of 50 CE for the composition of 1 Thessalonians is correct, 2 Thessalonians must have been written between mid-50 and mid-51 (for discussion of an alternate chronology, see the introduction to 1 Thessalonians).

An interval of only a few weeks or months, however, is indicated by the close continuity of circumstances behind the two letters. Second Thessalonians appears to deal with three main problems, all of which Paul addressed in some form in the earlier letter: (1) the church faces persecution (1:6; 2:2; 3:3; cf. 1 Thess. 1:6; 2:14–16); (2) they are confused about the parousia and day of the Lord (2:1–12; cf. 1 Thess. 4:13–5:11); and (3) some people in the church are not working but are being *ataktoi*, or "disorderly/disruptive" (3:6–15; cf. 1 Thess. 4:11–12; 5:14).

An overall reconstruction of the situation must be able to explain the continuity of circumstances as well as whether/how the three problems outlined above relate to one another. Among those who see the letter as authentic, most surmise a close continuity of circumstances between the two letters and a tight relation between each of the problems addressed in the second letter. According to Robert Jewett (1986), the Thessalonians exhibited an attitude characteristic of "millenarian radicalists." Believing that the new age had dawned, it came to them as a surprise when they discovered that persecution continued (xiii, 94). Although Paul had tried to ease their anxiety with his first letter to the church, that letter had not been effective. Based on a misinterpretation of 1 Thessalonians, they intensified their millenarian commitment and became increasingly perplexed by their persecution. Meanwhile, those to whom Paul refers as *ataktoi* were convinced that they were already experiencing the fullness of the new age. They began to proclaim that the day of the Lord had come (176), and together with those they persuaded, they ceased from their occupations (2 Thess. 3:6–15). In this way 2 Thessalonians reflects "both a condensation and an expansion of the earlier letter" (192), serving to "replace" the letter that had dealt with similar problems but that had exacerbated rather than alleviated them.

Like Jewett, Karl Donfried (2002) proposes a close continuity of circumstances behind the two letters and seeks to integrate all the main problems that 2 Thessalonians addresses. According to Donfried, persecution had intensified since Paul wrote previously. Misunderstanding the eschatological perspective of Paul's earlier letter and interpreting their persecution as a final tribulation, it occurred to them that perhaps the "day of the Lord" had already come. Salvation, however, had consummated for believers in a spiritual way. Consequently, the *ataktoi* committed themselves to charismatic activities, ceasing from work and claiming a right to support from the congregation on the pretext of their charismatic authority (62–64). According to this view, Paul wrote 2 Thessalonians to apprise them that the Day had not come but still lay in the future.

John Barclay (1993, 528–29) coordinates the pieces of the letter somewhat differently. According to Barclay, 1 Thessalonians had bolstered the church's eschatological beliefs, increasing their fervor to see God's wrath fall on those who harassed them. Persecution had intensified, and on the basis of some unspecified event, some within the church began to proclaim that God's wrath had fallen on the unbelieving. Dismayed by the descent of judgment on unbelieving friends and family, however, the Thessalonians (specifically the *ataktoi*, 5:14) retired from their occupations and committed themselves to full-time evangelism. According to this view, Paul wrote 2 Thessalonians both to encourage the church amid their vexing state of persecution and to curb their eschatological fervor by informing them that certain signs must precede before the day of the Lord will arrive.

Several treatments of the letter have focused attention more narrowly on the issue of eschatology. James Harrison (2002; 2011) has argued that the letter was intended to counter Roman propaganda about the eternal rule of Rome and the divine status of the emperor by presenting an eschatological gospel centering on the return and rule of the Son of God, Jesus Christ. Focusing on 2 Thess. 2:1–12, Harrison argues that the "man of lawlessness," with his outrageous claim to divinity (2:4), embodies the character of the emperor Caligula and that Paul seeks to subvert imperial rule by declaring Christ's supremacy and judgment on Rome, bringing an end to the present world order and relief to those who suffer under the current evil regime (1:7–8).

Also focusing on eschatology, Colin Nicholl (2004) considers the continuity of concern with eschatology in the two letters, proposing that 1 and 2 Thessalonians reflect "two stages of the *same single* crisis" (188). Just as Paul wrote 1 Thessalonians to allay the Thessalonians' despair over the deceased (4:13–18), Paul writes 2 Thessalonians, Nicholl proposes, to alleviate their fear that the day of the Lord had come (2:2) and that divine wrath was imminent (1:7–9; 2:8).

Not all interpreters agree that the main problems in 2 Thessalonians are related. Abraham Malherbe (2000, 351) has suggested that "the major reason for writing the letter" was to address consternation in the church over an increase in persecution. Malherbe, however, is not convinced that the problems of the *ataktoi* and the erroneous view that the day of the Lord had come are related to each other (350). Regarding the latter issue, he suggests that Paul's reference to a "letter" alleging that the day of the Lord had come (2:2) in fact refers to 1 Thessalonians, or a version of it. The letter had been circulated among other churches locally and regionally, and copies were made, discussed, and commented on. The result was a construal of 1 Thessalonians that, whether maliciously or innocently, misrepresented Paul's eschatology and reflected the view described in 2 Thess. 2:2. According to this view, Paul wrote 2 Thessalonians to clarify his eschatological position and to correct misinformation about it.

Several facts emerge from this discussion on which all interpreters agree. First, the situation behind the second letter is very similar to the situation behind the first, but the problems either have grown worse or their seriousness has more recently become evident. Apparently the church now faces more intense persecution than before and stands in need of encouragement. Their persecution continues to be related to the group's unwillingness to participate in the religious life of

Thessalonica, perhaps the imperial cult most specifically (see the introduction to 1 Thessalonians). Furthermore, while the subject of the "disorderly" (the *ataktoi*) received only passing attention in 1 Thessalonians, the problem now appears to be a major concern and occupies a large portion of 2 Thessalonians, and those who violate Paul's instructions are to be shut out from fellowship (3:6–15).

Second, Paul's discussion of the parousia and the day of the Lord in his first letter (1 Thess. 4:13–5:11) either caused or left open the possibility of a realized eschatology wherein the day of the Lord was believed to have already come. Paul therefore writes to correct and rebalance the church's eschatology, clarifying that, though the Day is near, signs that have not yet come to pass must precede it.

Disagreement about other points remains. Scholars do not agree on the source of the erroneous claim that "the day of the Lord has come." Did it stem from a pseudonymous letter attributed to Paul or from some other source? Moreover, scholars do not agree about whether the eschatological error was in any way generative of, or had any relation to, the habits of the *ataktoi*. These issues will be discussed at the appropriate points in the commentary.

The Content of the Letter

Genre and Style

As with any sensitive letter, 2 Thessalonians reflects a style that is—or that Paul judged to be—appropriate to the situation. Continuities with the situation in 1 Thessalonians, particularly the church's experience of persecution, necessitated a style of address similar to that of the earlier letter. Therefore, 2 Thessalonians contains many of the paraenetic elements of its earlier counterpart. Using the vocabulary of exhortation, Paul prays that God would give "comfort" (*paraklēsis*) to the Thessalonians and "encourage" (*parakalein*) and "strengthen" (*stērixai*) their hearts (2:17), Paul "boasts" in their "endurance" and "faith" (1:4), the first thanksgiving section aims to raise their spirits by pointing them to the assurance of eschatological justice (1:5–12), and the second by reminding them of their "election" (2:13–14). This letter, however, exudes less ardent warmth and a slightly sharper edge of advice, command, or admonition than the earlier letter. As Donfried (2002, 61) has noted, the term "exhort" (*parakalein*) appears eight times in 1 Thessalonians (2:12; 3:2, 7; 4:1, 10, 18; 5:11, 14) but only twice in 2 Thessalonians (2:17; 3:12). By contrast, the more advisory verb "instruct" (*parangellein*) occurs once in 1 Thessalonians (4:11) but four times in 2 Thessalonians (3:4, 6, 10, 12). Paul also censures those who are "walking disruptively" (3:6) and "not working but being busybodies" (3:11), and he demands that anyone who does not "obey" (*hypakouein*) his instructions be excluded from the community (3:14). Thus 2 Thessalonians can appropriately be considered to be a letter of "mixed" type, having elements of both "paraenetic" and "censorious" letters (cf. Jewett 1986, 81; Malherbe 2000, 361). While the older classification of the letter as "deliberative" (using a category from ancient rhetorical theory) is fitting in that it captures the letter's intent to exhort and advise (Hughes 1989, 55; Donfried 2002, 50), the use of rhetorical categories rather than epistolographic ones in the analysis of letters is now widely regarded as being inappropriate (see the introduction to 1 Thessalonians).

Themes in 2 Thessalonians

Readers who are familiar with Paul's other letters will notice a conspicuous absence in 2 Thessalonians of themes that feature prominently in those letters. Second Thessalonians makes no mention of Jesus's death or resurrection, of his defeat of sin, of believers' justification, of the general resurrection (cf. 2:1), or of "works of the law," and it reflects only minor interest in "participation" or being "in" Christ (see the introduction to 1 Thessalonians; cf. 2 Thess. 1:12; 2:14; 3:5). The main thematic point of contact with Paul's other letters, including 1 Thessalonians, is the letter's emphasis on Jesus's return and the day of judgment. This emphasis illustrates the letter's strong apocalyptic character. *The letter's purpose is to offer encouragement to a suffering church by pointing them to their future vindication and their unique relationship with God over against their persecutors, who are destined for destruction.*

Thus, most of the letter's major themes reflect an apocalyptic character:

1. *The lordship of Christ.* The term "Lord" (*kyrios*) occurs as a title for Jesus some twenty times in the letter (whether it refers to Jesus or God is sometimes ambiguous) and is combined in various ways with other titles, such as "our Lord Jesus Christ" (2:1, 14), "the Lord Jesus Christ" (1:2, 12; 3:12), "our Lord Jesus" (1:8, 12), or "the Lord Jesus" (1:7; 2:8). While Jesus's lordship is presumed to be a present reality, Paul places major emphasis on the confirmation of his lordship through his eschatological destruction of the unrighteous (1:7–9) and of the man of lawlessness (2:8).

2. *The parousia and the day of the Lord.* The parousia of Jesus is mentioned no less than four times in the letter (1:7, 10; 2:1, 8). In each case its mention serves to assure the Thessalonians of Jesus's final victory. The parousia occurs on the "day of the Lord" (cf. 2:2), when the Lord Jesus exacts vengeance on the unrighteous (1:7–9) and the "man of lawlessness" (2:8). This emphasis is accented by allusions to several OT texts that look ahead to God's impending wrath (2 Thess. 2:4//Dan. 11:36; 2 Thess. 2:8//Isa. 11:4; 30:27–28). Aus (1977, 552) proposes a list of nine different allusions to Isa. 66 in 2 Thess. 1–2.

3. *Group boundaries and moral antitheses.* The letter reflects a characteristic apocalyptic antithesis between insiders and outsiders, or more specifically, those who will be destroyed (1:7–10; 2:10–12) and those who will be glorified (1:10–12; 2:13–14). In 2:10–12 Paul poses a series of contrasts that together reinforce group identity and normative group behavior: "deceit" versus "truth," "perishing" versus "saved," "unbelief" versus "belief."

4. *Future salvation.* Although God "elected" (2:13) and "called" (2:14) the Thessalonians for salvation, Paul emphasizes that the acquisition of "glory" stands in the future (1:12; 2:14), when the Lord metes out final justice. Salvation is not a result of a one-off personal decision to place faith in Christ but comes in the future to those who have proved themselves worthy (1:5–7, 11). Paul's attention to the Thessalonian's "endurance" (1:4; cf. 3:5) and "faith" (1:3, 4, 11; 2:13; 3:2)—or as often appears to be the meaning of *pistis*, their "faithfulness" (1:3, 4, 11; 3:2)—is intended to spur the Thessalonians on to the end.

These thematic elements highlight the substantially paraenetic quality of the letter. God wins in the end through the Lord Jesus. Although the Thessalonians currently suffer at the hands of persecutors, in the future they will be saved and their persecutors destroyed. Negatively, Paul's emphasis on future judgment sounds a note of warning to those who would slacken in their faith and make themselves liable to destruction along with the unbelieving.

Outline of 2 Thessalonians

Scholars have outlined 2 Thessalonians according to various classification schemes. As noted in the introduction to 1 Thessalonians, through the 1980s and 1990s many interpreters devised outlines of Paul's letters by correlating the letters' parts with the parts of a speech as outlined in ancient rhetorical theory. Repeated attempts to outline 2 Thessalonians in this way were made during this period (Jewett 1986, 82–85; Holland 1988, 8–33; Hughes 1989; Menken 1990, 373–82; Wanamaker 1990, 48–52). It is now acknowledged that Paul's letters are more appropriately outlined according to the conventions of ancient epistolography (Klauck 2006, 388; Weima 2014, 55–59); 2 Thessalonians is, in the truest sense of the word, a letter, written under a particular set of circumstances to a remote audience with whom Paul had a personal relationship.

In simplest terms, then, 2 Thessalonians, as a letter, contains an opening, a body, and a closing. The *opening* (1:1–12) follows a fairly typical epistolary format, which includes a prescript (sender, recipient, health wish) and a proem (thanksgiving). The *body* of the letter contains two parts. The first part (2:1–12) features one of the main reasons for the letter's composition: to address and refute a circulating rumor that "the day of the Lord has come" (2:2). Paul's refutation of the claim is predicated upon the current non-fulfillment of certain historical prerequisites, including the occurrence of "the apostasy" (2:3) and the revelation of the "man of lawlessness" (2:3–9). The second part of the letter (2:13–3:5) begins, atypically for Paul, with a second thanksgiving section (2:13–14). The thanksgiving, together with a brief exhortation (2:15) and a wish-prayer (2:16–17), focuses on the Thessalonians' election by God, implicitly contrasting them with the unbelievers of the preceding verses, who are said to be "perishing" (2:10–12). This second part of the body also includes a second subsection consisting of some loosely related exhortations of a general nature (3:1–5). Like 1 Thessalonians (5:12–22), the body of 2 Thessalonians closes with a final exhortation (2 Thess. 3:6–15). Unlike the closings of many of Paul's other letters, however, the exhortation section does not consist of a series of succinct and generic exhortations (Rom. 16:17; 1 Cor. 16:13–18; 2 Cor. 13:11; cf. Eph. 5:1–6:17; Col. 4:2–6) but addresses at some length a concrete problem in the community: the problem of those who are "walking disruptively" (i.e., the *ataktoi*). The exhortation section closes with an admonition to obey Paul's instructions about such people and to exclude those who fail to comply. The letter's *closing* includes three elements and is fairly typical of Paul's letter closings: a wish-prayer (3:16), a greeting and signature (3:17), and a benediction (3:18).

Outline of 2 Thessalonians

Letter opening (1:1–12)

Prescript: Superscription, adscription, and greeting (1:1–2)

Proem (first thanksgiving): The Thessalonians' faith and God's justice (1:3–12)

Letter body (2:1–3:5)

First main part: Signs preceding the parousia (2:1–12)

Second main part: General exhortation (2:13–3:5)

Second thanksgiving and exhortation (2:13–17)

A prayer request, exhortation, and a wish-prayer (3:1–5)

Final exhortation: Admonition against irresponsible living (3:6–15)

Letter closing (3:16–18)

This outline further illustrates what "type" of letter 2 Thessalonians is and what its rhetorical purposes are. The substantial paraenetic quality of the letter is evident in that the letter, atypically, includes two thanksgiving sections (1:3–12; 2:13–14), in which Paul's review of God's actions both present and future serves indirectly to encourage the Thessalonians both in regard to their present status before God ("beloved") and in the assurance of final justice. This quality is evident also in the inclusion of two hortatory wish-prayers at structural junctures in the letter (2:16; 3:5) and in the relative absence of commands/instructions in the letter. Accordingly, the letter's first main part (2:1–12), while seeking to correct an eschatological error, is not censorious but, as its introductory marks reveal, has a paraenetic purpose: Paul reviews his previous eschatological teachings *so that* the Thessalonians *will not be "shaken"* by false claims (2:2). Only in the final exhortation (3:6–15) is Paul censorious or threatening. The shift in tone at that point is what makes the style of 2 Thessalonians somewhat "mixed," being both "paraenetic" and "censorious."

2 Thessalonians 1:1–12

Letter Opening

Introductory Matters

Paul's second letter to the Thessalonians, like his first, begins in a similar way to other Hellenistic letters. A prescript names the sender(s) and addressee and wishes health upon the latter (1:1–2); this is followed immediately by a proem (1:3–12), which comes—in contrast to other Hellenistic letters (Artz-Grabner 1994)—in the form of a thanksgiving (1:3–12). Quite out of the ordinary, the thanksgiving also runs on grammatically at great length. It takes little time to build up as Paul erupts right out of the gate with delight over his audience and then moves quickly into a review of final judgment, when vindication for the righteous and punishment for the wicked will occur. It is evident that Paul wishes to accomplish a lot through this section.

Two "critical" issues deserve attention by way of introduction. The first concerns the relevance of verses 1–12 to the question of the letter's authenticity. The second concerns the origins of the material in verses 5–10.

The letter opening and pseudonymity. Those who maintain that 2 Thessalonians is pseudonymous find evidence in the letter's opening lines.

1. It is claimed that the simple salutation of 1 Thess. 1:1 ("grace to you and peace") has been expanded in 2 Thess. 1:3 in conformity with the salutations of Paul's later letters, with which a forger would have been familiar.
2. It is pointed out that 2 Thessalonians contains two thanksgiving sections (1:3–12; 2:13–14), a feature seen elsewhere only in Paul's earlier letter to the same church (1:2–10; 2:13–16), suggesting that an imitator used 1 Thessalonians as a template.

Table 8. The Thanksgiving Sections in 1 and 2 Thessalonians

1 Thessalonians	2 Thessalonians
"Grace to you and peace" (1:1)	"Grace to you and peace from God our Father and the Lord Jesus Christ" (1:3)
"We give thanks to God always for all of you" (1:2)	"We are obligated to give thanks to God always for you" (1:3)
"the work of your faith and the labor of your love and the endurance of your hope in our Lord Jesus Christ" (1:3)	"your faith and . . . love is increasing . . . so that we boast in you because of your endurance and faith" (1:3, 4)
Two thanksgivings (1:2–10; 2:13–16)	Two thanksgivings (1:3–12; 2:13–14)

3. It is observed that the opening thanksgivings in both letters share some similar phrasing, specifically the terminology of "faith," "love," and "endurance," and that these similarities betray imitation.
4. It is alleged that different authorship explains the disparaties between the introductory formulas of 1 Thess. 1:2 and 2 Thess. 1:3.
5. It is maintained that the prayer in 2 Thess. 1:11–12 introduces significant structural parallels between the two letters, and that this too is to be explained on the basis of imitation.

Although an accumulation of literary arguments against the letter's authenticity should be taken seriously, for many interpreters none of these arguments are particularly compelling. Indeed, it appears that the arguments generally rest on a *presupposition* of inauthenticity, which is then used to interpret the data and reinforce the conclusion with which one began. For instance, if the *conformity* of the letter's salutation with conventional Pauline greetings is considered to be an argument for imitation by a pseudepigrapher, one would already have to have a bias in this direction, since as far as his letters indicate, this is how Paul actually wrote. Similarly, when conformity with Paul's other letters is viewed as merely good imitation (points 1, 2, 3, and 5 above) and the lack of conformity is considered botched imitation (point 4 above), one wonders what kind of evidence could possibly lead to a conclusion other than one's starting position.

The origins of verses 5–10. Second Thessalonians 1:5–10 has struck many readers as sounding unlike Paul. Besides the atypical emphasis on the Lord's vengeance in these verses, they also contain a somewhat different stock of vocabulary and stand out from Paul's more typical manner of syntax. Interpreters have offered a variety of explanations for these irregularities.

1. Some have concluded that the content of verses 5–10 (or vv. 6–10) did not originate with Paul, but that he either appropriated an early Christian hymn (Bornemann 1894, 329, 336–39) or has adapted Christianized Jewish apocalyptic material (Dibelius 1937, 41–43).

2. F. F. Bruce (1982, 148–49) argued that Paul drew from a "testimony book" that consisted of eschatological passages from the OT.
3. Roger Aus (1971, 113–14) argued that the peculiarity of the passage owes to Paul's complicated intertextual interaction with OT passages.

Although it is possible that Paul derived his material in more or less complete form from an earlier source, his own intertextual interaction with the Jewish Scriptures may alone be sufficient to explain the content. Particularly salient are allusions to Isa. 66 (Isa. 2:19, 21//2 Thess. 1:9; Isa. 66:4//2 Thess. 1:8; Isa. 66:5//2 Thess. 1:12; Isa. 66:15//2 Thess. 1:8). In 2 Thess. 1:10, there may also be allusions to Pss. 88:8; 67:36 LXX (89:7; 68:35 Eng.).

Tracing the Train of Thought

Prescript: Superscription, Adscription, and Greeting (1:1–2)

1:1–2. The superscription to 2 Thessalonians names the same three individuals as the first letter to the church (**Paul and Silvanus and Timothy**). As before, Paul refrains from adding an epithet to his name (see 1 Thess. 1:1); still now, he relates to them not as their "apostle" (Rom. 1:1; 1 Cor. 1:1; 2 Cor. 1:1; Gal. 1:1; Eph. 1:1; Col. 1:1; cf. 1 Tim. 1:1; 2 Tim. 1:1; Titus 1:1) but as an intimate acquaintance. The adscription too matches that of the first letter, except for the addition of "our" to qualify "Father": **the assembly of Thessalonians that is in God our Father and the Lord Jesus Christ.**

The rather simple salutation of the first letter ("grace and peace") is now expanded, reaching a form identical to what becomes the standard salutation in all of Paul's later letters: **Grace to you and peace from God our Father and the Lord Jesus Christ** (some manuscripts omit the word "our"). The reference to God and Jesus in verse 1 and then again in verse 2 is not so "ponderous" as to prove that a pseudepigrapher has imitated Paul awkwardly (Richard 1995, 297). Such double references are common in the openings of Paul's letters (Weima 2014, 439; citing 2 Cor. 1:2–3; Gal. 1:1, 3; Col. 1:2–3; Eph. 1:2–3). Moreover, the double reference is hardly redundant; each iteration serves a different purpose—the first to *qualify* the identity of the assembly, and the second to convey the *source* of its identity.

In Greek "God our Father" and "the Lord Jesus Christ" are here joined as objects of a single preposition. Although the construction itself need not be christologically significant (cf. Sollamo 1995, 16), the pairing is meaningful nonetheless

---

2 Thessalonians 1:1–12 in the Rhetorical Flow

▶ **Letter opening (1:1–12)**

   Prescript: Superscription, adscription, and greeting (1:1–2)

   Proem (first thanksgiving): The Thessalonians' faith and God's justice (1:3–12)

(see 1 Thess. 1:1; also 1 Thess. 3:11–12; 2 Thess. 2:16; cf. 1 Thess. 1:8). Both here and in verse 12, "grace" and/or "peace" are said to derive "from" both God and Jesus. In his letters, Paul affirms that people "receive" grace from God (2 Cor. 6:1), that it is a "gift" from God (Rom. 5:15; 2 Cor. 8:1–2), and that people are "justified by" God's grace (Rom. 3:24). On the other hand, Paul frequently speaks of "the grace of the Lord Jesus" (Rom. 16:20; 1 Cor. 16:23; Phil. 4:23; 1 Thess. 5:28), "the grace of our Lord Jesus Christ" (Gal. 6:18), or "the grace of Christ" (Gal. 1:6), using "Jesus" and his titles as a genitive of source (grace comes *from* him). Though people are "justified *by*" God's grace as a gift, Paul indicates that their justification occurs "*through* the redemption that is in Christ Jesus" (Rom. 3:24) and that God's grace is "given *in* Christ Jesus" (1 Cor. 1:4). Likewise, Paul can refer to both the "God of peace" (Rom. 15:33; 16:20; 1 Cor. 14:33; Phil. 4:7, 9; 1 Thess. 5:23) and the "peace of Christ" (Col. 3:15); or to the peace that believers have "*with* God *through* our Lord Jesus Christ" (Rom. 5:1). That Paul in some instances assigns Jesus an instrumental role, then, suggests that he considered Jesus to be an *intermediate source* of grace and peace and as the instrument through which grace and peace flow from God.

Proem (First Thanksgiving): The Thessalonians' Faith and God's Justice (1:3–12)

In accordance with his usual practice, Paul adds to the prescript a "thanksgiving" (see "1 Thessalonians 1:1–10: Letter Opening"). The shared phrasing of 2 Thess. 1:2 ("grace to you . . . from God our Father and the Lord Jesus Christ") and 1:12 ("the grace of our God and the Lord Jesus Christ") creates an *inclusio* that marks off verses 3–12 as a discrete unit. Grammatically, the thanksgiving section consists of only two loosely constructed Greek sentences (vv. 3–10, 11–12), which most English translations break into three or more sentences (3 in NASB, 4 in ESV, 5 in NAB and NRSV, 7 in NIV). Thematically, the two sentences divide into three sections: verses 3–4 (Paul's gratitude for the increase of the Thessalonians' faith and love), verses 5–10 (eschatological justice), and verses 11–12 (a prayer for the Thessalonians).

The thanksgiving section is replete with the language of gift-giving: "grace" (also rendered "gift"; v. 12), "obligated" (v. 3), "worthy" (v. 3), "deem worthy" (v. 5), "make worthy" (v. 11), "give back" (v. 6), "give" (v. 8), "repay" (v. 9), and "honor" (v. 12). As usual (see 1 Thess. 1:1–10), the thanksgiving also anticipates themes that will be amplified in the letter's body: faith (2 Thess. 1:3, 4, 11; 2:13; 3:2) and love (1:3; 2:10; 3:5); the day of the Lord (2:2–3) / parousia (1:7, 10; 2:1, 8) / eschatology (1:5–10; 2:1–12); the distinction between insiders and outsiders (1:6–10; 2:10–14); and the Thessalonians' endurance under persecution (1:4; 3:5).

1:3–4. In place of the frequently occurring formula "I/we give thanks to God" (Rom. 1:8–15; 1 Cor. 1:4–9; Phil. 1:3–11; Col. 1:3–14; 1 Thess. 1:2–10; Philem. 4–7), Paul here writes, **We are obligated to give thanks to God always for you,**

"Fitting Thanks" and 2 Thess. 1:3

Inscriptions from Greek associations often express "fitting thanks" for the benefactions bestowed upon them by their benefactors (cf. "as is fitting," 2 Thess. 1:3). In these cases "fitting" thanks is, literally, a kind of thanks that is "worthy" of the gifts received.

"They give back fitting thanks [axias charitas] *for the benefactions."* (IG II² 1262)

"They will see to thanks worthy [charitas kataxias] *of the gifts that they gave."* (IG II² 1284)

---

brothers and sisters, as is fitting. The language of "obligation" has been variously understood by interpreters. Some take the language to mean that Paul was admonishing the Thessalonians ("no, we *really ought* to give thanks"). Others suggest that overwhelming emotions had given rise to a compulsion to speak ("we *can't help but* give thanks"). Others see the language as evidence that the letter was written pseudonymously, feeling that the language of obligation sounds more formal and frigid, indicating a level of detachment from the audience that cannot have characterized Paul's relationship with that church.

These explanations, however, incorrectly identify the significance of the "obligation" language. While Roger Aus (1973) has convincingly argued that this language was common in "liturgical" contexts in Hellenistic-Jewish and early Christian literature, it should be added that the specific cultural domain from which this language stemmed was that of gift-giving (Brookins forthc. b). All the basic elements of the system are implied (see comments on 1 Thess. 3:9): (1) God is the ultimate Benefactor; (2) a gift requires a fitting "return"; (3) the return is an "obligation," or something that one "owes"; (4) God's gifts ought to be returned with the gift of gratitude; and (5) gratitude is the only kind of return that one is able to render to God, although (6) the return of gratitude will never match the abundance of the gift.

Far from reflecting a coldly formal tone, the thanksgiving section here establishes a tone of intimacy and warmth. Indeed, Paul not only addresses the Thessalonians as his **brothers and sisters** (here, and not in 1 Thess. 1:2, where it is never said that his tone is "cool"), but he also feels "obligated" to render thanks to God on behalf of God's work in *their* lives, not even in his own. This dynamic actually reflects a sense of deep connection with his audience. David Briones (2010) has noticed a similar dynamic at work in 2 Corinthians. According to Briones, Paul sees himself and his churches as "brokers" who mediate God's grace to one another. Because a *koinōnia* (community) exists in the divine economy of God-Paul-churches, Paul and his churches can mediate both the gift of God's grace to each other *and* thanks to God on *behalf* of each other.

Paul next states *why* thanks are "fitting": for your faith is increasing and the love of each and every one of you toward one another is abounding (1:3). By giving God thanks, Paul conveys the idea that God is the one responsible for the Thessalonians' progress. The terms "faith" and "love" may focus, respectively, on the "inner aspect of Christian life" and "the outer action within the Christian community" (Best 1979, 251; see also comments on 1 Thess. 3:6). In Paul's letters, faith is invariably oriented toward God (cf. Morgan 2015), and love (almost) invariably toward other people (note an exception in Rom. 8:28). Despite Paul's celebration of the Thessalonians' faith and love, he will later ask that God might increase it further (3:5; cf. 1 Thess. 3:1–13).

The *result* of their increase in faith/love is this: **that we for our part boast in you in all the churches of God concerning your endurance and faith in all the persecutions and afflictions that you are bearing** (1:4). Paul's boasting "among the churches of God" recalls 1 Thess. 1:6–8, where he happily reported that the Thessalonians' endurance of affliction had become an example to those in Macedonia and Achaia and that the churches had spread the report abroad. Here Paul is responsible for the report. In his earlier letter he said that the Thessalonians had earned him a right to "boast" at the *judgment* (2:19), and he now finds personal grounds for "boasting" among the *churches* (2 Thess.1:4). Yet he also confesses that the church's "endurance and faith" (1:4) are the result of the increase of "faith and love" for which thanks are due to God (v. 3). Moreover, since his boasting concerns the *church's* endurance of affliction—not his own—it is intended to elevate not Paul but the church, and to elevate them as a model that is suited to inspire others (see also 2 Cor. 9:2).

Paul's remarks about the Thessalonians' endurance have clear paraenetic intentions. In the first place, they serve to encourage the Thessalonians to press through the trials that oppose them and likely are wearing on them. Their suffering is not in the past: they "*are* enduring" suffering. In 1 Thess. 3:7 Paul used the word pair

"Faith," "Love," and "Endurance" in the Thessalonian Letters

Although the terms "faith," "love," and "endurance" appear in both 1 Thess. 1:3 and 2 Thess. 1:3–4, the verbal coincidence is not so extensive or exact as to suggest the imitation of a forger. These terms appear together frequently in the Thessalonian letters (and other letters of Paul), and in various combinations. The three terms "faith," "love," and "endurance" fall into pairs on three occasions in 2 Thessalonians, with each term occurring once with each of the others: faith and love (1:3); endurance and faith (1:4); love and endurance (3:5). These terms also occur together in 1 Thessalonians: faith, love, and "hope of *endurance*" (1:3); and faith and love (3:6). Moreover, the coordination of the terms "faith" and "love" appears to have been quite traditional in Christianity (see comments on 1 Thess. 3:6 for references in the letters of both Paul and Ignatius).

"distress and affliction" (*ananke* and *thlipsis*) to describe their experiences; now he uses the pair "*persecution* and affliction" (*diōgmos* and *thlipsis*, 2 Thess. 1:4). These terms sometimes occur together as synonyms (Rom. 8:35; Matt. 13:21; Mark 4:17), and both could be used in reference to suffering experienced for religious reasons. In Paul's letters, *thlipsis* is sometimes used in this way; *diōgmos* invariably has this sense (Rom. 8:35; 2 Cor. 12:10; cf. 2 Tim. 3:11 [2×]). While the Thessalonians' suffering surely involved social oppression, the terms *diōgmos* and *thlipsis* almost certainly indicate that it also involved the experience of physical violence (see introduction), as these terms often indicate in the NT (*diōgmos* in Acts 8:1–3; 2 Tim. 3:11–12; cf. Acts 13:50; the verb *diōkein* in Matt. 23:34; Luke 11:49; 21:12; Acts 7:52; 22:4; 26:11; Gal. 1:13; *thlipsis* in 2 Cor. 6:4; Rev. 7:14). That Paul refers to "all" their persecutions and afflictions, moreover, suggests that he refers not just to a single event but to an ongoing experience (Weima 2014, 457).

Paul's praise of the Thessalonians' endurance is also intended to assure them that others are benefiting from it. In Paul's letters the term "endurance" (*hypomonē*) is frequently used to mean steadfastness in the face of difficulties resulting from commitment to Christ (Rom. 5:3; 12:12; 2 Cor. 6:4). The endurance of suffering as a model for imitation is a common theme in Paul's letters. Those who suffer, especially unjustly, imitate Christ in his suffering (Rom. 8:17). These in turn become an example to others. This view of suffering resonates to some extent with Stoic paraenesis about suffering. Seneca (*Prov.* 6.3) affirms that the endurance of hardships by the virtuous provides examples for others to follow. Christian martyr literature of later centuries, influenced by the language of Stoicism, presented the "endurance" of the martyrs as examples for other Christians to imitate (*Mart. Pol.* 1.2; see esp. *The Martyrs of Lyons*), though as for Paul, the model they aimed to follow was Jesus Christ.

1:5–10. The next six verses constitute a distinct unit focused on final judgment. This unit emphasizes that God is just and will repay to each according to their works, but that rectification holds off until the "day" when Jesus "comes." Although this section constitutes a single sentence in Greek, conceptually the sentence breaks down into two parts: (1) an affirmation of the principle of retributive justice (vv. 5–7a) and (2) an application of this principle to two different groups (vv. 7b–10): (a) first the persecutors (vv. 7b–9) and then (b) the persecuted (v. 10). This section is not just an informative review of Christian theology but also serves a paraenetic purpose. Although the Thessalonians currently suffer at the hands of persecutors, Paul assures them that the injustice they experience is only temporary. Justice will be served. Thus Paul's emphasis on God's wrath (1:6) and the Lord's judgment (1:7–9; 2:8) is intended, not to fuel hatred, but to encourage those who are weary and at risk of crumbling under the pressure of affliction.

Verse 5 is laden with interpretive difficulties. (1) At the beginning of the verse the term *endeigma* stands in apposition to something that precedes, though it is unclear exactly what. (2) *Endeigma* could mean either "evidence" or "grounds." (3) It is unclear whether God's "judgment" occurs at the present time or at the end. (4) The syntactical function of the infinitive (*kataxiōthēnai*) is unclear. (5) *Kataxiōthēnai* could mean either "deem worthy" or "make worthy."

The following interpretation offers a coherent solution to this set of problems. Paul considers the Thessalonians' *endurance* of suffering to be *proleptic* **evidence of the rightness of God's judgment.** Here God's judgment concerns his eschatological decision to deem the Thessalonians worthy of the kingdom (judgment **to deem you worthy of the kingdom of God**), granting them that for which they suffered (**for which very thing you also suffer,** 1:5). In other words, the fact that they have endured suffering is evidence that God will be "right" when on that final day he deems them worthy to enter the kingdom (on the "kingdom of God," see comments on 1 Thess. 2:12). God will be rewarding them according to their faithfulness. This decision by God will be "right," Paul continues (2 Thess. 2:6–7a), since God will then be acting according to his character (this is the kind of thing that God "does") by seeing fit to reward faithfulness and punish wickedness (**if indeed God sees fit to repay with affliction those who afflict you and give relief to you who are afflicted,** 1:6).

While the notion of postmortem judgment is almost completely absent from the Hebrew Bible (though see Dan. 12:2–3), Jewish texts in the apocalyptic tradition place heavy emphasis on a final judgment that would occur once and for all on some climactic day in the future (cf. 1 Thess. 5:3). Coming out of a pagan background, the Thessalonians would also have been familiar with the notion of postmortem judgment. Popular mythology affirmed that each individual upon death would stand trial before the bar of Minos and Rhadamanthus in the underworld and receive recompense according to their deeds (Cicero, *Tusc.* 1.5.10; Lucian, *The Downward Journey, or The Tyrant*). Ancient philosophy in the tradition of Plato had speculated about the postmortem judgment of souls and the sentencing of each to fitting rewards and punishments (Plato, *Phaed.* 113D–114B). In popular thinking, however, the prospect of *reward* was not as favorable as the prospect of punishment (see comments on 1 Thess. 5:9). Most philosophers, moreover, denied the prospect of postmortem recompense, holding that philosophy itself was sufficient to produce the perfect and happy life now, even in the present. To the Thessalonians, then, Paul's theology of judgment would have seemed somewhat novel in focusing on an eschatological rather than an individual judgment and emphasizing—for believers anyway—*rewards* rather than punishments.

Now 2 Thess. 1:7b–8a introduces an application of the affirmations made in 1:5–7a. Aid will come from the sky, **at the revealing of the Lord Jesus from heaven together with his mighty angels in a flame of fire** (on the descent of Jesus from heaven, see comments on 1 Thess. 4:16). The image of "fire" serves various symbolical purposes in biblical literature. Often it is associated with "theophanic" events (Exod. 3:2; 19:18; Deut. 5:4; Dan. 7:9–10). If there is an allusion here to Isa. 66:15, then fire may also function as a manifestation of the Lord's power, an interpretation that receives support in Paul's reference here to "his *mighty* angels" (on the role of angels in the judgment, see comments on 1 Thess. 3:13).

It is not the "flame of fire" that takes vengeance (not: "in a flame of fire that gives vengeance to those . . ."), but the Lord himself ("at the revelation of the Lord Jesus . . . **when he gives vengeance**"). Two substantival participles specify the objects of his vengeance: **those who do not know God and who do not obey the gospel of our Lord Jesus** (2 Thess. 1:8b–c; on "the gospel of Christ," see comments on 1 Thess. 1:5). In verse 6 Paul had affirmed that God will repay "those who afflict you"; here the descriptions reveal that the object of the Lord's vengeance is not limited to the church's persecutors but threatens to fall upon all nonbelievers. The two substantives need not distinguish gentiles (who are ignorant) from Jews (who are disobedient). While gentiles are often described in both the OT and NT as "ignorant" of God (Jer. 10:25; Ps. 79:6; Rom. 1:21; 1 Thess. 4:5) and were so described in 1 Thessalonians (4:5), Jews could also be described in this way, both in the OT (Jer. 4:22; 9:6; Hosea 5:4; cf. John 8:55) and in Paul's letters (Rom. 10:16). Conversely, while Jews could indeed be described as "disobedient" to God (Isa. 66:4), Paul also describes gentiles in this way (Rom. 10:16; 11:30). The two substantives, then, most likely function synonymously. This conclusion gains support not only from the widespread use of coordinated synonyms in Paul's letters ("indignation and wrath," Rom. 2:8; "my word and my preaching," 1 Cor. 2:4; "wickedness and evil," 5:8; "fear and trembling," 2 Cor. 7:15; etc.), including elsewhere in 2 Thessalonians ("persecution and affliction," 1:4; "perverse and evil men," 3:2), but also from the reappearance of synonymous parallelism in both 1:9b and 10 (see comments below).

Nonbelievers **will pay the penalty of eternal destruction** (1:9; cf. 1 Thess. 5:3). Paul gives no indication that their punishment will be restorative. Rather, it is retributive. However, the adjective "eternal" could indicate either *duration* ("forever and ever") or *finality* ("once and for all"). Fourth Maccabees describes "eternal torment" (13:15). It also clearly depicts postmortem punishment as a process (18:5) and explicitly refers to punishment that is "unceasing" (10:11 NRSV) and occurs "throughout all time" (12:12 NRSV). A great many Jewish texts, on the other hand, can be seen as affirming annihilation (*Pss. Sol.* 14.9; 15.12; Wis. 2:1–5). The phrase "everlasting destruction" occurs frequently in the literature from Qumran (*lklt ʿôlm* in 1QS V.13; *wklt ʿôlmîm* in 1QM I.5; IX.5–6; cf. *Pss. Sol.* 15.12), and in apparent accord with the theology of the community, probably describes total annihilation.

The meaning of the term "eternal" in 2 Thess. 1:9 is partly dependent on the significance of the prepositional phrase that follows (*apo prosōpou tou kyriou kai apo tēs doxēs tēs ischyos*), where the preposition could indicate either *space* or *cause*. Possible allusions here to Isa. 2:19, 21 may argue in favor of the spatial interpretation ("eternal ruin *from* the face of the Lord"; Malherbe 2000, 393). Several factors, however, point strongly toward a causal interpretation. First, even if allusions to Isa. 2:19, 21 are present, the change of syntax (from "*hide* away from") renders a spatial meaning more problematic (i.e., "*destruction* away from"). Moreover, in both the OT and NT, theophanic encounters, or "face-to-face"

Table 9. The Antitheses between Believers and Nonbelievers

"at the revelation of the Lord Jesus from heaven" (1:7b)	"on that day" (1:10c)
"ignorant and disobedient" (1:8b)	"saints and believers" (1:10a)
"vengeance" (1:8b)	"to be glorified in him and to marvel at him" (1:10a)

encounters with the Lord, are depicted as highly dangerous, even fatal. Isaiah exclaims his own destruction when he stands before the Lord's throne (Isa. 6:5). In Exodus it is said that no one could see the "face" of the "Lord" and live (33:20). Clearly alluding to this text, in 2 Corinthians Paul solemnly states that no one could gaze at the "face" of Moses because of the "glory" that he derived from face-to-face encounters with the Lord (3:7). Later in 2 Thessalonians, Paul predicts that Jesus will "destroy" the man of lawlessness with the breath of his mouth (2 Thess. 2:8). Finally, the scene that Paul sets here is quite inconsistent with a spatial interpretation: Paul visualizes Jesus *descending* from heaven with *mighty* angels in a *flame of fire* to "*give* vengeance"—a very unfitting description if destruction implies "separation." Rather, this surely implies an *encounter*. The causal meaning, then, should be preferred: it is destruction **at the sight of the Lord and the glory of his might** (1:9).

After applying the retributive principle to nonbelievers (vv. 7b–9), Paul next applies it to believers (v. 10). All of this—the "revelation" of Jesus and his "vengeance" on the ungodly—will happen **when he comes to be glorified in his holy ones and to be marveled at among all those who believed** (1:10). As in verse 8, two substantival participles probably refer to a single group: "the holy ones" are "saints," the same people who also "believed" (in the aorist tense, i.e., "who put their faith in Jesus while still living"). While the term "holy ones" (*hagioi*) sometimes designates angels (1 Thess. 3:13), the emphasis in verses 5–10 is on contrasting groups of *people* and their respective fates: on the one hand, the "ignorant" and "disobedient" will pay the penalty of destruction at Jesus's coming; corresponding to them, on the other hand, the "saints" and "believers" will share in his glory and marvel at him. The addition of **for our testimony to *you* was believed as well** is parenthetical: Paul is making it a point to mention that the Thessalonians too are counted among "those who believed." Here the tie between "belief" and Paul's "testimony *toward*" suggests that the *pist-* language ("all those who *believed*") does not here connote "faithfulness" but rather "assent" to the message that Paul directed "toward" them. The final phrase **on that day** completes a fairly complex conceptual parallel that has developed across verses 7b–10: at the "revelation" of Jesus, the "ignorant" and "disobedient" will be subject to the Lord's "vengeance"; "on that day," the "saints" and "believers" will "marvel at" him.

1:11–12. A concluding "prayer report" parallels the introductory thanksgiving formula that occurred in verse 3; having first said, "We ought to give thanks to God for you always" (v. 3), Paul now says, **For this reason we also pray for**

you always (1:11a). The adverb "also" therefore implies *prayer in addition to thanksgiving*. In other letters Paul's thanksgivings conclude with similar prayer reports (Phil. 1:9–11; Col. 1:9–14; cf. Rom. 1:10b). These serve indirectly but quite clearly to exhort the audience as to how they should conduct themselves (Weima 2014, 479).

The syntax of verse 11 presents two difficulties. First, verse 11 connects with what precedes by means of a preposition and a relative clause (*eis ho*), and it is not clear how the preposition functions or what the referent of the pronoun is. Second, it is unclear whether the *hina* clause that follows indicates the purpose of Paul's prayer or its content.

The best solution to these problems seems to be that the relative pronoun refers generally to the eschatological scenario described across verses 5–10: God will punish and reward. Introduced by the preposition *eis*, the relative clause then indicates the *grounds* of Paul's prayer activity: he prays because not all will be among the saved. After stating the *grounds* of his prayer, Paul finally indicates *to what end* he prays: in order that they specifically (with the pronoun "*you*" fronted for emphasis) might not be among the objects of the Lord's vengeance but rather among the saved: thus, **that our God might make *you* worthy of the calling** (1:11b).

The term rendered "*make* worthy" (*axioun*) is cognate with the term rendered "*deem* worthy" in verse 5 (*kataxioun*). Whereas *axioun* would normally mean "*deem* worthy" (with the compound form *kataxioun* being slightly more emphatic), the context here requires "*make* worthy." This is shown by at least two considerations. First, if Paul's prayer could persuade God to "*consider*" someone worthy (that person as opposed to someone else), God's response to do so would seem to be arbitrary unless he made his decision in concurrence with a real change in the subjects' orientation and behavior, or put differently, unless they had in fact become or been "*made*" worthy. Second, the adjoining of the words **and powerfully fulfill every good pleasure of your goodness and fulfill the work of your faith** (1:11c) reveals that Paul's emphasis is on producing a life that, indeed, *is* worthy of the call. The expression "good pleasure of goodness" refers not to God's good pleasure but to a *person's* good pleasure in doing good. Likewise, the "work of faith" refers to *human* work produced by faith (on "the work of faith," see comments on 1 Thess. 1:3). Although these human behaviors "make" the subjects "worthy" of the calling, Paul does not fail to note that God is the one who has so made them ("powerfully"). Paul's prayer, in short, is that God's power would *produce* in them a life worthy of the call.

The final clause of the sentence (vv. 11–12), like the preceding *hina* clause, indicates purpose (**in order that**), though this time the purpose clause is introduced not by *hina* but *hopōs*. The change of conjunction is not merely stylistic but rather indicates that the two purpose clauses do not serve parallel functions. Whereas the *hina* clause indicates the purpose of *praying* (so that they too will be made worthy of the kingdom), the *hopōs* clause conveys why Paul asks that

---

Honor and Mutual Benefit

"Tell me, if a man has attained so much eminence as to be renowned throughout the world by reason either of his eloquence or of his justice or his military prowess, if he has been able to encompass his father also in the greatness of fame, and by the glory of his name to dispel the obscurity of his birth, has he not conferred upon his parents a benefit that is beyond all estimate?" (Seneca, *Ben.* 3.2, trans. Basore, LCL)

Cornelia Gracchus *"often reproached her sons because the Romans still called her the mother-in-law of Scipio, but not yet the mother of the Gracchi."* (Plutarch, *Ti. C. Gracch.* 8.6, trans. Perrin, LCL)

God might *make them worthy*: **so that the name of our Lord Jesus might be glorified in you and you in him** (1:12a). This last assertion stands parallel to verse 10 ("glorified . . . marveled at"), and as in verse 10, the meaning is eschatological (Weima 2014, 485). The scene implicitly depicts the presence of witnesses apart from the Lord Jesus and the Thessalonian believers, thus recalling a common theme in Jewish apocalyptic literature: that of the public vindication of the righteous before the wicked (*1 En.* 27.3; 108.11–15; 2 Esd. [*4 Ezra*] 7:83; *2 Bar.* 30.4; 51.1–6). In short, Jesus is glorified *in* them and they *in* Jesus *in the presence of* nonbelievers.

The language of glorification has strong resonances with cultural discourse about honor and shame. In the Roman patron-client system, it was the responsibility of clients to promote the name, or prestige, of their benefactors (Barclay 2015, 35–39). Often this happened by honoring the benefactor directly—by commissioning an inscription, setting up a statue, or singing their praises in public. In other cases, this happened indirectly. Patron and client were associated in such a way that the honor or shame accruing to the one also accrued to the other. The relationship was a partnership, or *koinōnia*. Thus, if the patron was glorified, the client was glorified "in" him; and if the client was glorified, the patron in turn was glorified "in" him. This framework helps explain why Paul here uses not *doxazein* but the uncommon, compound verb form *endoxazein*: the prepositional prefix *en-* adds *local* significance to the verb. The name of Jesus is glorified "in" the Thessalonian believers. Like patron and client, Jesus and believers are united in a *koinōnia*. Reference to Jesus not as "*the* Lord Jesus" but "*our* Lord Jesus" highlights this relational emphasis further. Although the "participation Christology" that is so important in Paul's later letters is far from salient in 2 Thessalonians, verse 12 shows that in some form it was already present in his theology when he wrote this letter (see also comments on 1 Thess. 4:17).

The final phrase of the verse describes the cause (or source) of their glorification: they are glorified in the Lord Jesus **according to the grace of our God and**

"Our God and the Lord Jesus Christ" (1:12)

In the Greek text of 1:12, both "God" and "the Lord Jesus Christ" are united under one definite article (*tou*). This construction has sometimes been used to argue that the author presents God and Jesus as being ontologically identical (Turner 1965, 13–17). Dobschütz (1909, 258) even used this interpretation to support his claim that the letter was the product of a later author, who lived when, ostensibly, Christian theology had begun to articulate a higher Christology. This construction, however, need not imply the synonymous identity of the two subjects. The article occurs with the name "God" according to Paul's general usage, for "*the* God" is his preferred expression (cf. 1 Cor. 8:5–6); the article would be required in any event due to the qualifying personal pronoun. The expression "Lord Jesus Christ," on the other hand, routinely lacks the article in Paul's letters, since Paul generally treats "Lord" as a name. Thus the article is used ("*the* God") and then not used ("Lord") here according to Paul's regular usage with each name. Consequently, the use of a single article does not in itself have implications for the ontological unity of God and Jesus.

---

the Lord Jesus Christ (1:12b; see sidebar). Although they themselves are to live in a way that will merit their glorification before nonbelievers, it is from grace that they so live.

Theological Issues

An Emphasis on the Present

It is a common practice, when consoling people, to point them to the future. Christians remind each other that a more blessed life awaits on the other side of death. We will rest from our labors. Pain will cease. Weeping will give way to laughter. In 2 Thess. 1:3–12, Paul likewise has the future in view. Upon closer look, however, Paul does not just point the Thessalonians *to* the future but, assuming the *vantage point* of the future, also points them back to the present. He speaks *from* the time when God "deems them worthy of the kingdom" (v. 5), when the Lord Jesus "gives vengeance" to those who disobey God (v. 8), and "when Jesus comes" to be glorified in his people (v. 10). While Paul's approach indeed implies that blessings await, his retrospective view sets the focus on the life lived *now*, the life that *paves the way* to the hoped-for end. God will "deem them worthy" of the kingdom because he has looked back on their endurance through what they are still presently suffering (vv. 4–5). Paul, moreover, prays that God will "*make* them worthy" of the calling, precisely because it is possible still to become an object of the Lord's wrath. The eschatological framework, then, is a presupposition used in service of paraenesis. Because God's kingdom awaits those who are obedient, the Thessalonians should make all the more certain that they continue to endure and become worthy of God's calling.

God's Work in the Present

Anyone who has experienced suffering—whether prolonged or short-lived—knows the importance of perspective. What we think we *can* do sometimes depends on our frame of mind. We can endure pain for a few seconds, for a few days, or even for years, but everything can change with a change in perspective. A sudden switch, and panic sets in: we decide that our bodies can take no more, we can no longer do it on our own, and we finally despair from the pain.

As Paul wrote, the Thessalonian believers were burdened under the weight of persecution and affliction. Paul's approach in 2 Thess. 1:3–12 reflects subtle awareness that their situation might have rendered them psychologically fragile. Conceivably some of them stood at a breaking point. Wearied as they were, Paul did not urge them to "stand firm" and "keep laboring in the Lord." Rather, he focused on the enabling work of God. *They* may feel that they can do no more, but there is one who can empower them. Although Paul "boasts" in the church (v. 4) and is "thankful" for the increase of their faith and love, his thanks (to God) implies that God is somehow responsible for their progress. Moreover, while Paul's prayer on the church's behalf in verses 11–12 undoubtedly communicates that the Thessalonians themselves must *live* worthily of God's call, his emphasis remains on God's initiative: God is the subject of the two main actions ("that *God might make you* worthy and *fulfill* . . ."), and it is by the grace of "our God and the Lord Jesus Christ" that their lives will meet the intended goal. This, then, is Paul's strategy: not to tell the suffering Thessalonian believers what *they must do* but to remind them of what *God is doing*.

2 Thessalonians 2:1–3:5

Letter Body

Introductory Matters

After a twelve-verse opening (1:1–12), the body of the letter begins. The body contains two main parts. The first (2:1–12) discusses certain eschatological events centering around a figure called "the man of lawlessness," in response to concerns that the Thessalonians have been "shaken" by reports that "the day of the Lord has come" (2:2). The second part comprises a loose assemblage of hortatory material that breaks down into three paragraphs: the first presents a new thanksgiving section (2:13–14); the second exhorts the Thessalonians to hold fast to the traditions that they have received (2:15), followed by a wish-prayer (2:16–17); the third consists of a prayer request (3:1–2), some general exhortation (3:3–4), and another wish-prayer (3:5), all tied loosely together.

The body reprises themes anticipated in the letter's opening: faith (1:3, 4, 11; 2:13; 3:2) and love (1:3; 2:10; 3:5); the day of the Lord (2:3) / parousia (1:7, 10; 2:1, 8) / eschatology (1:5–10; 2:1–12); the distinction between insiders and outsiders (1:6–10; 2:10–14); and the Thessalonians' endurance under persecution (1:4; 3:5). Like the letter's opening, the body also evinces intense paraenetic concerns. Although Paul's discussion of the man of lawlessness and his relation to the day of the Lord is undoubtedly informative in nature, Paul's introduction to 2:1–12 reveals a primary aim of alleviating his audience's consternation over the pertinent eschatological questions (2:2, "so that you are not *shaken* . . . nor *disturbed*"). Moreover, Paul wishes to assure his audience that God is faithful (3:3) and that, in contrast to "those who are perishing," they themselves have been "chosen" by God and "called" to obtain glory. Finally, he urges them on to behavior that suits their status as called people (2:15–17; 3:3–5).

The body of the letter has invited rich discussion about Paul's eschatology and, overlapping with this issue, the letter's authorship. A brief word will be offered about these issues before tracing Paul's train of thought.

"The man of lawlessness" and "the restraining thing / restrainer." Paul's tantalizingly obscure references to "the man of lawlessness" and "the restraining thing" or "the restraining one" in 2:1–12 have provoked lively debate about the intended referents. Paul's description of the man of lawlessness fits a number of candidates, including OT, intertestamental, and contemporary figures. More obscure are the references to the "restraining thing" (neuter substantive) and "the restraining one" (masculine substantive). Paul provides no further description of these entities, and little if any precedent for this language appears in prior sources. The possible referents of these expressions will be discussed in the commentary below.

> **2 Thessalonians 2:1–3:5 in the Rhetorical Flow**
>
> Letter opening (1:1–12)
>
> ▶ Letter body (2:1–3:5)
>
> > First main part: Signs preceding the parousia (2:1–12)
> >
> > Second main part: General exhortation (2:13–3:5)
> >
> > > Second thanksgiving and exhortation (2:13–17)
> > >
> > > A prayer request, exhortation, and a wish-prayer (3:1–5)

Second Thessalonians 2:1–12 and pseudonymity. Advocates of the view that 2 Thessalonians is pseudonymous discern abundant evidence for their view in the letter's body. Key arguments include the following:

1. Extensive structural and verbal parallels with 1 Thessalonians reveal that the author has used the earlier letter as a template.
2. Discrepancies between the eschatology of 1 Thess. 4:13–5:11 and that of 2 Thess. 2:1–12 indicate that the author of the latter (and later) epistle objected to the eschatology of the former letter and aimed to replace it with his own eschatology under the guise of the person whose eschatology he aimed to replace (i.e., Paul).
3. The author's warning about "a letter as if through us" (as most interpreters render the Greek) is just the sort of thing a liar wanting to be trusted as a truth-teller would say.

These points merit a fuller assessment than can be given here. In addition to the comments that touch directly or indirectly upon them below, the reader is directed to the introduction to 2 Thessalonians for further discussion.

Tracing the Train of Thought

First Main Part: Signs Preceding the Parousia (2:1–12)

This first part of the body addresses the timing of the day of the Lord (2:1–12). Mention of the parousia in 2:1, 8 reprises a theme anticipated in the letter's opening, where Paul referred to Jesus's "revelation" (1:7) and "coming" (1:10). Now Paul predicts that two events must precede: the "rebellion" (*apostasia*) and the revelation of "the man of lawlessness" (2:3). Although Paul speaks of these future events with clairvoyance, his predictions remain cryptic in the details, and despite his confidence about the signs that precede the end, his general outline of events can hardly be considered a precise "timetable." Moreover, the sequence of events described across verses 5–12 is muddled not only by the nonsequential description of the events (the destruction of the man of lawlessness is mentioned before his activities) but also by the use of verb forms in all tenses (past, present, and future), which do not always seem to be situated relative to the author's anchoring point in the present: the revelation and destruction of the man of lawlessness are described in the future tense (v. 8) but his parousia in the present tense (v. 9), the "perishing" of nonbelievers is described in the present tense and their refusal of the truth in the past tense (v. 10), God's sending of deception is described in the present tense (v. 11), and, finally, those who are perishing are described, in the past tense, as having not believed and having not been pleased with the truth (v. 12).

2:1–2. A transition from the opening of the letter to its body is signaled by the conjunction *de*, together with a meta-comment formula (*erōtōmen de hymas*) and a vocative of address (*adelphoi*): **Now we ask you, brothers and sisters** (an expression occurring elsewhere in the NT only in 1 Thess. 5:12). Taking up his first issue (2:1–12), Paul speaks **regarding the parousia of our Lord Jesus Christ and our gathering to him** (2:1). The term "gathering" (*episynagōgē*) echoes the prophetic prediction that God would regather the Jews of the dispersion into Palestine (Ps. 106:47 [105:47 LXX]; Isa. 27:13; Ezek. 28:25; Zech. 2:6–7; Tob. 14:7; 2 Macc. 1:27; 2:7–8). The NT appropriates this word to refer to the gathering of the church at the parousia (Matt. 24:31; Mark 13:27; cf. *Apoc. Ab.* 31.1). In 1 Thessalonians the gathering at the parousia is clearly described as a resurrection (4:14, 16; cf. 4:17). Here, the use of a single definite article to coordinate "parousia" and "gathering" suggests, likewise, that the two actions are part of a single event.

Paul writes on this topic so that the Thessalonians would **not be quickly shaken from good sense, nor disturbed, neither through a spirit nor a report nor a letter** (2:2a). Commentators generally agree that "a spirit" refers to a prophetic spirit—the supposed spiritual *source* behind a prophecy (cf. 1 Cor. 14:32). Evidently this would be a spirit of *false* prophecy (whether the prophet intended it as such or not). Next, it is agreed that the second and third sources refer respectively to an oral (lit., "a word," *logos*) and written source ("a letter"). It is debated, however, whether the phrase that follows (**as if through us**) qualifies one, two, or all three of the sources identified. It could be read as qualifying all three: "a spirit as if through us," referring either to a prophecy attributed to Paul or to an allegedly inspired interpretation of his teaching (whether offered by others or discerned by the Thessalonians themselves); "a report as if through us," indicating a report purportedly stemming from Paul; and "an epistle as if through us," referring to an epistle attributed to him, whether spurious or (though misinterpreted) authentic.

That the phrase "as if through us" qualifies one or more of these items is a supposition that all have taken for granted and that has consequently been left unexamined. The usual assumption is that the qualifying phrase marks Paul as the *alleged original* source behind certain *intermediate* sources: a "prophetic utterance deriving from Paul," a "report deriving from Paul," or a "letter deriving from Paul." The grammar, however, does not demand this reading. In the first place, this reading assigns a different qualifying function to the final preposition than to the first three, despite the fact that the same preposition is used in all four instances (*dia*). That is, in the first three instances the prepositional phrases are taken as describing the source of the teaching ("shaken by [a *teaching* received] *through a spirit, word, or letter*"), while in the final instance, the phrase is taken as modifying one or more of the other three prepositional phrases ("through a *spirit, word, or letter* as if *through* us, etc.").

An alternative, however, is to take the fourth prepositional phrase not as qualifying the first three, but as parallel to them (Brookins forthc. a). Read in this way, "as if through us" sets in contrast a spirit, a report, and a letter as three possible sources of information on the one hand, and Paul himself as the source of information on the other: that is, the Thessalonians should not be deceived by what they may have received "through a spirit, nor through a report, nor through a letter," as if these sources trumped what they have heard through *Paul*. "As if through us," then, would not indicate Paul's challenge to the supposition that the sources *derived* their information from Paul, but simply that the source—no matter whence it derived its information—was not *Paul* (the same argument used in Gal. 1:8). In verse 15, indeed, Paul reaffirms the "word" that *he* originally shared with them during his founding visit. If this reading is correct, then Paul's remarks about "an *epistle* as if" need not be taken as a reference to an epistle spuriously attributed to him, an epistle that either he was aware was in circulation or he suspected could be in existence. Rather, such an epistle could have been written by anyone or attributed to anyone. That was not his point. The problem was that this hypothetical epistle—no matter its author—taught what Paul himself did not: **that the day of the Lord has come** (2:2b).

With regard to the refuted claim, a present-perfect translation of the verb (*enestēken*) certainly captures the meaning: the day "has come and is here." Disputing this translation, some interpreters take the verb to express imminence ("the day is near at hand") on the grounds that the Thessalonians cannot have believed the day had come since they would be aware that Christ had not returned with fanfare and they had not been raptured (1 Thess. 4:13–18). However, the lexical evidence for usage of this verb, in the perfect tense, weighs heavily in favor of a present-perfect meaning. Moreover, it would be understandable if the Thessalonians interpreted their experiences of "persecution and affliction" (1:4) as evidence that the "day" had come, perhaps viewing it as a period of final tribulation before the parousia itself (Wanamaker 1990, 240). The claim that the day had come would, moreover, become more credible on a certain (misreading) of 1 Thessalonians, where Paul describes the falling of wrath on the Jews in the past tense (2:16), affirms that Satan is presently at work (2:18), and describes the day of the Lord in the present tense (5:1–5). As to the point that the unmissable occurrences of the parousia and their own resurrection had not occurred, it need only be supposed that the Thessalonians viewed the Day as occurring non-simultaneously with these events. It would be this last point, then, that Paul sought to correct. Indeed, verses 1–2 suggest that Paul is trying to *reassociate* events that were conceived separately in his audience's minds. As already observed, Paul presents "the parousia-and-gathering (resurrection)" as closely associated, if not simultaneous. In this regard, it should not be missed that in his very appeal to them "*regarding* the parousia and gathering" he asks that they not be shaken by claims about "the *day of the Lord.*" He speaks "regarding" these things when teaching about the day of the Lord, in short, because these events occur together.

2:3–4. After citing the claim that the day of the Lord has arrived (made by unidentified people), Paul proceeds to prove that the claim is wrong, introducing his remarks with a grave word of caution: **Let no one deceive you in any way.** Although it is others who perpetrate the deception (wittingly or unwittingly), Paul's emphasis is on the Thessalonians' volition: they ought not *allow* themselves to be deceived, **for** (*hoti*) they have already been instructed on these matters (see v. 5). He reminds them that the day of the Lord cannot have come, for two things must first precede: **if the apostasy does not come first and the man of lawlessness is not revealed.**

Having mentioned the "apostasy" (*apostasia*), Paul quickly leaves it behind and is drawn into a series of appositives that amplify the character of the "man of lawlessness." Yet, as the discussion continues, it becomes evident that the *apostasia* consists in a kind of religious "rebellion" (hence "apostasy") against God and the Lord Jesus, stirred up by the man of lawlessness and constituted by those whom he has led astray with signs and wonders energized by Satan himself (vv. 9–10).

Mysteriously, the man of lawlessness is identified only by a series of epithets: the man of lawlessness, **the son of destruction, the one who opposes** . . . (2:3b–4a). "Man of lawlessness" and "son of destruction" are Semitic constructs, although neither construct occurs in known Semitic sources (cf. "son of lawlessness," Ps. 89:22 [88:23 LXX]; "sons of lawlessness," Justin, *Dial.* 16.5; 132.3; "son of destruction," John 17:12 ESV; "children of destruction," Isa. 57:4 LXX; "sons of darkness," 1QM I.1–7; III.6–9; 1QS I.9–10; "sons of the pit," CD VI.15). The genitive noun in the first title expresses a characteristic: "the *lawless* man," meaning the man who incites rebellion against God. In the second title, the genitive indicates either what the man produces or the man's destination or end, i.e., "the son *destined for* destruction" (cf. v. 8). The substantive that follows, "the one who opposes," attributes to the same man an activity that gives Satan his name, "the Opponent," or "the Adversary" (in Hebrew and Aramaic, *Śāṭān*; see Job 1:6–2:7;

1 Chron. 21:1; Zech. 3:1–2; so also *ho antikeimenos* in early Christian literature: *1 Clem.* 51.1; *Mart. Pol.* 17.1). His opposition to God reaches its most brazen extreme in his claim to divinity: he **exalts himself above everything named as a divinity or object of worship** (2:4b). The result of his arrogance is that he **sits in the temple of God in order to display himself as being a god** (2:4c; in *LAE* 15.3 Satan is the figure who exalts himself in heaven and declares himself equal to God).

The question of the "man's" identity has exercised biblical interpreters for millennia. A great number of figures fit his description, from the kings of Tyre (Ezek. 28:2) and Babylon (Isa. 14:4, 13–14) in the OT; to the Greek king Antiochus IV Epiphanes (2 Macc. 5:11–17; Dan. 9:27; 11:31, 36–37; 12:11) and the Roman general Pompey (*Pss. Sol.* 2.2–3, 29; 17.11) of the intertestamental period; to contemporary Roman rulers like Caligula and Nero (*Sib. Or.* 3.33–34, 63–74, 93–110, 137–54). In some sources Satan himself is described similarly (*LAE* 15.3; cf. *Barn.* 18.2). To be sure, Paul's prediction of this future individual does not directly *refer* to any earlier figure, though his description of the man obviously interacts intertextually with texts where such figures are described (esp. Dan. 11:36). Nor (assuming Pauline authorship) can Paul's prediction refer to a contemporary figure (like Caligula), for his point is that the figure has yet to be revealed and that the day of the Lord cannot have come for precisely this reason. In any case, with Paul's description matching so many figures from across Jewish history, it cannot be doubted that the description is prototypical, even if it is based primarily on a single individual. Wanamaker (1990, 245) says it is Pompey,

---

"The Temple of God" in 2 Thess. 2:4

Paul's reference to "the temple of God" could be construed in several different ways. (1) Throughout church history, it was commonly believed that "temple" referred to the church (cf. 1 Cor. 3:16–17 [3×]; 2 Cor. 6:16 [2×]; Eph. 2:21), into the midst of which the antichrist would come and lead its members into apostasy. (2) Based on abundant examples in the OT and other Jewish literature (Ps. 11:4; Isa. 66:1; *1 En.* 14.10–22; etc.), others take "temple" in reference to the heavenly temple, in which God is said to have his throne (Frame 1912, 257). (3) The appearance of the definite article before both "temple" and "God" ("*the* temple of *the* God") has led most interpreters to conclude that the reference is to the Jerusalem temple. Since the Jerusalem temple was destroyed in 70 CE, however, some have been moved to conclude either that Paul's prediction was wrong and can no longer be considered theologically valid (Wanamaker 1990, 248) or that the temple in Jerusalem will evidently need to be rebuilt (R. Thomas 1978, 322). More likely, "temple" here serves as a figurative expression in which Paul uses the typical theme of the Jerusalem temple's desecration (see below) to describe, not an event that takes place in the actual temple in Jerusalem, but rather the lawless one's usurpation of God's authority and status (Weima 2014, 522).

The Evil Opponent in Apocalyptic Literature

To call Paul's "man of lawlessness" "the antichrist" would be a bit of an anachronism. In Paul's day there was not yet a standard antichrist concept. In a lengthy monograph, L. J. L. Peerbolte (1996) has traced the antecedents of the concept in Jewish and Christian literature in the period between 200 BCE and 150 CE. As Peerbolte demonstrates, Jewish and Christian apocalyptic literature depicted the rise of various evil persons at different stages of the eschatological drama. The various entities depicted this way in Jewish apocalyptic provided inspiration for the development of evil eschatological entities in early Christian literature. In Christian literature such entities include, among others, false prophets/messiahs (Mark 13; *Acts Pet.* 4–7), antichrists (1 and 2 John), a dragon and a beast (Rev. 12–14), the deceiver of the world (*Did.* 16), the eschatological tyrant (*Barn.* 4), Beliar (*Martyrdom and Ascension of Isaiah*), and the man of lawlessness (2 Thess. 2:4). By about 150 CE, a unified concept of "the antichrist" had crystallized. Peerbolte concludes: "Since all the eschatological opponents in the earliest Christian speculation were counterparts of one single person, namely Christ, they could easily coalesce as time went by. The various notions gradually merged into the concept of Antichrist as the single eschatological opponent" (345).

Malherbe (2000, 420) says it is Antiochus IV Epiphanes, and Harrison (2011, 71) says it is Caligula.

Many interpreters see Paul not as identifying a particular figure and actions he will perform but as describing an impersonal force or personification of lawlessness (Lightfoot 1904, 112; Malherbe 2000, 432) that will thrive in the last days. Others are confident that Paul / the author must have a concrete individual in mind (Best 1979, 288; Peerbolte 1996, 89), especially given the extensive parallels in the description between the man of lawlessness and Jesus: as Jesus will be "revealed" from heaven (1:7), so the man of lawlessness will be "revealed" (2:3); as Jesus will have his "parousia" (2:1, 8), so also will the man of lawlessness (2:9); and as Jesus will be revealed on "the day of the Lord" (2:1–2), so the man of lawlessness will be revealed "in his time" (2:6). Whether these parallels suggest that the man has supernatural origins is not clear, but such a reading is possible. Some Jewish apocalyptic texts speak of the Messiah as being "revealed," having previously existed with God in heaven (see comments on 1 Thess. 4:16). The "revelation" of the man of lawlessness, then, could suggest his preexistence, though this is far from certain (see comments on 2:9 below).

2:5–10. Having begun to say that the widespread apostasy and the revelation of the man of lawlessness are prerequisite to the day of the Lord ("for unless . . ."), Paul fails to complete his sentence, breaking off as he trails into a description of the man of lawlessness. The break, however, is no indication that the digression has gotten him off track or that he is employing ellipsis. Rather, Paul stops himself because, as he goes on to say, his audience has already been instructed on these matters—the apostasy, the man of lawlessness, and so on: **Do you not remember that while I was still with you, I was saying these things to you?** (2:5; an instance of *aposiopesis*, leaving a thought incomplete; cf. Lausberg 1998, §§887–88). It is quite significant that Paul points them back—as he has so often done in the two Thessalonian letters (cf. 1 Thess. 3:4; 4:2, 6, 11; 2 Thess. 3:4,10)—to his original teaching. They should not heed what they may have heard about the day of the Lord through a spirit or a report or a letter (v. 2) but hold fast to what they learned from *him* while he was among them, about which he had taught them repeatedly ("*was saying* these things"). That he has covered this ground before explains why he is able to be speak so cryptically. *They* know what he means.

Paul proceeds to preview the events in which the man of lawlessness will participate: his restraint, his release and revelation, his works of deception, and finally his destruction. Verse 6 extends the question of the previous verse: **and do you not know that now there is something restraining him, so that he is not revealed until his time?** (2:6). The pronouns here are most naturally taken as referring to the man of lawlessness. The question therefore sets in contrast the present "restraint" of the man and his "revelation" in the future. That is, he is being restrained *now* so that he will not be revealed until the *appointed time*.

Indeed, **the mystery of lawlessness is already at work** (2:7a). In the Greek text, the word "mystery" occurs first and is separated from "of lawlessness" (*anomias*), which appears at the end of the clause. This arrangement highlights the word "mystery," setting it in contrast with "revealed" in the previous verse. Thus, the man of lawlessness has not yet been revealed; that is, the lawlessness that is now at work is a "mystery," for it is known as lawlessness to believers but is not understood as such by unbelievers. "Mystery of lawlessness" and "man of lawlessness," therefore, complement one another: the mystery is at work now, in a hidden way, and the man of lawlessness will set to work at an appointed time in the future, after he is revealed (Weima 2014, 529–30).

The final part of verse 7 presents a major interpretive crux. The first difficulty is that the thought contains an ellipsis: *monon ho katechōn arti heōs ek mesou genētai*. One must supply either "the mystery must continue to work" after *monon* or "will continue to restrain" after *ho katechōn*. The former better accounts for the sequence of thought. That is, the mystery of lawlessness remains a mystery only for a time, before it is revealed, and it remains a mystery only while there is "something restraining" the man of lawlessness. Thus the mystery is now at work, **though only until the one restraining him is moved aside** (2:7b).

The second, and much more perplexing question, concerns the identity of "the one who restrains," or the so-called Restrainer. This label recalls the expression "the thing restraining" from verse 6. Both expressions use the same verb, in participial form; however, the first instance occurs in the neuter (*to katechon*), while the second occurs in the masculine (*ho katechōn*). There is no precedent for either substantive in ancient literature, though we find the Latin equivalent, *qui tenet*, in *LAB* 51.5 (of uncertain date). Because Paul's description is tantalizingly vague, interpreters have found no consensus as to his meaning, though there has been no shortage of proposals. Some identify the restrainer as a good being (God, an angel, Paul), others as a neutral power (the Roman emperor as governing authority) or an evil entity (Satan or some possessing spirit). Among all possible solutions, the most satisfactory is that proposed by Colin Nicholl (2000), who argues that the restrainer is an angel, probably specifically Michael, and that the restraining thing is also Michael, though with an emphasis on his qualities rather than on Michael as an individual. Based on known traditions about Michael in Jewish literature, Nicholl says, only Michael could be responsible for the actions that Paul attributes to the restrainer: he restrains the eschatological rebel's revelation, executes God's will, and is then removed from the action.

And then—when the restrainer has moved aside—**the lawless one will be revealed** (2:8a). Paul immediately adds, **whom the Lord Jesus will destroy with the breath of his mouth** (2:8b), skipping entirely over the events that intervene, before backtracking to cover them in verses 9–10. The eschatological destruction of evil powers by God (*1 En.* 38.3; 46.5; 48.8; 53.5; 54.2) or the Messiah (*2 Bar.* 40.1–4) or God's people (1QM) was a common motif in Jewish apocalyptic theology. As in 2 Thess. 1:7–9, Paul here makes Jesus the agent of judgment. In predicting the destruction of the man of lawlessness by the "breath" of Jesus's mouth, Paul assigns to Jesus an activity that in the OT is attributed to God (Isa. 11:4; 30:27–28; through the Messiah in 2 Esd. [*4 Ezra*] 13:10–11, 32). The final clause of 2 Thess. 2:8 is synonymous with the clause that precedes: whom he "will destroy with the breath of his mouth" **and bring to naught at the appearance of his parousia.** The parallelism suggests that "appearance of his parousia," like the "breath of his mouth," is the *means* by which Jesus brings about the lawless man's destruction (see comments on "destruction" in 1:9). The terms "appearance" and "parousia" could potentially be synonymous, but to avoid redundancy, it seems better to take the "parousia" as referring to Jesus's arrival and his "appearance" as referring to the splendor of his presence, which the man of lawlessness cannot withstand.

Although in verse 8 Paul referred to the man's appearance and destruction using verbs in the future tense, in verse 9 he uses a futuristic present, as if speaking prophetically. Now Paul sharpens the antithesis between Jesus and the man of lawlessness by attributing a "parousia" not only to the former but also to the latter: **whose own parousia is attended by the working of Satan.** Clearly the man of lawlessness is not Satan, since the two are here differentiated (cf. *Apoc. Ab.* 24.5, where "the lawless one" and "Satan" are the same person). When the man of lawlessness is revealed (and he has not yet been revealed, according to vv. 6–8), Satan's power will manifest itself (*tou Satana* as a subjective genitive), evidently through the man of lawlessness. Paul now further develops the antithesis between Jesus and the man of lawlessness: just as Jesus at his parousia will be attended "by the angels of his power" (1:7), the parousia of the man of lawlessness will be attended by the "working of Satan." While this could indicate that the man of

Table 10. The Lord Jesus and the Man of Lawlessness Compared

The Lord Jesus	The Man of Lawlessness
"parousia" of (2:1, 8)	"parousia" of (2:9)
"revealed" (1:7)	"revealed" (2:3, 6, 8)
revealed on "the day of the Lord" (2:2)	revealed "in his time" (2:6)
"with the angels of his power" (1:7)	"by the power of Satan" (2:9)

lawlessness is a supernatural being (see comments on 2:4 above), Jewish apocalyptic literature as well as early Christian literature sometimes depicts human beings as agents of Satan's work (1QM I.1–17). In many sources, the agents of demonic power are identified as human rulers (*1 En.* 55.4; *Mart. Pol.* 17.1–2; *Acts Pet.* 5, 6; Origen, *Cels.* 8.65; Eusebius, *Hist. eccl.* 5.1).

Satan's working consists of "power" (*dynamis*), "signs" (*sēmeia*), and "wonders" (*terata*). "Signs and wonders" (*sēmeia kai terata*) appears to have been a fixed pair in both Jewish and Christian theology (Matt. 24:24; Mark 13:22; passim in the LXX and NT). While all three terms—powers and signs and wonders—are often coordinated in the NT (Acts 2:22; Rom. 15:19; 2 Cor. 12:12; Heb. 2:4), here "signs and wonders" is in apposition to the first term, "power" (cf. Rom. 15:19), and specifies the kind of power that Satan will work: **consisting in every power—both signs and wonders—that serves falsehood** (2:9b). That his power "serves falsehood" does not mean that the signs and wonders are mere illusions. In the OT and NT, the expression "signs and wonders" refers to authentic activities of God (Exod. 7:3; Deut. 4:34; 6:22; Isa. 8:18; 20:3; Jer. 32:20–21), Jesus (John 4:48), or the apostles (Acts 2:43). The NT predicts the coming of those who would deceive people with their "signs and wonders," including false prophets (Mark 13:22; Rev. 19:20) and a "beast" (Rev. 13:13–14; 20:10); yet in all cases the emphasis is not on the illegitimacy of the miracles performed but on their power to lead people astray. In the non-Christian world, miracles were reportedly performed commonly, for instance, by "divine men" (Philostratus, *Vita Apollonii*), Roman emperors (Tacitus, *Ann.* 4.81), or Jewish rabbis (Josephus, *Ant.* 8.2.5). Early Christians commonly gave credence to the wonders purportedly performed through non-Christians, only they attributed their works to the power of Satan or of demons (Origen, *Cels.* 1.60; 2.51; 7.69; 8.36; *Acts of Peter*). In the second-century work the *Acts of Peter*, Simon Magus appears to be modeled after the man of lawlessness. Simon performs what sometimes appear to be authentic miracles (4), which are not discredited but rather attributed to the power of Satan (6, 7). Disapproval of the miracles stems not from their inauthenticity but from the fact that they "deceive" people (6, 7; cf. 8, 12, 16, 17, 24, 28) or turn them aside from the gospel. In the same way, the wonders performed by the man of lawlessness are not "false," but rather point people to what is false.

2:10–12. The first portion of verse 10 runs parallel with "in every power of falsehood" (v. 9): Satan's power consists also **in every deceit that derives from unrighteousness** (2:10a). At this point Paul shifts attention from the man of lawlessness to the people receptive to his deceptions, describing them as **those who are perishing** (a dative of disadvantage). Verses 10–12 add to the antitheses of the preceding verses by contrasting the fates of believers and nonbelievers and the basis for their respective fates:

"deceit of unrighteousness" (2:10) and "believe the lie" (2:11) *versus* "love of truth" (2:10)

"perishing" (2:10) *versus* "saved" (2:10)

"so that they might believe the lie" (2:11) *versus* "so that they might be saved" (2:10)

"were pleased with unrighteousness" (2:12) *versus* "believe the truth" (2:12)

"The lie" is the anti-gospel, for the "truth" is synonymous with the gospel itself (cf. 2 Cor. 4:2; 13:8; Gal. 5:7). The correlation between "deceit / the lie" on the one hand and "unrighteousness" on the other suggests that the "truth" here is not merely propositional but is a lived truth (cf. *Jos. Asen.* 8.8): those who have a "love of truth" live righteously just as those who "believe the lie" live unrighteously.

Undoubtedly, verses 10–12 describe the "apostasy" to which Paul made reference in verse 3: a massive "rebellion" against God, resulting from the deceptive works of the man of lawlessness. In this regard, the *logical* relationships between several propositions in these verses seem clear: "those who are perishing" perish **since** (in the past) **they did not receive the love of truth that is required for them to be saved** (2:10b); it is since they did not receive the love of truth (**and for this reason**) also that **God is sending to them the working of deception so that they might believe the lie** (2:11b; cf. Rom. 1:18–27); finally, God sends this deception so that **all those who did not believe the truth but were pleased with unrighteousness might be condemned** (2:12). Part of the *chronological* sequence is also clear: some did not believe and consequently are perishing; God then sends the working of deception; finally, these people are condemned (i.e., at the final judgment).

Not clear is the temporal relationship between God's working of deception and the deceitful works of the man of lawlessness. Does God "send" the deception *prior to* the working of the man of lawlessness; that is, God leads people astray and as a result they are deceived when the man of lawlessness begins to work? Or does God's deception *consist in* the working of the man of lawlessness; that is, God's "working of deception" (i.e., the "power of falsehood") is worked by the man of lawlessness?

The present tense of the verb "is sending" could support the former interpretation: God is sending deception *now* on those who have rejected the truth—these people being, specifically, the nonbelievers in Thessalonica (Weima 2014, 542).

Paul's use of the present tense, however, is not conclusive since Paul also uses the present tense in reference to the parousia of the man of lawlessness (v. 9), who plainly has not yet been "revealed" (vv. 3–8). Supporting the alternative interpretation, moreover, are several points. First, it is most natural to take all of verses 7–12 as referring to the future, since Paul's rhetorical aim, as indicated by verses 1–2, is to show that the *still-future* events that must occur *before* the day of the Lord have not yet happened. Second, the terms used to describe the working of the man of lawlessness (*pseudos*, "falsehood," 2:11; cf. 2:9; *apatē*, "deceit," 2:10) and the term used to describe the working of God (*planē*, "deception," 2:11) are not clearly distinguishable and, in the absence of a good reason to the contrary, should probably be taken as synonymous. Third, Paul describes both the man of lawlessness and God as "working" (*energeian*, 2:9, 11) deceit, and both for the same purpose, to lead people astray. The word order in this regard reveals a deliberate attempt to set Satan and God in parallel, where the juxtaposition of *ho theos* and *energeian planēs* in verse 11 highlights a change in the implied agent: "according to the working of *Satan*. . . . And . . . *God* a working of deception is sending." Fourth, the notion of a "spirit of deceit" sent or implanted by God is not unknown in Jewish theology of this period. The Qumran *Rule of the Community* explains human behavior as a result of God's setting within each person "two spirits, one of truth and one of deceit" (*hnh rôḥôt h 'mt wh 'wl*; 1QS III.18–26, esp. 18–19). A "spirit of deceit" (from God?) motif is also common in the *Testament of the Twelve Patriarchs* (Peerbolte 1996, 88). Finally, Paul presents the whole series of events here, including the coming of the man of lawlessness, as unfolding according to God's providence: there is something/someone (Michael?) restraining the man of lawlessness, which/whom God will later remove, so that the man of lawlessness can be revealed "in his time." So regardless of whether God's "working of deception" is due to his direct agency or is carried out through the man of lawlessness, it seems best to conclude that God's "deception" refers to the same type of activity as the "power of falsehood" and "deceit" associated with the "working" of the man of lawlessness. Consequently, Paul speaks in the "present" tense in verses 10–12 from the *perspective* of the future, at which time the man of lawlessness has begun to work. At that time there will be some who *are* perishing because they did not *previously* believe, and at *that* time God *sends* a working of deception, consisting in the activities carried out by the man of lawlessness.

Second Main Part: General Exhortation (2:13–3:5)

Second Thanksgiving and Exhortation (2:13–17)

Here begins the second of two main parts of the letter's body (2:1–12; 2:13–3:5). Notably, this part begins with a thanksgiving formula, thus introducing a second thanksgiving section into the letter (1:3–12; 2:13–14), an anomaly seen elsewhere in Paul's letters only in 1 Thessalonians (1:2–10; 2:13–16). Following the thanksgiving is a short exhortation (2:15), followed by a wish-prayer (2:16–17) and some loosely related exhortations of a general nature (3:1–5).

This part of the letter exhibits several structural similarities with 1 Thessalonians: a second thanksgiving section (2 Thess. 2:13–14; 1 Thess. 2:13–16) followed by exhortation (2 Thess. 2:15; 1 Thess. 2:17–3:10) and then a wish-prayer (2 Thess. 2:16–17; 1 Thess. 3:11–13), and a transition introduced by the rare adverbial substantive *to loipon* (2 Thess. 3:1; cf. 1 Thess. 4:1). Moreover, at two points this section shares verbal similarities with content in 1 Thessalonians (2 Thess. 2:14//1 Thess. 5:9; 2 Thess. 2:16–17//1 Thess. 3:13; cf. 2 Thess. 2:14//1 Thess. 2:12). On the potential significance of these parallels, see the discussion in the introduction to 2 Thessalonians.

2:13–14. Paul now renews his thanksgiving (see 1:3–12). Though anomalous outside the Thessalonian letters, the occurrence of a second thanksgiving section is natural in the context. Paul has described nonbelievers in the preceding verses as adherents of the falsehood perpetrated by the man of lawlessness, those who have rejected the truth and are pleased with unrighteousness, who consequently are gradually perishing and destined finally to be "condemned" (2:10–12). Now Paul expresses relief that the Thessalonian believers, by contrast, have been chosen by God and are called to receive salvation and glory (cf. "chose . . . called . . . for the acquisition of glory" here; and "predestined . . . called . . . glorified" in Rom. 8:29–30).

Apart from a few small differences, the introductory formula in 2:13a, **But we ought to give thanks to God always for you,** matches the formula found at 1:3 (see comments there). (1) The conjunction *de* occurs in none of the other thanksgiving formulas in Paul's letters and here serves to introduce a contrast between nonbelievers (2:10–12) and believers (2:13–14): "But." (2) The addition of the emphatic subject *hēmeis* does not serve the contrast but rather indicates a change in the topical frame (or subject) from nonbelievers back to the letter's author(s). (3) Paul's switch from the vocative "brothers and sisters" in the first thanksgiving (1:3) to **brothers and sisters beloved by the Lord** here has both contextual and theological significance (2:13b). Contextually, it serves to highlight the contrast between the audience and the nonbelievers described in verses 10–12: the latter will be "condemned" by God (2:10), but the former are "beloved by the Lord."

The ambiguity of Paul's reference to "the Lord" may have theological significance. The same vocative formula occurred in 1 Thess. 1:4, where the loving agent was named as *God* ("brothers and sisters, beloved by God"). God, moreover, is the explicit subject of the actions described here—of both the condemnation of nonbelievers (vv. 11–12) and the election of believers (v. 13)—yet the title "Lord" usually refers to Jesus in Paul's letters. Just as Paul can speak of God's love for humanity (Rom. 5:5, 8; 8:39; 2 Cor. 9:7; 13:13; Eph. 2:4; Col. 3:12; 1 Thess. 1:4), so he can also speak of Christ's love (Rom. 8:35; 2 Cor. 5:14; Gal. 2:20). Indeed, just three verses later Paul appears to make God and Jesus the joint agents of love (2 Thess. 2:16). Furthermore, just as 2:11–12 says that God is the agent in "condemning," 2:8 states that Jesus is the agent of "destruction." Finally, while the mention of "God" both before and after "Lord" here could point to God as the referent, in the next verse "Lord" refers explicitly to Jesus. In sum, the points seem evenly balanced, and ultimately the intended referent for "Lord" in 2:13 cannot be decided with certainty.

The way in which Paul expresses his grounds for thanks is manifestly parae-netic. First, he says that he gives thanks **because God chose** them **as a firstfruit for salvation** (2:13c; cf. 1 Thess. 1:4). The language of election now extends the contrast with nonbelievers (who will be "condemned") and places stress on God's initiative and agency in salvation. Implicitly, this language assures the Thessalo-nian believers of their capacity to persevere through trial and persecution (Best 1979, 312). At the same time, it reminds the Thessalonians that their avoidance of the fate assigned to nonbelievers is not by their own merit (Gaventa 1998, 121).

Paul qualifies salvation as that which happens **through sanctification of the Spirit and through belief in the truth** (2:13d). The two instruments of salvation perhaps distinguish the *works* (sanctification) and the *belief* (faith) that are needed for salvation to be completed. The term *pneuma* could refer either to the human spirit ("through the spirit's sanctification") or to the Holy Spirit ("sanctification wrought by the Spirit"). In support of the latter interpretation, Paul frequently identifies the Holy Spirit as the agent of sanctification and does so twice in 1 Thes-salonians (1:4–5; 4:7–8; Rom. 15:16; 1 Cor. 6:11–12; cited by Weima 2014, 552). This interpretation reveals a complementary emphasis on what God does (sanctify) and what the human agent does (believe). As in 2 Thess. 1:10, the reference to "belief" (*pistis*) likely puts emphasis on the cognitive component of *pistis*; indeed, while faith as Paul sees it always manifests itself in action (e.g., 1:3, 4, 11), he here presents an emphatic antithesis between "falsehood" (2:9, 11), "deception"

"Firstfruit" or "from the Beginning"? (2:13)

At 2 Thess. 2:13, the manuscripts vary between the reading "firstfruit" and the reading "from the beginning," which in Greek differ essentially only in the division of letters (*aparchēn* versus *ap' archēs*). While the variant reading "from the beginning" would fit well with the theme of election (2:13) and has fairly strong support in the manuscript tradition (‭א‬ D others), several points speak in favor of the alternative reading: (1) Paul nowhere else uses the expression "from the beginning" in his letters; (2) he rarely uses the word *archē* to mean anything other than "ruler," "authority"; and (3) he fairly frequently uses the word *aparchē*, or "firstfruit" (see Weima 2014, 550). If the reading "firstfruit" is correct, then the noun's anarthrous force is indefinite: the Thessalonians are not *the* first believers in Macedonia (note the earlier founding of the Philippian church: 1 Thess. 2:2), much less in the world; rather, they are *"a* firstfruit," being a part of the first crop in what Paul expected to become a much larger harvest.

(2:10), "belief in falsehood" (v. 11), and *lack* of "belief in the truth" (v. 12) on the one hand and "love of truth" on the other hand (v. 10). Here, in other words, it is "belief" in "the truth," as opposed to "falsehood," to which Paul refers.

Verse 14 runs parallel to verse 13 both syntactically and thematically. God's initiative in "electing" is now described in terms of "calling" (**for which God also called you**; cf. 1 Thess. 2:12; 5:24); the previous construction "through sanctification of the Spirit and faith in the truth" is now paralleled by **through our proclamation** (2:14b; on "our gospel," see comments on 1 Thess. 1:5); and in parallel with "for salvation" (2 Thess. 2:13) is **for the acquisition of the glory of our Lord Jesus Christ** (2:14c). The final portion of the verse presents glory as something that will be "acquired" in the future, presumably following the parousia and the day of the Lord (2:1–12). This portion of the verse adumbrates what will become (or will become more prominently) an important theological motif in Paul's later letters: believers "participate" in Christ (see comments on 1 Thess. 5:10; 2 Thess. 1:12). Accordingly, Paul refers to *Christ's* glory (cf. 2 Thess. 1:9) in which those *in* Christ will participate, thus making Christ's glory also the believers' own (see comments on 1 Thess. 2:12). Thus Paul presents the "acquisition of glory" differently from how it is often presented in Greek sources of antiquity (see sidebar). Glory is not achieved by exploits of war, hard work, public service, or even through virtue, but rather is a *transferred* property derived from Christ.

2:15. Paul continues with a general exhortation grounded loosely in the reality described in verses 1–14. The Thessalonians have been elected for salvation (through sanctification!) and should be wary that destruction awaits the unfaithful: **Therefore, brothers and sisters, stand fast and keep to the traditions that you were taught** (2:15a). Implied in Paul's command is the admonition that it is possible to fall and become like those who are duped by falsehood and destined to be condemned in the judgment.

The Phrase "Acquiring Glory" in Greek Writers

Paul's reference to the "acquisition of glory" is abundantly paralleled in Greek writers, using the equivalent verb form *peripoiein* (to acquire) + *doxan* (glory). In these writings, "to acquire glory" frequently refers to the acquisition of glory through public works or exploits in war.

"To acquire glory" through public service (Diodorus Siculus, *Bib. hist.* 1.56.1.7; 9.1.3; cf. *ID* 1519; *Miletos* 22)

"To acquire glory" through war (Diodorus Siculus, *Bib. hist.* 11.39.2; 11.41.3; 15.29.2; Polybius, *Hist.* 20.4.2; Josephus, *Ant.* 12.350)

"To acquire glory" through virtue (Diodorus Siculus, *Bib. hist.* 1.2.3.6)

"To acquire glory" through hard work (Plutarch, *Lib. ed.* 12C.10)

Earl Richard's (1995, 355–68) view that a pseudonymous author is exposed here as trying, specifically, to "combat apocalyptic fervor" by appealing to apostolic tradition in institutionalized form ("the traditions that you were taught") could only be reached by prejudice as to the letter's authorship. Reference to "the traditions" betrays the hand of a pseudepigrapher only if the term is predetermined to have a more restricted sense. There is no reason why this expression cannot refer simply to what Paul himself had taught or "handed over" to them. In the philosophical schools, "tradition" was what teachers passed on (*trans* + *ditum* = "give over") to their students, whether in the form of precepts/doctrines (Philo, *Fug.* 200; Ps.-Dionysius, *Rhet.* 8.8.19) or exempla (Plutarch, *Mor.* 119D). Although this activity could consist in the transfer of material to succeeding generations (Plutarch, *Mor.* 119D), it could also refer to knowledge transferred directly from teachers to students (Philo, *Fug.* 200; cf. 2 Thess. 2:15). Similar language occurs in Paul's Letter to the Romans, where he urges his listeners to "watch out" for those who lead them "away from the *teaching*" (*didachē*) that they "learned" (Rom. 16:17). Again, while the word *didachē* could indicate "received tradition" passed on through the generations (notably as in the early Christian work *Didache*), it is significant that no interpreter argues for this meaning in Romans as evidence of the epistle's pseudonymity. Finally, Paul uses the language of tradition twice in his previous letter to the Thessalonian church, and in both cases the language refers to what Paul had passed to them directly: in 1 Thess. 2:13, Paul refers to what he had passed on and the Thessalonians had "received" from him (*paralabontes*); and in 1 Thess. 4:1–2 he refers to what they had "received" (*paralambanein*) from him, using the technical term for "precepts" (*parangelia*).

The final part of 2:15 echoes 2:2, where Paul warned about misinformation received "through a spirit," "through report," or "through a letter," though this time Paul makes no reference to the first item, saying only: **whether orally or through our letter.** While the personal pronoun follows only the second item, it evidently applies to both: "through *our* word or through *our* letter." The oral instruction to which Paul refers must be what he had imparted during his founding visit. While "our letter" is generally taken as a reference to 1 Thessalonians, it makes better sense as a reference to the present letter, which has just addressed the relevant topic, the day of the Lord (2:1–12), doing so in a more direct way than does 1 Thessalonians. By doing this, Paul is not *prioritizing* the theological content of this letter (as Lindemann 1977 thinks a pseudepigrapher has done) but simply drawing attention to the content of this letter as clarifying the specific issue at hand. Ultimately, Paul's point is that the Thessalonians should keep anchored to traditions that stem directly from *him* (thus reference to "a spirit" is not appropriate here). They should not believe what they hear from *other* sources (2:2) if it contradicts what he himself has taught (cf. Gal. 1:8).

2:16–17. With a minor transition in the discourse (**now**), Paul expresses a wish-prayer, a literary form found twice in 1 Thessalonians (3:11–13; 5:23) and three times in 2 Thessalonians (2:16–17; 3:5, 16). The prayer here shares some fairly significant verbal parallels with the wish-prayer in 1 Thess. 3:11–13. A key difference is the reversal of elements from "our God and Father and our Lord Jesus" to **our Lord Jesus Christ and God our Father** (2:16a). While rarer, this order appears elsewhere in Paul's letters (Gal. 1:1; 2 Cor. 13:13). Here the order could be constrained by the long appositive phrase that Paul uses to describe God, to which "our Lord Jesus Christ" could not have been naturally appended. The appositive itself describes actions that are, to be sure, used together elsewhere to describe activities of Christ: **who loved us and gave . . .** (2:16b; cf. "who loved me and gave himself for me," Gal. 2:20; "loved us and gave himself for us," Eph. 5:2; Christ's "love" in Rom. 8:35; 2 Cor. 5:14; "who gave himself for our sins," Gal. 1:4). Yet the two actions here more aptly describe God. Paul frequently refers to God's "love" for humanity (Rom. 5:5, 8; 2 Cor. 13:13; 1 Thess. 1:4; 2 Thess. 3:5). Moreover, in other texts Christ is said to have given "himself," whereas here the object of giving is **eternal comfort and good hope** (2:16c); God is the one who gives comfort in Paul's letters (Rom. 15:5; 2 Cor. 1:3, 4). And while Christ *is* the hope of believers (Col. 1:27; 1 Thess. 1:3), God is the "God of hope" (Rom. 15:13), or the God who *gives* hope. Both actions here are put in the past tense, indicating that God *acted* in love through what he accomplished in Christ and that comfort and hope are things that believers already have in hand. Paul's reminder is paraenetically motivated, aiming to encourage the Thessalonians amid trying circumstances. In this respect, both comfort and hope attach not only to the present but also to the future: their comfort is "eternal," and present hope, insofar as it is "good," will have definite fulfillment in the future. Paul adds that God has given these things **in his grace**, grace being the intention that motivated God to act.

As in 1 Thess. 3:11, Paul makes Christ and God subjects of a singular verb (may Christ and God **comfort *your* hearts and strengthen** them; 2:17a). The singular form does not in itself indicate that the subjects are identical (see comments on 1 Thess. 3:11), though it surely indicates that they cooperate closely. The verb "encourage" (*parakalesai*) is cognate with the noun "comfort" (*paraklēsis*) from the previous verse, making the appositive description of God in verse 16 "thematic": as he is "the one who gave comfort," he is able now to "comfort" specifically, "*your* hearts." The personal pronoun "your" precedes the head noun so as to put it in focus, as Paul switches from first-person plural to second-person plural: "may God . . . who loved and gave *us* eternal comfort . . . comfort *your* hearts."

This exhortation provides a fitting conclusion to 2:1–15. Having been "shaken" by rumors about the day of the Lord (v. 2), they are to find *comfort* now in Paul's assurance that the Day has not come; that when he comes, the man of lawlessness will come to naught; and that they themselves have been elected for salvation and called to inherit Christ's glory. Finally, having warned that those who are "pleased with unrighteousness" will be "condemned," Paul asks God to *strengthen* the Thessalonians **in every good work and word** (2:17b), so that they do not meet the same end. A symmetry of word order indicates that their "works" and "words" are to be consistent with their "hope": as God gave *hope* that is good (*elpida agathēn*), they ought to *do* and *say* what is good (*ergō kai logō agathō*).

A Prayer Request, Exhortation, and a Wish-Prayer (3:1–5)

3:1–5. The address **finally, brothers and sisters** marks a transition to a new paragraph and seems to indicate that the body of the letter is winding down (see comments on *to loipon* at 1 Thess. 4:1). This final paragraph lacks tight coherence, although its various strands evidently tie loosely together.

First, Paul asks for the Thessalonians' prayers (3:1–2; see also 1 Thess. 5:24), making two specific requests. (a) He asks them to pray **that the word of the Lord might race on and win the glory** (cf. Col. 4:3, where he requests prayer for an "open door" for the gospel). In this way, Paul depicts the gospel as a runner traveling at swift speed, triumphing by arriving successfully at a distant destination where the good news is celebrated by those who receive it. **As it did also** [i.e., race] **toward you** refers the listeners back to Paul's founding visit, when the gospel had made its way successfully into their own hearts. (b) Paul also (**and**) asks them to pray **that we might be delivered from the perverse and evil men.** "Perverse" (*atopoi*) and "evil" (*ponēroi*) are synonyms, though this does not make their coordination superfluous; rather, the subtle semantic difference between the two adjectives serves to intensify the expression for more emotive effect (cf. Lausberg 1998, §651; cf. "bad and evil," 1 Cor. 5:8). Where Paul requests prayer for deliverance in his other letters, he has in mind opposition to his mission in specific locations (Judea in Rom. 15:31; Asia in 2 Cor. 1:8–11); here the use of the definite article may suggest that he has even a specific group in mind. Neither this letter nor the Corinthian letters openly refers to external opposition in Corinth (whence he writes), but Acts 18:5–6, 12–17 reports opposition from "the Jews."

In the final clause of verse 2, Paul leaves behind the topics of his prayer request, jumping from his description of "perverse and evil men" to the general observation that **not everyone has the faith** (3:2b). This remark (**for**) provides the grounds for Paul's previous description of the evil men by suggesting that to be "perverse and evil" means "not having faith," a point that bears slight mention since the terms "perverse and *faithless*" (*ponēros* and *apistos*) are often coordinated as synonyms in Greek literature (Demosthenes, *Or.* 19.109; Plato, *Phaed.* 89D; Josephus, *J.W.* 3.372). If a similar semantic relationship is in view here, then Paul's reference to "the faith" probably refers to a quality of life rather than simply to a set of Christian beliefs.

Next, in another quick change of direction, Paul swings from the general fact that some people are faithless to the general and contrary fact that "the Lord" is faithful (**But faithful is the Lord,** 3:3). Mention of the Lord's faithfulness now becomes an opportunity for Paul to assure the Thessalonians that, in his faithfulness, **he will strengthen** them **and guard** them **from the evil** (see below). Reference to "the evil" in turn creates an arc back to "evil men," tying the paragraph together with yet another loose connection.

Verse 3 contains two significant ambiguities. The expression "the Lord is faithful" substitutes here for the more common "God is faithful" (1 Cor. 1:9; 10:13; 2 Cor. 1:18; cf. 1 Thess. 5:24). "The Lord" (*ho kyrios*) usually refers to Jesus in Paul's letters and indeed refers to him unambiguously in 2:14, 16; and 3:6. However, the referent is ambiguous both here and in 2:13; 3:1, 4, and 5. Also problematic is the term *tou ponērou*. This form could be either masculine or neuter and, consequently, could refer either to "the Evil (One)" or to "evil" more generally. Elsewhere in the Thessalonian letters, Paul makes mention of "the Satan" (1 Thess. 2:18; 2 Thess. 2:9) and "the Tempter" (1 Thess. 3:5), though not "the Evil One." In Second Temple literature, the neuter adjective *to ponēron* often appears in reference to "the evil (impulse)" in the heart of humanity (Dibelius 1937, 53), but it rarely occurs in the masculine form in reference to an evil being. It does occur in this sense, however, in *1 En.* 69.15, and it commonly occurs in this sense in early Christian writings (Eph. 6:16; cf. Matt. 13:19; 1 John 2:13–14; 5:18–19; *Barn.* 4.13; *Acts Pet.* 8). Common usage, then, moderately favors Jesus as the referent of *kyrios* and "the Evil One" as the referent of *tou ponērou*. This interpretation is strengthened by the juxtaposition of the two: Jesus and the Evil One can be seen as direct opponents in the same way that Jesus was pitted against the man of lawlessness and Satan in 2:3–12. In short, the sense here is that the Lord (Jesus) will guard the Thessalonians from the Evil (One).

A minor transition occurs in verse 4 (*de*, **now**), though a continuous train of thought is discernible. Having stated that "not all have the faith" (v. 2), Paul now says, **We are confident in the Lord regarding you,** a comment that serves to provoke his audience to live up to his assessment and avoid lapsing to join the faithless (3:4a). The identity of "the Lord" is again not explicitly clarified (nor again in 3:5), although the term will refer explicitly to "the Lord Jesus Christ" in 3:6. Notably, Paul's confidence does not rest "in" the *Thessalonians* but "in" the *Lord* "with *regard* to" the Thessalonians (cf. Rom. 15:14; 2 Cor. 3:4–5; Gal. 5:10).

Paul is confident of this: **that the things we are instructing you to do you also are doing and will do** (3:4b). Paul's use of positive reinforcement is paraenetic, resembling statements made in 1 Thessalonians where he asks the church to continue to act in the way they are already acting (1 Thess. 4:1, 10; 5:11). Paul affirms that they have remembered his instructions, probably without direct confirmation of the fact, though his show of confidence would stir up their desire not to let him down. Whether the "instructions" refer to what precedes or to what follows is debatable. The reference could point ahead to Paul's instructions about work in 3:6–13, since he uses the same verb again in verse 6 (*parangellein*), where he follows with instructions about the *ataktoi*. This interpretation, however, would be more convincing if verse 4 introduced a new section. Because verse 4 belongs instead with verses 1–3, the reference to instructions makes better sense with reference to what precedes. But to how much of the preceding? The instructions

"The Lord" in 2 Thess. 3:1–5

Ho kyrios (the Lord) occurs four times in these verses, always without qualification (3:1, 3, 4, 5).

1. It occurs first in the expression "the word of the Lord" (v. 1), where "word" evidently functions as an equivalent of "gospel." The referent cannot be determined in this case because Paul frequently refers both to the "gospel of God" and the "gospel of Christ" (see comments on 1 Thess. 1:5).
2. In verse 3 Paul uses the expression "faithful is the Lord." Here God may more likely be the referent, since Paul commonly uses the expression "faithful is God" (1 Cor. 1:9; 10:13; 2 Cor. 1:18; cf. 1 Thess. 5:24), and never (unless one counts 2 Tim. 2:13) refers to Christ as "faithful" (*pistos*).
3. The expression "we are persuaded in the Lord" in verse 4 is paralleled in Rom. 15:14 with "I am persuaded in the Lord Jesus," which could indicate that Jesus is also the referent here (see also Phil. 1:13–14).
4. Parallels between the verbiage of the wish-prayer in verse 5 and the verbiage of the wish-prayers elsewhere in the Thessalonian letters again render the referent of "the Lord" ambiguous. Whereas "the Lord" alone is the subject of the wish-prayer here (also in 3:16), God alone is the subject in 1 Thess. 5:23–24, and both God and Jesus are the subjects in 1 Thess. 3:11–13 and 2 Thess. 2:16–17.

could concern Paul's request (*erōtōmen de hymas*) for the Thessalonians not to allow themselves to be "shaken" by reports about the advent of the day of the Lord (2:1–2) and, in view of the condemnation of those who believe the lie, to "stand fast and keep to the traditions" they were taught (v. 15). But it would more naturally occur to the listener to take his "instructions" as referring to the immediately preceding demand for prayer ("*Pray* for us"): Paul grants that they are already praying for him and asks them to continue doing so. There is nothing at all in verses 1–5 that would imply that Paul has obedience to "the traditions" in mind. Consequently, there is little merit to Earl Richard's (1995, 376) speculation that an emphasis on "instructions" exposes the interests of a pseudepigrapher, who was concerned to enforce an established body of "apostolic tradition."

De occurs with transitional force again in verse 5, now marking a shift to a conclusion to the paragraph—and indeed to the body of the letter—in the form of a final wish-prayer: **And may the Lord direct your hearts to the love of God and to the perseverance of Christ** (3:5). The coordination of "love" and "endurance" here recalls 1 Thess. 1:3, where Paul referred to "the work of faith," "labor of *love*," and "hope of *endurance*." Here, however, it is not the Thessalonians' love and endurance but God's love (subjective genitive) and Christ's endurance (subjective genitive) that Paul has in view. Still, Paul may intend to point the audience to God's love as the source from which they should derive their love for one another (cf. Rom. 5:5; 2 Cor. 5:14). Similarly, the reference to Christ's endurance may reflect the notion of "participation" with Christ (see 1:12). The word "endurance" surely refers to perseverance through opposition and suffering. In 1 Thess. 1:6 Paul noted that the Thessalonians became "imitators" of Christ precisely in that they endured suffering with joy. In being "directed" to the "endurance of Christ," then, they take on the very quality that Christ displayed when he suffered. This idea stands in remarkable tension with Paul's earlier affirmation that they would acquire "the *glory* of Christ" (2:14). In that respect, the Thessalonians participate now in Christ's endurance through *suffering* and will participate later in his *glory* (cf. Phil. 2:8–9).

Theological Issues

Expecting "the Antichrist"

For many individuals and groups across church history, 2 Thess. 2:1–12 has provoked frenzied apocalyptic speculation. The notion of a semidivine figure and embodiment of evil who rises up at the climax of history and leads God's people astray by the power of Satan understandably excites fervor and fear in the hearts of many. Paul's discussion of the "man of lawlessness" has put many on the alert to identify this figure: perhaps he is one of the popes, Napoleon, Hitler, Paul McCartney, Barack Obama, or any of thousands of others. While the appropriateness of individual examples can be debated, the fact that Christians have identified so many people with this role is telling and perhaps not out of place. The temptation to identify "*the* Antichrist" may be difficult to resist, but there is perhaps some benefit in looking instead for "*an* antichrist," the *kind* of character who opposes Christ and what he stood for, a character who appears not just once and for all but in various places and at all times. In this respect, Paul's words apply not just to the end of days but to now as well. Christians should always be wary of the destructive potential of the powerful, should always be alert against deception, and should always be mindful of their susceptibility to temptation. They should always, in short, resist the "spirit of antichrist."

Why Eschatology Matters

For Paul, a person's salvation was not secured in an instant of personal decision. Although he assures the Thessalonians that God has "elected" and "called" them (2:13, 14), he also indicates that God has elected and called them *for* salvation and *for* the acquisition of glory. That is, God's initial act marked the beginning of a process that is leading up to a goal yet to be reached. Significantly, Paul's "thanks" for the Thessalonians' election and calling comes on the heels of his prophetic prediction of a great "apostasy" precipitated by Satan's deception.

This juxtaposition tacitly warns the Thessalonian believers of their own vulnerability. It is possible to fall. They must "hold fast" to the traditions (2:15). They must be "exhorted" to do good deeds (2:17). They must be "strengthened" and "guarded from the Evil One" (3:3). Salvation is not yet in hand. They must be faithful until the end.

2 Thessalonians 3:6–15

Final Exhortation: Admonition against Irresponsible Living

Introductory Matters

Paul has one final issue to discuss, and it appears to be among his primary reasons for writing the letter. Rounding out the letter's body, 2 Thess. 3:6–15 addresses a problem that concerns those who "are not keeping busy with work but are being busybodies" (3:11). After imparting instructions on this subject, at last Paul closes the letter (3:16–18), offering a wish-prayer (3:16); a personal greeting, together with an intriguing comment about how to determine his letters' authenticity (3:17); and finally, a benediction (3:18).

The occasion behind 2 Thess. 3:6–15. In 2 Thess. 3:6–15 Paul addresses a group of individuals whom he describes as *ataktoi*, a term that in its root sense means "disorderly." This group is also mentioned very briefly in 1 Thess. 5:14 ("admonish the disorderly"). While the term receives no elaboration in 1 Thess. 5:14, in 2 Thess. 3:6–15 Paul describes the *ataktoi* as people who are "not working but being busybodies." In this way they are violating a precept that he had taught them repeatedly during his founding visit: "If anyone does not want to work, let them also not eat" (3:10). The common reference to the *ataktoi* in the two letters, combined with common references to Paul's own "labor and toil" (1 Thess. 2:9//2 Thess. 3:8) and a directive either to "be quiet and work" (1 Thess. 4:11) or to "work quietly" (2 Thess. 3:12), has led many interpreters to believe that what had been (or Paul believed to be) only a minor issue when Paul wrote 1 Thessalonians has now become more serious and calls for sterner action.

Various theories have been proposed as to why the *ataktoi* were not working: (1) they believed that the parousia was imminent (Best 1979, 334; cf. Bruce 1982, 209), (2) they believed that eschatological blessings were already present in spiritual form (Beale 2003, 251), (3) they had dedicated all their time to vigorous and aggressive evangelism (Barclay 1993), (4) they believed that they could rely on the support of wealthy patrons (Russell 1988; Harrison 2011, 327–28) or were busy with client duties (Winter 1994), or (5) they believed they shared the apostolic right to demand financial support (Jewett 1986, 105).

Although most interpreters treat the element of "disorderliness" as secondary to the problem of idleness ("not working"), the "disorderliness" too requires some explanation.

> **2 Thessalonians 3:6–15 in the Rhetorical Flow**
>
> Letter opening (1:1–12)
>
> Letter body (2:1–3:5)
>
> ▶ Final exhortation: Admonition against irresponsible living (3:6–15)

Explanations of this issue can be divided into two categories: (1) disorderliness consisted in violation of the command to work, so that they were "out of order" or "out of line" with group norms; or (2) disorderliness amounted to "disruptiveness" in the social life of the community, of the city, or a combination of these. These options are further considered in the commentary below.

Second Thessalonians 3:6–18 and the letter's authorship. For those who view 2 Thessalonians as pseudonymous, the final exhortation (3:6–15) and closing (3:16–18) of the letter add several further planks in the argument. The appearance of a wish-prayer prior to the closing (2 Thess. 3:16) is taken as further evidence that 2 Thessalonians is dependent on 1 Thessalonians, since the latter also includes a wish-prayer near its conclusion (1 Thess. 5:23–24). Verbal parallels between the two letters occur where Paul / the author discusses his own "work" for the Thessalonians' benefit (1 Thess. 2:9//2 Thess. 3:8) and where he instructs the church to "work quietly" (1 Thess. 4:11; 2 Thess. 3:12). Both letters address problems with a group described as *ataktoi*. Moreover, the author's stress on "the tradition" (3:6) is seen as evidence of postapostolic authorship, working on the premise that "tradition" implies the existence of a well-defined and widely accepted body of teaching. Finally, and most significantly, the author's intriguing comment in the final two verses about how to determine his letters' authenticity (3:17) strikes many readers as an over-earnest attempt to prove that he really is Paul and thus as evidence that he is being disingenuous about his identity.

The structural and verbal arguments have been given some attention in the commentary's introduction. Regarding the argument from the author's reference to "the tradition," the comments made earlier on 2:15 apply equally here. The discussion below provides further treatment of Paul's comments in 3:17 about determining his letters' authenticity.

Tracing the Train of Thought

A transitional formula in 3:6 introduces a new section, which brings the body of the letter to a close. In conformity with Paul's other letters (Rom. 16:17; 1 Cor.

16:13–18; 2 Cor. 13:11; cf. Eph. 5:1–6:17; Col. 4:2–6), this final section is hortatory; yet uniquely, it does not consist of a brief collection of exhortations. Rather, it focuses extensively on a single issue—that of work.

3:6–9. The formula introducing the section (**now, we instruct you, brothers and sisters in the name of our Lord Jesus Christ**) is worthy of comment. Similar formulas occur at several points in the Thessalonian letters: "we ask and exhort you" (1 Thess. 4:1), "we exhort you" (1 Thess. 4:10; 5:14), and "we ask you" (1 Thess. 5:12; 2 Thess. 2:1). While the force of the relevant verbs may vary with context, generally the verb that is used in the formula here (*parangellein*) has more authoritative connotations. The addition of "in the name of the Lord Jesus Christ," moreover, backs Paul's words with the authority of Jesus (cf. 1 Thess. 4:1). Thus it is evident that Paul's mode of address has moved on the spectrum from paraenesis toward command (though see below on Paul's personal example), and so we translate "we *instruct* you."

Paul instructs them **to keep away from every brother or sister who walks disruptively** (3:6a). The meaning of this is not initially evident, though Paul has instructed them on this topic before (**and not according to the tradition that they received from us**, 3:6b). According to UBS⁵/NA²⁸, the tradition is what "*they* received," although there is good manuscript support for the second-person plural "*you all* received." Ultimately the decision between the two options makes little difference. In the given reading it is the "brothers" who received the tradition, but the ensuing verses show that the tradition had been passed on to the Thessalonians as a whole, both in the form of Paul's example (vv. 7–10) and as a precept about work (v. 10). These "brothers," moreover, are later identified as members of the Thessalonian church (vv. 11–12). In short, both "they" and the Thessalonians received the tradition.

The coordination of the ideas "*walks* disruptively *and not* according to the *tradition*" shows that Paul refers not to ritual or doctrinal tradition but to ethical tradition (see comments on 2:15). The tradition is what the church received from Paul in the form of his exemplum (see 1 Thess. 1:6–8), or the pattern of life that he modeled while he was among them. This reading is verified by what immediately follows: **For you yourselves know in what way you should walk to imitate us** (3:7a). The conjunction "for" (*gar*) indicates that Paul's example "explains" the "tradition" that they "received" from him. The expression "you yourselves know" occurs in Paul's letters only here and in 1 Thess. 2:1; 3:3; 5:2. Here, as in 1 Thess. 2:1, it refers the audience to Paul's previous conduct and example.

The conjunction **that** (*hoti*) resumes "in what way" (*pōs*), reexpressing "how you should walk so as to imitate us" with a specific description of the actions to be imitated: that **we did not walk in disruptive fashion when we were among you** (3:7b). Here one begins to gain clarity about what Paul means by "disruptive" behavior (*ataktōs*, v. 6). The adverb *ataktōs* appears only here and in 3:11 in the NT, and the corresponding adjective (*ataktos*) only in 1 Thess. 5:14. In its root sense, the term denotes a lack of proper "order," as in behavior that does

Table 11. Contrast between Paul and the *Ataktoi*

Paul	The Disruptive
"*working*" (3:8)	"*not working* but being busybodies" (3:11)
"nor did we *eat anyone's bread* freely" (3:12)	"that they should *eat their own bread*" (3:12)
"we did *not act disruptively among you*" (3:7)	"some *are walking disruptively among you*" (3:11)

not conform, for example, to institutional regulations or social conventions (see comments on 1 Thess. 5:14). Now in 3:7 Paul uses the cognate verb, *ataktein*. What is not clarified by the semantics of this word group is clarified in verse 8 and following. With "we did not walk in disruptive fashion" Paul coordinates **nor did we eat bread from anyone free of charge, but rather working night and day so as not to burden any of you** (3:8). This addition closely associates "disruptive" conduct with freeloading (eating bread "free of charge"), living off others' resources rather than earning one's own livelihood. This connection is clarified further in verse 11. Here Paul's reference to his own work finds a virtually exact parallel in 1 Thess. 2:9 (oddly, to the extent of thirteen words in the same order), though Paul now gives a different reason for his policy. In 1 Thess. 2:9 he expressed a desire to alleviate the Thessalonians of the burden of supporting him (also in 2 Cor. 11:9; 12:13–16) as an act of love for them. In his First Letter to the Corinthians (1 Cor. 9:3–18), Paul gives still another reason for working. There he establishes his "right" to take pay or sustenance for his ministry on the authority of Jesus himself (1 Cor. 9:14; Matt 10:10//Luke 10:4–8; cf. *Did.* 13.1–2), but maintains that he resolved to work anyway "so as not to give any hindrance to the gospel of Christ" (1 Cor. 9:12), presumably by making his ministry appear mercenary. Here Paul's passing comment about his "right," **Not that we did not have a right to do so** (3:9a), apparently alludes to the "right" of support mentioned in 1 Cor. 9; but now he presents yet another (a third) reason for his choice to work: it is to model self-sufficiency for the church: **but we did this so that we might present ourselves as an example to you, so that you might imitate us** (3:9b). Although this comment might appear to exalt behavior that for most people is an ordinary expectation (most people had to work for a living), Paul's passing reference to his "right" highlights the true nature of his labor, not as a necessity, but as a choice. As members of the lower classes, the Thessalonians had little choice but to work for a living. Paul had a choice not to work, but for their sake he did. If he was going to ask them to work, he would inspire them by his own example.

3:10. After basing his instructions to "keep away from the disruptive" on his personal *example* in verses 7–9, now in verse 10 he offers further grounds in the form of a *precept* (on *exempla* and *praecepta*, see comments on 1 Thess. 1:6–8; 4:1–2): **for also when we were with you, we were enjoining this upon you: that if someone wishes not to work, let them also not eat.** Although in his previous letter (1 Thess. 4:11) Paul had urged the Thessalonians to "work quietly with their own hands," he elects to refer them back not to his earlier letter but to his teaching during his founding visit. In part, this must be because the instructions in his letter to "work quietly" were substantially more succinct than what he taught them over the weeks of his visit. He reaches back to his visit undoubtedly also to underscore that this teaching is neither new nor added as an afterthought but something he emphasized from the very beginning. In addition to the early priority of this teaching, several other considerations reveal that he considered this issue to be of great importance. Paul's use of the imperfect tense ("we *were enjoining*") indicates that he had given these instructions repeatedly (cf. "we were saying to you," 1 Thess. 3:4; "I was saying these things to you," 2 Thess. 2:5). Moreover, semantically the verb *parangellō* has moderately authoritarian connotations (also in 2 Thess. 3:4, 6, 12), making it somewhat out of place in the generally paraenetic context of the Thessalonian letters (though he had used the same verb in regard to work in 1 Thess. 4:11). Finally, the succinct nature of the work-to-eat saying suggests that it may have been a maxim, conveying a common if not universal sentiment. Parallels occur in the Jewish Scriptures and in rabbinic sources (cf. "You shall eat your bread by the sweat of your brow," Gen. 3:19; cf. Prov. 10:4; *Gen. Rab.* 2.2), perhaps suggesting that the teaching was a popular Jewish proverb that the early church then incorporated into its catechetical tradition (Best 1979, 338).

There is no reason to limit the scope of concern here to members' contributions to the "communal meal" (Jewett 1993). The instructions are expressed about work in general. It would be a serious mistake, on the other hand, to generalize the instructions as applying to all those who *do not* work. Rather, the instructions concern those who "do not *wish*" to work. Presumably this would exclude those prevented from working due to health or complicating circumstances. Despite a trend in scholarship toward seeing the culprits as "clients" living off the support of their patrons (Russell 1988; Winter 1994), doubts could be raised about whether either patrons saw clients or clients saw themselves as "not working." Although clients discharged their duties as a "gift" to their patrons in some sense, sources describe these obligations in the language of commercial exchange ("owe," "debt," "return," "pay," "wages," "deserve," etc.). Those who *chose* not to work were familiar characters in the urban environment, like the Cynic philosophers, who idealized the ascetic lifestyle and unashamedly demanded charity from the public (Diogenes of Sinope, *Cynic Epistles* 34). In the second century, sources describe professed Christians who sponged off the community in this way: some of a Cynic stamp (Lucian, *Peregr.* 13, 16), some self-professed prophets (*Did.* 11.1–12; 13.1–7; *Herm. Mand.* 43.12 [11.1]). Such figures were sometimes itinerant (Lucian, *Peregr.* 13; *Did.* 11.4–5), but often they were residents or members of the local community (Lucian, *Peregr.* 13, 16; *Did.* 13.1–7), as they apparently were in Thessalonica (see 2 Thess. 3:11–12). The activities of the Thessalonian *ataktoi* are spelled out further in the next verse, where Paul says not only what they are *not* doing but also what they *are* doing.

3:11–13. Paul now explains why he has repeated his instructions. They have been violated: **For we hear that there are some among you who are walking disruptively.**

Voluntary Mendicants

"Do not complain to my associates, Olympias, that I wear a worn-out cloak and make the rounds of people begging for barley meal. For this is not disgraceful, nor as you claim, suspect behavior for free men. Rather, it is noble and can be armament against the appearances which war against life. Now I did not learn these lessons from Antisthenes first, but from the gods and heroes and those who converted Greece to wisdom, like Homer and the tragic poets." (Diogenes of Sinope, *Cynic Epistles* 34.1)

"He [Peregrinus] left home, then, for a second time, to roam about, possessing an ample source of funds in the Christians, through whose ministrations he lived in unalloyed prosperity." (Lucian, *Peregr.* 16)

Paul's presentation of the report as something he has "heard" need not imply that it was only rumor or that he did not give full credence to the report. The harsh command that precedes, in no way qualified as a hypothetical, indicates that this is a solemn announcement, as if to say: "It has come to my attention that . . ." At this point the meaning of *ataktoi* becomes more apparent: "walking disruptively" means **not keeping busy with work but being busybodies** (3:11b). There is a play on words in the Greek (a figure of speech known as paronomasia), as the words "keeping busy with work" (*ergazesthai*) and "being busybodies" (*periergazesthai*) employ the same verbal root (*ergaz-*).

Some sense of the prevalence of "busybodies" in the Greco-Roman social milieu can be gathered from the fact that Plutarch composed an entire treatise on the subject, known in modern scholarship by the title "On Being a Busybody" (*Peri polypragmosynē*). *Periergazesthai* and its noun cognate *periergia* are used throughout the treatise to describe busybodies and their business. Busybodies, Plutarch observes, are unable to endure the quiet life; they pry into others' affairs while neglecting their own; they are attentive to the affairs of paupers no less than princes and of strangers no less than their own; they take joy at others' misfortune, seeking to expose problems rather than to assist in solving them; and by being so occupied, they are distracted from more valuable pursuits, such as philosophical contemplation (or perhaps in Paul's terms, "the things of the Lord," 1 Cor. 7:32).

Such activity would require a certain degree of leisure. Since the Thessalonian *ataktoi* do not *want* to work, their fondness for meddling appears to be the cause of their unemployment rather than their unemployment the cause of their meddling. Like Plutarch's busybodies, they are unable to "work quietly" but have to be in other people's business at all times (2 Thess. 3:12; cf. Plutarch, *Mor.* 518E–519A; 1 Thess. 4:11). Paul does not say whether the locus of their activity was the believing community or the general civic environment, though his show of concern about work in his previous letter—where he advises the Thessalonians to "walk presentably toward outsiders" (1 Thess. 4:12)—suggests that the culprits' activities among outsiders are probably among his (highest?) concerns.

Paul's original description of these people as *ataktoi* can now be put in sharper focus. The *ataktoi* are likely "disorderly" in that they transgress the boundaries of expected social roles (insinuating themselves into business inappropriate to their relationships) and upset communal or societal stability (stirring up rumors, inciting fear, provoking discord). Paul's charge to **such people** is firm, so that he again appeals to his audience using the somewhat commanding verb **instruct** (v. 12). Two items, however, relax the confrontational tone. First, by adding the verb **exhort** immediately afterward, Paul shifts down the tone from that of command to that of paraenesis (cf. Weima 2014, 620). Although the connotations of the verbs *parangellein* and *parakalein* could overlap, it is telling that Paul sets a similar pair in contrast with each other in his Letter to Philemon ("although having boldness in Christ to *command* what is fitting on you, I prefer to *exhort* you on account of love," 8–9). Second, while the qualifying phrase **in the Lord Jesus Christ** (*en kyriō Iesou Christō*, 3:12) could indicate the authority by which Paul speaks (cf. 1 Thess. 4:1; Eph. 4:17; 6:1), far more often in Paul's letters this expression indicates the common sphere of existence that believers share "in the Lord" (e.g., "those in the Lord," Rom. 16:11; "faithful in the Lord," 1 Cor. 4:17; "to be married in the Lord," 1 Cor. 7:39; "servant in the Lord," Eph. 6:21; Col. 4:7; "brothers in the Lord," Phil. 1:14) or activities that believers do to or with one another because of their common sphere of existence "in the Lord" (e.g., "welcome in the Lord," Rom. 16:2; "greet in the Lord," Rom. 16:8; 1 Cor. 16:19; "agree in the Lord," Phil. 4:2).

Characteristically (cf. 1 Cor. 5:1; 2 Cor. 2:5; 10:2, 12; Gal. 1:7; 2:12), Paul does not name the offenders here but identifies them only as "some people" (*tines*), "such people" (*toioutoi*), or with the singular "someone" (*tis*). Several points indicate that these people were probably members of the local church. First, immediately following Paul's review of what he had taught on his *founding visit*, he turns to the lamentable fact that some "among" them have violated his instructions (v. 11). Second, Paul's instructions are directed not just at the community but indirectly

Plutarch on "Busybodies"

"But busybodies ruin and abandon their own interests in their excessive occupation with those of others. Only rarely do they visit the farm, for they cannot endure the quiet and silence of being alone. . . . And the busybody, shunning the country as something stale and uninteresting and undramatic, pushes into the bazaar and the market-place and the harbours: 'Is there any news?' 'Weren't you at market early this morning? Well then, do you suppose the city has changed its constitution in three hours?'" (Plutarch, *Mor.* 518E, 519A)

at the offenders themselves ("instruct and exhort such people to work quietly"). Third, despite Paul's unusual practice of carrying his occupation from place to place, the expectation that these people should "work" for a living (**to work quietly and eat bread that they have earned themselves**) is more understandable if they are residents rather than transients (v. 12). They would have needed a stable income to work for a consistent *living*, and if they were transients, Paul can hardly have objected to extending hospitality to them in principle (see 1 Thess. 4:9–10). Finally, Paul's injunction not to "associate" with such people (v. 14) but still to regard them as a "brother or sister" (v. 15) surely implies the likelihood of routine encounters. These points render it unlikely that we have to do here with itinerant prophets or false prophets. Rather, these are members of the Thessalonian community who occupy their time in meddling rather than working.

Verse 13 is continuous with what precedes (not the beginning of a new section, contra Malherbe 2000, 457). The initial word of the verse puts the second-person plural (emphatic *hymeis*) in focus as the new subject, signaling a contrast with the initial word of the previous verse ("such [people]"). This cohesive tie links together the subject matter of verses 6–12 with that of verse 13. Paul has issued instructions for "such people" (the *ataktoi*) to work. While these people are apparently included within the scope of the church, Paul now turns to the church as a whole: **And for your part, brothers and sisters, do not grow weary of doing good** (3:13). The verb form "doing good" is semantically vague (*kal-* + *poie-* = "good-doing"). The LXX uses the counter term *kakopoiein* (*kak-* + *poie-* = bad-doing) and the compound construction *kalōs poiēsai* (to act in a good way) in reference to evil deeds and good deeds, respectively (both occur in Lev. 5:4 LXX). At least two points, however, suggest that the verb here refers not to good works generally but specifically to works of *benefaction*. First, the verb's Greek roots parallel the Latin roots *bene-* (= *kal-*) and *fac-* (= *poie-*), which together constitute the word *beneficia*, meaning "services," "favors," "offerings," "gifts," or "benefactions." Second, the complementary tie between "such people" (who should work) and "you" (who should not grow weary of doing good) suggests that the two principles correlate, with the conjunction *de* showing that the second principle answers the first. In short: "Direct these people to work, *but* do not grow weary of offering assistance."

3:14–15. Verses 14–15 offer concluding instructions, in which Paul explains how to handle such a person (**anyone**) who **does not heed our message given through this epistle.** Paul refers literally to "*the* epistle," though undoubtedly the reference is to the present letter and not to 1 Thessalonians, for which some reference to the past would be expected (note the use of the aorist in 1 Cor. 5:9, "I wrote," in reference to an epistle written prior to 1 Corinthians; and *ante scripsi*, "I wrote before," in Cicero, *Att.* 1.2.1; 1.14.1; 1.20.4; passim). Although it would be possible to take this comment as referring to the *whole* content of 2 Thessalonians, it is most naturally taken as a reference to the instructions given about the *ataktoi* in 3:6–13. Indeed, apart from Paul's brief request for prayer (3:1–2), the content of the letter prior to 3:6–13 can hardly be viewed as "instructions" to be "obeyed," including his "request" that the Thessalonians not be "*shaken*" regarding the day of the Lord (2:1–2). Moreover, Paul's identification of the disobedient person here as "someone" (*tis*) audibly echoes his description of the *ataktoi* as "some" (*tines*) or "such people" (*toioutoi*) and his description of an *ataktos*, likewise, as "someone" (*tis*) who "does not want to work" (3:10–12). Finally, 3:14 ("so as not to associate with this person") essentially restates Paul's instruction in 3:6 ("Keep away from every brother or sister who walks disruptively"), thus creating an *inclusio* around 3:6–14/15. The opening conjunction (*de*) in verse 14, then, is less transitional than it is continuative (**and**) and evidently introduces a final set of comments on the subject of the *ataktoi*.

Paul advises that if any do not heed his message, the church should **mark such persons so as to avoid associating with them** (3:14b). The true graciousness of this policy should not be overlooked. The extreme measure of exclusion was to take place only after violation not only of the instructions given during Paul's founding visit (repeatedly), but also of the instructions reiterated in the present letter. Violations of his instructions at that point must be viewed as determination to flout them. Two further items deserve notice. First, it is apparent that Paul's policy was not intended to be punitive, but rather restorative. By excluding the offenders, his hope was **that they might be brought to shame**, that is, that they might experience *remorse* and restore themselves to order (3:14c). **Furthermore**, he asks the Thessalonians not to **regard such a person as an enemy, but to admonish that individual as a brother or sister** (3:15). Exclusion, in other words, did not amount to "excommunication" from the household of faith but was intended only as a temporary disciplinary measure.

Paul's discussion of the *ataktoi* and their potential exclusion from the community is strikingly consistent with his discussion of the adulterous man in 1 Cor. 5:1–13, which shares four significant points of contact with the present text: an indefinite reference to the offender ("someone"), an order not to "associate" with the offender (*synanamignysthai*), the restorative purpose of exclusion, and the need still to regard the offender as an insider (see the comparison table). As in 1 Cor. 5:3–5, it is the community itself, and not just its leaders, who are asked to take responsibility for action (2 Thess. 3:14–15 is addressed unrestrictedly to the second-person plural). There is no reason to see exclusion as being restricted to the context of community meals (Jewett 1993). Paul's concern, rather, is with community boundaries. No doubt the perceptions of outsiders are among his concerns, as is evident from his comments about work in 1 Thess. 4:11–12. In a group-oriented culture, social exclusion was a common means of maintaining group norms, as seen in both the Greco-Roman practice of exile and in sectarian excommunication practices. The former was not generally seen as restorative but as a means of cleansing the state of "cancerous" individuals (Lee 2006, 40–41). Excommunication as practiced at Qumran was grounded in a principle of community purity (1QS IX.3–6). As offenders of community norms threatened that

Table 12. 2 Thess. 3:14–15 and 1 Cor. 5:1–11 Compared

2 Thess. 3:14–15	1 Cor. 5:1–11
"some are walking disruptively" (2 Thess. 3:6)	"someone has his father's wife" (1 Cor. 5:1)
"so as to avoid associating with them" (2 Thess. 3:14)	"that the one who did this deed might be removed from your midst.... I wrote to you not to associate with anyone called a brother who is a fornicator. ..." (1 Cor. 5:2, 9)
"so that they might be brought to shame" (2 Thess. 3:14)	"hand over such a person to Satan for destruction of the flesh, so that the spirit might be preserved in him on the day of the Lord" (1 Cor. 5:5)
"do not regard them as an enemy but admonish them as a brother or sister" (2 Thess. 3:15)	"Is it any business of mine to judge outsiders? Should you not rather judge insiders?" (1 Cor. 5:12)

purity, rules stipulated probationary measures, temporary excommunication, and in some cases final excommunication (1QS VI.24–VII.27). In this sense, the book of Deuteronomy stipulates excommunication for those who compromise the purity of the community, frequently repeating the refrain: "Purge the evil from your midst" (Deut. 17:7b; 19:19; 21:21; 22:24; 24:7; cf. Matt. 18:17–18). Paul stops short of this extreme. His addition of the directive not to regard the offender as an "enemy" could be prompted by a desire to offer an improvement on the Deuteronomic policy of the death penalty for excommunicable offenses (Deut. 17:7; 21:21; etc.).

Theological Issues

Group Identity

Like other portions of the letter, 2 Thess. 3:6–15 reflects a deep concern with Christian identity. However, in its framing, this section is not about the identity of individuals as believers but the identity of the community and the individual's identity as *embedded within* that community. This is why Paul stipulates *exclusion* from the community as the penalty for violations of group norms. The purpose of this exclusion is to bring the individual to repentance and to restore the offender to the *group*.

Exclusion also serves to preserve the integrity of the group. While Paul does not here express concern regarding the perceptions of outsiders (cf. 1 Thess. 4:11–12), this is implicit in the nature of group-identity formation. The group does not act in such and such a way. By acting differently, they are perceived differently, that is, as a distinct kind of people. In this case, the imperative to work and not to be "busybodies" addresses a concern that believers should not appear as social delinquents or public nuisances but as valuable members of society and model citizens.

Applying Paul's Instructions

Just because Paul's instructions to his churches have enduring practical relevance does not mean that they should be woodenly replicated. The transformation of culture over the centuries and the varying circumstances according to time and place require that applications vary. Paul would have advised this himself. For Paul, ethics consisted not in compliance with a set of rigid rules but in the creative application of a Christ-centered theological framework by means of sensitive discernment that is guided by wisdom or, put differently, inspired by the Spirit (Rom. 8:5, 14; 1 Cor. 2:16; Gal. 5:18, 25).

The need for discernment is all the more important since Paul's "precepts" (as we have often called them in this commentary) sometimes stand in tension with each other. For instance, while Paul's approach of "tough love" may still be a successful way of restoring members of the believing community in some contexts (and perhaps should be practiced more often today), in other contexts such an approach might not induce "shame" so much as resentment and permanent defection from the church. If restoration of wayward members is (or ought to be) the church's goal, Paul surely would have agreed that other, potentially more effective methods should be tried. Such methods, however, would also need to take into account the importance of preserving the integrity of the group as a church, an entity that acts or is meant to act distinctly as the people of God. In some situations, unconditional *inclusion* of members who persist in egregious behavior may be more damaging than helpful to the church, not to mention to the individual. Finding an appropriate balance, or rather an appropriate application, of these principles requires discernment.

To take another example, Paul's affirmation of both a work-to-eat and a continue-to-give principle shows that he was aware of the potential for an imbalance between a kind of indolence that is enabled by welfare on the one hand and a kind of severity that refuses to lend a helping hand on the other. The fact that the principles of "work" and "give" stand in tension with one another was not lost on Paul. Rather, he must have expected that applications would be determined situationally. Given the centrality of grace in Paul's message, it seems inconceivable that he would have enforced "eating" restrictions against those who *could not* work (2 Thess. 3:10). In cases of a persistent and willful idleness within the community, he might generally, if not always, have objected to charity, as the work-to-eat principle suggests. However, he might have encouraged charity as a way to help meet the needs of those whose financial situation was in jeopardy, so long as the recipients were working as they could. Determining when people are "working as they can," however, may be difficult. Could they afford to work just a little more? What constitutes too much or too little work? Who gets to decide? Could the struggling individual change professions and find better pay? Remembering that Paul was not addressing state-controlled welfare (here or anywhere in his letters) but was urging charity practiced by the believing community or individuals within it, no doubt he would have advised reliance on prayerful wisdom and the Spirit's moving to navigate such questions.

2 Thessalonians 3:16–18

Letter Closing

Introductory Matters

The closing of the letter contains several elements, all of which have parallels in the closings of one or more of Paul's other letters: a wish-prayer (3:16a; Rom. 16:20; Phil. 4:19; 1 Thess. 5:23–24); a benediction, along with a second benediction (2 Thess. 3:16b, 18; Rom. 16:20; 1 Cor. 16:23; 2 Cor. 13:13; Gal. 6:18; Eph. 6:24; Phil. 4:23; Col. 4:18; 1 Thess. 5:28; 1 Tim. 6:21; 2 Tim. 4:22; Titus 3:15; Philem. 25); a personal greeting (v. 17a; 1 Cor. 16:21; Col. 4:18); and a reference to his own handwriting (v. 17b–c; 1 Cor. 16:21; Gal. 6:11; Col. 4:18; Philem. 19).

Tracing the Train of Thought

3:16–18. The wish of peace in verse 16 could be interpreted as referring to the specific issue that precedes: Paul wishes for peace between the *ataktoi* and the rest of the church. However, the salient issue in verses 6–13 is the failure of some within the community to work, not dissension within the community (perhaps in contrast to 1 Thess. 5:12–13). Thus the UBS[5] (against the segmentation of the NA[28]) correctly identifies verse 16 as a final benediction, not concluding the discussion of the *ataktoi* but rather transitioning

> **2 Thessalonians 3:16–18 in the Rhetorical Flow**
>
> Letter opening (1:1–12)
>
> Letter body (2:1–3:5)
>
> **Final exhortation: Admonition against irresponsible living (3:6–15)**
>
> ▶ Letter closing (3:16–18)

to conclude the letter as a whole: **Now may the Lord of peace himself give you peace always in every way** (3:16).

Three times the closing mentions the "Lord" (vv. 16 [2×], 18), twice without qualification and once in explicit reference to "our Lord Jesus Christ." The final occurrence could suggest that reference is to Jesus also in the other occurrences. Although Paul elsewhere uses the expression "*God* of peace" and never "the *Lord* of peace" as here, he does speak elsewhere of the "peace of Christ" (see comments on 2 Thess. 1:2). Perhaps not insignificantly, Paul also repeats the phrase "with you all" in verses 16 and 18: **The Lord . . . the Lord of peace be with you all** (v. 16); **The grace of our Lord Jesus Christ be with you all** (v. 18). This shared phrasing "with you all" after wishes of grace and peace from either the "Lord" or "the Lord Jesus" could suggest that both grace *and* peace are here associated with "the Lord Jesus." With the conjoining of grace and peace, the letter comes full circle to the salutation, where Paul had wished the audience "grace and peace" (1:2).

Much ado has been made of verse 17, though the content finds partial parallels in the closings of several of Paul's other letters. A personal "greeting" similar to the one here (**this greeting in my own hand, Paul's**, 3:17a) occurs at the conclusion of 1 Corinthians (16:21), Galatians (6:11), Colossians (4:18), and Philemon (19), where Paul makes a concluding reference to his "own hand." A reference to one's own handwriting at the closing of a letter was not unusual in the ancient world. Since many people wrote through an amanuensis, including those among the literate and highly educated (Klauck 2006, 55), the sender often took the pen in closing (Klauck 2006, 16, 138). This need not have been for the purpose of authentication. Rather, there was something in the very handwriting that brought the sender nearer, as it provided "real traces, real marks, of an absent friend" (Seneca, *Ep.* 40.1; cf. Chariton, *Chaer.* 8.4.5–6).

More unusual is Paul's concern to provide his audience with the means of authenticating his letters: **This greeting is an earmark in every epistle; thus I write** (3:17b). It is the greeting specifically *in that handwriting* that served as an earmark of his epistles, not that every epistle included a personal "greeting," as in fact they did not. Many scholars regard the added certification as "suspicious" (Klauck 2006, 393) inclining toward the position that those who insist that they are not liars should be regarded as being such. There is some justification for this view, for affirmations of the author's veracity are a common feature in Jewish pseudepigraphic literature (see sidebar), that is, works that are manifestly pseudonymous.

The other possibility is that this is really how Paul wrote, and he found it important that the church knew that. Why Paul felt this to be important could have a range of explanations. (1) He was aware or suspicious of the possibility of a spurious letter written in his name; (2) he was aware of a misleadingly revised version of one of his letters, most likely a copy of 1 Thessalonians; or (3) he wished to guard preemptively against the future contingency of a spurious letter. Among those who accept 2 Thessalonians as authentic, the first explanation

Pseudepigraphic Reaffirmations of Truthfulness

"All who will inherit this narrative will, I think, find it incredible. To tell lies concerning matters which are being chronicled is inappropriate: If I were to make a single error, it would be impious in these matters. On the contrary, we narrate things as they happened, eschewing any error. I therefore, heartily accepting the force of their argument, have tried to present from the record the details of events at the audiences with the king and at the banquets." (Aristob. 296–98, trans. Shutt, *OTP* 2:32)

"God himself, the great eternal one, told me to prophesy all these things. These things will not go unfulfilled. Nor is anything left unaccomplished that he so much as puts in mind, for the spirit of God which knows no falsehood is throughout the world." (*Sib. Or.* 3:696–701, trans. J. Collins, *OTP* 2:377)

"I am Sibylla born of Circe as mother and Gnostos as father, a crazy liar. But when everything comes to pass, then you will remember me and no longer will anyone say that I am crazy, I who am a prophetess of the great God. . . . The first things happened to him [Noah] and all the latter things have been revealed, so let all these things from my mouth be accounted true." (*Sib. Or.* 3.815–29, trans. J. Collins, *OTP* 2:380)

See also *1 En.* 104.10–11.

is most prevalent. The second option (Abraham Malherbe 2000, 429–30, 463) is also plausible, though somewhat more speculative. Though rarely considered, the third possibility is also not without merit. Wanamaker (1990, 40), for instance, suggests that Paul may have "simply considered the possibility" of a forgery. The circulation of spurious letters during the lifetime of the alleged authors was not uncommon, especially letters purportedly written by important persons (Cicero, *Att.* 11.16.1; *Fam.* 3.11.5; Suetonius, *Aug.* 51, 55); the existence of such letters is sometimes mentioned by the affected individuals as no more than a possibility (Cicero, *Fam.* 3.11.5). Whatever the reason may have been in this case, any one of these three explanations is sufficiently plausible to obviate recourse to the premise that a pseudepigrapher affirmed his truthfulness in order to dispel doubts that he was lying.

Bibliography

Adams, Edward. 2009. "First-Century Models for Paul's Churches: Selected Scholarly Developments since Meeks." Pages 60–78 in *After the First Urban Christians*. Edited by Todd Still and David Horrell. Edinburgh: T&T Clark.

Artz-Grabner, Peter. 1994. "The 'Epistolary Introductory Thanksgiving' in the Papyri and in Paul." *Novum Testamentum* 36:29–46.

Ascough, Richard S. 2000. "The Thessalonian Christian Community as a Professional Voluntary Association." *Journal of Biblical Literature* 119:311–28.

———. 2003. *Paul's Macedonian Associations: The Social Context of Philippians and 1 Thessalonians*. Wissenschaftliche Untersuchungen zum Neuen Testament 2/161. Tübingen: Mohr Siebeck.

———. 2015. "Thessalonians." *Oxford Bibliographies Online: Biblical Studies*. Rev. ed.

Aus, Roger D. 1971. "Comfort in Judgment: The Use of the Day of the Lord and Theophany Traditions in Second Thessalonians 1." PhD diss., Yale University.

———. 1973. "Liturgical Background of the Necessity and Propriety of Giving Thanks according to 2 Thess. 1:3." *Journal of Biblical Literature* 92:432–38.

———. 1977. "God's Plan and God's Power: Isaiah 66 and the Restraining Factors of 2 Thess 2:6–7." *Journal of Biblical Literature* 96:537–53.

Barclay, John M. G. 1992. "Thessalonica and Corinth: Social Contrasts in Pauline Christianity." *Journal for the Study of the New Testament* 47:49–74.

———. 1993. "Conflict in Thessalonica." *Catholic Biblical Quarterly* 55:512–30.

———. 2015. *Paul and the Gift*. Grand Rapids: Eerdmans.

———. 2016. "'That You May Not Grieve, Like the Rest Who Have No Hope' (1 Thess 4.13)." Pages 217–35 in *Pauline Churches and Diaspora Jews*. Grand Rapids: Eerdmans.

Baur, F. C. 1845. *Paulus: der Apostel Jesu Christi*. Stüttgart: Becher & Müller.

———. 1875–76. *Paul the Apostle of Jesus Christ: His Life and Work, His Epistles and His Doctrine*. Translated by Allen Menzies. 2nd ed. 2 vols. London: Williams & Norgate.

Beale, G. K. 2003. *1–2 Thessalonians*. IVP New Testament Commentary. Downers Grove, IL: InterVarsity.

Best, Ernest. 1972; repr. 1979. *A Commentary on the First and Second Epistles to the Thessalonians*. Black's/Harper's New Testament Commentaries. New York: Harper & Row.

Bjerkelund, C. J. 1967. *Parakalō: Form, Funktion und Sinn der parakalō-Sätze in den paulinischen Briefen*. Oslo: Universitetsforlaget.

Bockmuehl, Markus N. A. 2001. "1 Thessalonians 2:14–16 and the Church in Jerusalem." *Tyndale Bulletin* 52:1–31.

Boring, Eugene. 2015. *1 and 2 Thessalonians*. New Testament Library. Louisville: Westminster John Knox.

Bornemann, Wilhelm. 1894. *Die Thessalonicherbriefe*. Meyer kritisch-exegetischer Kommentar über das Neue Testament 10. Göttingen: Vandenhoeck & Ruprecht.

Briones, David E. 2010. "Mutual Brokers of Grace: A Study in 2 Corinthians 1.3–11." *New Testament Studies* 56:536–56.

Brookins, Timothy A. 2018. "A Tense Discussion: Rethinking the Grammaticalization of Time in Greek Indicative Verbs." *Journal of Biblical Literature* 137:141–65.

———. Forthcoming a. "The Alleged 'Letter Allegedly from Us': The Parallel Function of ὡς δι' ἡμῶν in 2 Thess. 2.2." *Journal for the Study of the New Testament*.

———. Forthcoming b. "An Obligation of Thanks (2 Thess 1,3): Gift and Return in Divine-Human Relationships." *Zeitschrift für neutestamentliche Wissenschaft und die Kunde der älteren Kirche*.

Bruce, F. F. 1982. *1 & 2 Thessalonians*. Word Biblical Commentary 45. Waco: Word Books.

Campbell, Douglas. 2014. *Framing Paul: An Epistolary Account*. Grand Rapids: Eerdmans.

Collins, Raymond F. 1984. *Studies on the First Letter to the Thessalonians*. Bibliotheca ephemeridum theologicarum lovaniensium 66. Leuven: Leuven University Press.

———. 1988. "The Second Epistle to the Thessalonians." Pages 209–41 in *Letters That Paul Did Not Write: The Epistle to the Hebrews and the Pauline Pseudepigrapha*. Good News Studies 28. Wilmington, DE: Michael Glazier.

Cosby, Michael R. 1994. "Hellenistic Formal Receptions and Paul's Use of ΑΠΑΝΤΗΣΙΣ in 1 Thessalonians 4:17." *Bulletin for Biblical Research* 4:15–33.

Crüsemann, Marlene. 2010. *Die pseudepigraphen Briefe an die Gemeinde in Thessaloniki: Studien zu ihrer Abfassung und zur jüdisch-christlichen Sozialgeschichte*. Beiträge zur Wissenschaft vom Alten und Neuen Testament 191. Stuttgart: Kohlhammer.

———. 2018. *The Pseudepigraphical Letters to the Thessalonians*. London: Bloomsbury.

De Vos, Craig Steven. 1999. *Church and Community Conflicts: The Relationships of the Thessalonian, Corinthian, and Philippian Churches with Their Wider Civic Communities*. Society of Biblical Literature Dissertation Series 168. Atlanta: Scholars Press.

Dibelius, Martin. 1937. *An die Thessalonicher I, II*. Handbuch zum Neuen Testament. Tübingen: Mohr Siebeck.

Divjanović, Kristin. 2015. *Paulus als Philosoph: Das Ethos des Apostels vor dem Hintergrund antiker Populärphilosophie.* Neutestamentliche Abhandlungen, Neue Folge 58. Münster: Aschendorff.

Dobschütz, E. von. 1909. *Die Thessalonicher-Briefe.* Meyers Kritisch-exegetischer Kommentar über das Neue Testament 10. Göttingen: Vandenhoeck & Ruprecht.

Donfried, Karl P. 1985. "The Cults of Thessalonica and the Thessalonian Correspondence." *New Testament Studies* 31:336–56.

———. 2002. *Paul, Thessalonica, and Early Christianity.* Grand Rapids: Eerdmans.

Doty, William G. 1973. *Letters in Primitive Christianity.* Philadelphia: Fortress.

Downing, F. Gerald. 1992. *Cynics and Christian Origins.* Edinburgh: T&T Clark.

Dunn, James D. G. 1998. *The Theology of the Apostle Paul.* Minneapolis: Fortress.

Edson, Charles. 1948. "Cults of Thessalonica." *Harvard Theological Review* 41:153–204.

Faw, Chalmer E. 1952. "On the Writing of First Thessalonians." *Journal of Biblical Literature* 71:217–25.

Finney, Mark T. 2010. "Honor, Rhetoric and Factionalism in the Ancient World: 1 Corinthians 1–4 in Its Social Context." *Biblical Theology Bulletin* 40:27–36.

Foster, Paul. 2012. "Who Wrote 2 Thessalonians? A Fresh Look at an Old Problem." *Journal for the Study of the New Testament* 35:150–75.

Frame, James E. 1912. *The Epistles of St. Paul to the Thessalonians.* International Critical Commentary. Edinburgh: T&T Clark.

Friedrich, G. 1976. "Die erste Brief an die Thessalonicher." Pages 203–51 in *Die Briefe an die Galater, Epheser, Philipper, Kolosser, Thessalonicher und Philemon.* Edited by J. Becker, H. Conzelmann, and G. Friedrich. 14th ed. Das Neue Testament Deutsch 8. Göttingen: Vandenhoeck & Ruprecht.

Friesen, Steven J. 2010. "Second Thessalonians, the Ideology of Epistles, and the Construction of Authority: Our Debt to the Forger." Pages 189–210 in *From Roman to Early Christian Thessalonikē.* Edited by L. Nasrallah, C. Bakirtzis, and S. Friesen. Cambridge, MA: Harvard University Press.

Funk, Robert W. 1967. "The Apostolic *Parousia:* Form and Significance." Pages 249–69 in *Christian History and Interpretation: Studies Presented to John Knox.* Edited by W. R. Farmer, C. F. D. Moule, and R. R. Niebuhr. Cambridge: Cambridge University Press.

Furnish, Victor Paul. 2007. *1–2 Thessalonians.* Abingdon New Testament Commentaries. Nashville: Abingdon.

Gaventa, Beverly Roberts. 1998. *First and Second Thessalonians.* Interpretation. Louisville: John Knox.

Gilliard, Frank D. 1989. "The Problem of the Antisemitic Comma between 1 Thessalonians 2.14 and 15." *New Testament Studies* 35:481–502.

Goguel, Maurice. 1925. *Introduction au Nouveau Testament.* 4 vols. Paris: Leroux.

Gorday, Peter, ed. 2000. *Colossians, Thessalonians, 1–2 Timothy, Titus, Philemon.* Ancient Christian Commentary on Scripture: New Testament 9. Downers Grove, IL: InterVarsity.

Gorman, Michael. 2009. *Inhabiting the Cruciform God: Kenosis, Justification, and Theosis in Paul's Narrative Soteriology*. Grand Rapids: Eerdmans.

Gregson, R. 1966. "A Solution to the Problems of the Thessalonian Epistles." *Evangelical Quarterly* 38:76–80.

Grotius, Hugo. 1679. *Operum Theologicorum*. Amsterdam: Blaev.

Gupta, Nijay. 2019. *1–2 Thessalonians*. Zondervan Critical Introductions to the New Testament Series. Grand Rapids: Zondervan Academic.

Harnack, Adolf von. 1910. "Der Problem des zweiten Thessalonicherbriefes." Pages 560–78 in *Sitzungsberichte der königlich preussischen Akademie der Wissenschaften*. Philosophisch-Historische Klasse. Berlin: Verlag der Akademie der Wissenschaften.

Harrison, James R. 2002. "Paul and the Imperial Gospel at Thessaloniki." *Journal for the Study of the New Testament* 25:71–96.

———. 2011. *Paul and the Imperial Authorities at Thessalonica and Rome: A Study in the Conflict of Ideology*. Wissenschaftliche Untersuchungen zum Neuen Testament 273. Tübingen: Mohr Siebeck.

———. 2019. *Paul and the Ancient Celebrity Circuit: The Cross and Moral Transformation*. Tübingen: Mohr Siebeck.

Harrison, James R., and Benjamin Schliesser. Forthcoming. *Philippi and Thessalonica*. Vol. 14 of *New Documents Illustrating Early Christianity*. Grand Rapids: Eerdmans.

Harrison, James R., and L. L. Welborn. Forthcoming. *Thessalonica*. Vol. 7 of *The First Urban Churches*. Atlanta: SBL Press.

Hendrix, H. L. 1984. "Thessalonicans Honor Romans." PhD diss., Harvard University.

———. 1992. "Benefactor/Patron Networks in the Urban Environment: Evidence from Thessalonica." *Semeia* 56:39–58.

Hock, Ronald F. 1980. *The Social Context of Paul's Ministry: Tentmaking and Apostleship*. Philadelphia: Fortress.

Holland, G. S. 1988. *The Tradition That You Have Received from Us: 2 Thessalonians in the Pauline Tradition*. Hermeneutische Untersuchungen zur Theologie 24. Tübingen: Mohr Siebeck.

Holtz, Traugott. 1986. *Der erste Brief an die Thessalonicher*. Evangelisch-katholischer Kommentar zum Neuen Testament 13. Zurich: Benziger.

Hope, Valerie M. 2009. *Roman Death: Dying and the Dead in Ancient Rome*. London: Continuum.

Horrell, David. 2005. *Solidarity and Difference: A Contemporary Reading of Paul's Ethics*. New York: T&T Clark.

Hughes, Frank W. 1989. *Early Christian Rhetoric and 2 Thessalonians*. Journal for the Study of the New Testament Supplement Series 30. Sheffield: JSOT Press.

Jensen, Matthew. 2019. "The (In)authenticity of 1 Thessalonians 2.13–16: A Review of Arguments." *Currents in Biblical Research* 18:59–79.

Jewett, Robert. 1969. "The Form and Function of the Homiletic Benediction." *Anglican Theological Review* 51:18–34.

———. 1971. *Paul's Anthropological Terms: A Study of Their Use in Conflict Settings*. Arbeiten zur Geschichte des antiken Judentums und des Urchristentums 10. Leiden: Brill.

———. 1986. *The Thessalonian Correspondence: Pauline Rhetoric and Millenarian Piety*. Forschungen und Fortschritte. Philadelphia: Fortress.

———. 1993. "Tenement Churches and Communal Meals in the Early Church: The Implications of a Form-Critical Analysis of 2 Thess 3:10." *Biblical Research* 38:23–43.

Johnson, Luke Timothy. 1989. "The New Testament's Slander and the Conventions of Ancient Polemic." *Journal of Biblical Literature* 108:419–41.

———. 2001. *The First and Second Letters to Timothy*. Anchor Bible 35. New York: Doubleday.

Judge, Edwin A. 1971. "The Decrees of Caesar at Thessalonica." *Reformed Theological Review* 30:1–7.

Kim, Seyoon. 2005. "Paul's Entry (εἴσοδος) and the Thessalonians' Faith (1 Thessalonians 1–3)." *New Testament Studies* 51:519–42.

Klauck, Hans-Josef. 2006. *Ancient Letters and the New Testament: A Guide to Context and Exegesis*. Waco: Baylor University Press.

Knox, John. 1954. *Chapters in a Life of Paul*. London: SCM.

Koester, Helmut. 2010. "The Egyptian Religion in Thessalonikē: Regulation for the Cult." Pages 133–50 in *From Roman to Early Christian Thessalonikē*. Edited by L. Nasrallah, C. Bakirtzis, and S. Friesen. Cambridge, MA: Harvard University Press.

Korner, Ralph J. 2017. *The Origin and Meaning of Ekklēsia in the Early Jesus Movement*. Leiden: Brill.

Krentz, Edgar M. 1992. "Thessalonians, First and Second Epistles to the." Pages 515–23 in *Anchor Bible Dictionary*. Vol. 6. Edited by D. N. Freedman. 6 vols. New York: Doubleday.

———. 2009. "A Stone That Will Not Fit: The Non-Pauline Authorship of 2 Thessalonians." Pages 456–63 in *Pseudepigraphie und Verfasserfiktion in frühchristlichen Briefen*. Edited by J. Frey et al. Wissenschaftliche Untersuchungen zum Neuen Testament 256. Tübingen: Mohr Siebeck.

Lausberg, Heinrich. 1998. *Handbook of Literary Rhetoric: A Foundation for Literary Study*. Leiden: Brill.

Lee, Michelle. 2006. *Paul, the Stoics, and the Body of Christ*. Society for New Testament Studies Monograph Series 137. Cambridge: Cambridge University Press.

Lightfoot, J. B. 1904. *Notes on Epistles of St. Paul*. London: Macmillan.

Lindemann, Andreas. 1977. "Zum Abfassungszweck des zweiten Thessalonicherbriefs." *Zeitschrift für die neutestamentliche Wissenschaft* 68:34–47.

Long, A. A., and D. N. Sedley, eds. 1987. *The Hellenistic Philosophers*. 2 vols. Cambridge: Cambridge University Press.

Longenecker, Bruce W. 2009. "Exposing the Economic Middle: A Revised Economy Scale for the Study of Early Christianity." *Journal for the Study of the New Testament* 31:243–78.

Longenecker, Bruce W., and Todd D. Still. 2014. *Thinking through Paul: An Introduction to His Life, Letters, and Theology.* Grand Rapids: Zondervan.

Lüdemann, Gerd. 1984. *Paul, Apostle to the Gentiles: Studies in Chronology.* Translated by E. S. Jones. Philadelphia: Fortress.

Lütgert, W. 1909. *Die Volkommenen in Philipperbrief und die Enthusiasten in Thessalonich.* Beiträge zur Förderung christlicher Theologie 6. Gütersloh: Bertelsmann.

Lutz, Cora E. 1947. *Musonius Rufus, the Roman Socrates.* Yale Classical Studies 10. New Haven: Yale University Press.

Malherbe, Abraham J. 1970. "'Gentle as a Nurse': The Cynic Background to 1 Thessalonians 2." *Novum Testamentum* 12:203–17.

———. 1983. "Exhortation in First Thessalonians." *Novum Testamentum* 25:238–56.

———. 1987. *Paul and the Thessalonians: The Philosophic Tradition of Pastoral Care.* Philadelphia: Fortress.

———. 1989. "Hellenistic Moralists and the New Testament." Pages 267–333 in *Aufstieg und Niedergang der römischen Welt: Geschichte und Kultur Roms im Spiegel der neueren Forschung.* Part 2, *Principat*, 26.1. Edited by H. Temporini and W. Haase. Berlin: de Gruyter.

———. 1995. "God's New Family at Thessalonica." Pages 116–25 in *The Social World of the First Christians: Studies in Honor of Wayne A. Meeks.* Edited by L. Michael White and O. Larry Yarbrough. Minneapolis: Fortress.

———. 2000. *The Letters to the Thessalonians.* Anchor Bible 32B. New York: Doubleday.

———. 2013. *Light from the Gentiles: Hellenistic Philosophy and Early Christianity; Collected Essays, 1959–2012.* Edited by Carl R. Holladay, John T. Fitzgerald, James W. Thompson, and Gregory E. Sterling. 2 vols. Supplements to Novum Testamentum 150. Leiden: Brill.

Manson, Thomas W. 1962. "The Letters to the Thessalonians." Pages 259–78 in *Studies in the Gospels and Epistles.* Edited by Matthew Black. Manchester: Manchester University Press.

Marshall, I. Howard. 1983. *1 and 2 Thessalonians.* New Century Bible Commentary. Grand Rapids: Eerdmans.

Masson, C. 1957. *Les deux épitres de Saint Paul aux Thessaloniciens.* Commentaire du Nouveau Testament XIa. Neuchâtel: Delachaux & Niestlé.

McNeel, Jennifer Houston. 2013. "Feeding with Milk: Paul's Nursing Metaphors in Context." *Review and Expositor* 110:561–75.

———. 2014. *Paul as Infant and Nursing Mother: Metaphor, Rhetoric, and Identity in 1 Thessalonians 2:5–8.* Atlanta: SBL Press.

Meeks, Wayne. 1983; 2nd ed., 2003. *The First Urban Christians.* New Haven: Yale University Press.

Menken, M. J. J. 1990. "The Structure of 2 Thessalonians." Pages 373–82 in *The Thessalonian Correspondence.* Edited by Raymond F. Collins. Bibliotheca Ephemeridum Theologicarum Lovaniensium 87. Leuven: University Press-Peeters.

———. 1994. "Getransformeerde traditie: Christologie in 2 Tessalonicenzen." Inaugural address, Catholic University of Utrecht. Utrecht: Katholieke Theologische Universiteit.

Milinovich, Timothy. 2014. "Memory and Hope in the Midst of Chaos: Reconsidering the Structure of 1 Thessalonians." *Catholic Biblical Quarterly* 76:498–518.

Mitchell, Margaret M. 1989. "Concerning *peri de* in 1 Corinthians." *Novum Testamentum* 31:229–56.

———. 1992. "New Testament Envoys in the Context of Greco-Roman Diplomatic and Epistolary Conventions: The Example of Timothy and Titus." *Journal of Biblical Literature* 111:641–62.

Morgan, Teresa. 2015. *Roman Faith and Christian Faith: Pistis and Fides in the Early Roman Empire and Early Churches.* Oxford: Oxford University Press.

Morton, A. Q., and James McLeman. 1964. *Christianity in the Computer Age.* New York: Harper & Row.

Munro, Winsome. 1983. *Authority in Peter and Paul: The Identification of a Pastoral Stratum in the Pauline Corpus and 1 Peter.* Cambridge, MA: Harvard University Press.

Murphy-O'Connor, Jerome. 1996. *Paul: A Critical Life.* Oxford: Oxford University Press.

Newman, Robert J. 2008. "*In Umbra Virtutis: Gloria* in the Thought of Seneca the Philosopher." Pages 316–34 in *Seneca.* Edited by John G. Fitch. Oxford Readings in Classical Studies. Oxford: Oxford University Press.

Nicholl, Colin R. 2000. "Michael, the Restrainer Removed (2 Thess 2:6–7)." *Journal of Theological Studies* 51:27–53.

———. 2004. *From Hope to Despair in Thessalonica: Situating 1 and 2 Thessalonians.* Society for New Testament Studies Monograph Series 126. Cambridge: Cambridge University Press.

Nicklas, Tobias. 2019. *Der zweite Thessalonicherbrief.* Meyers Kritisch-Exegetischer Kommentar über das Neue Testament 10.2. Göttingen: Vandenhoeck & Ruprecht.

Nigdelis, Pantelis M. 2006. *Επιγραφικά Θεσσαλονίκεια: Συμβολή στην πολιτική και κοινωνική ιστορία της απαρχαίας Θεσσαλονίκης.* Epigraphica Thessalonicensia: Contribution to the Political and Social History of Ancient Thessalonikē. Thessaloniki: University Studio Press.

Oakes, Peter. 2005. "Re-mapping the Universe: Paul and the Emperor in 1 Thessalonians and Philippians." *Journal for the Study of the New Testament* 27:301–22.

———. 2009a. "Contours of the Urban Environment." Pages 21–35 in *After the First Urban Christians.* Edited by Todd Still and David Horrell. Edinburgh: T&T Clark.

———. 2009b. *Reading Romans in Pompeii.* Minneapolis: Fortress; London: SPCK.

Pahl, M. W. 2009. *Discerning the "Word of the Lord": The "Word of the Lord" in 1 Thessalonians 4:15.* Library of New Testament Studies 389. London: T&T Clark.

Pearson, Birger A. 1971. "1 Thessalonians 2:13–16: A Deutero-Pauline Interpolation." *Harvard Theological Review* 64:79–94.

Peerbolte, L. J. L. 1996. *The Antecedents of Antichrist: A Traditio-Historical Study of the Earliest Christian Views on Eschatological Opponents.* Leiden: Brill.

Rabens, Volker. 2017. "Paul's Mission Strategy in the Urban Landscape of the First-Century Roman Empire." Pages 99–122 in *The Urban World of the First Christians.* Grand Rapids: Eerdmans.

Raeburn, David A., trans. 2004. *Ovid: Metamorphoses; A New Verse Translation*. London: Penguin.

Redalié, Yann. 2011. *La deuxième épître aux Thessaloniciens*. Commentaire du Nouveau Testament 9c. Geneva: Labor et Fides.

Richard, Earl J. 1991. "Early Pauline Thought: An Analysis of 1 Thessalonians." Pages 39–52 in *Pauline Theology*. Vol. 1. Augsburg: Fortress.

———. 1995. *First and Second Thessalonians*. Sacra Pagina 11. Collegeville, MN: Liturgical Press.

Riesner, Rainer. 1994. *Die Frühzeit des Apostels Paulus: Studien zur Chronologie, Missionsstrategie und Theologie*. Wissenschaftliche Untersuchungen zum Neuen Testament 71. Tübingen: Mohr Siebeck.

———. 1998. *Paul's Early Period: Chronology, Mission Strategy, Theology*. Translated by D. Stott. Grand Rapids: Eerdmans.

Rigaux, B. 1956. *Saint Paul: Les épitres aux Thessaloniciens*. Études bibliques. Paris: Gabalda.

Roetzel, Calvin J. 1986. "Theodidaktoi and Handiwork in Philo and 1 Thessalonians." Pages 324–31 in *L'Apôtre Paul: Personnalité, style et conception du ministere*. Edited by A. Vanhoye. Leuven: Leuven University Press.

———. 1991. "The Grammar of Election in Four Pauline Letters." Pages 211–33 in *Pauline Theology*. Vol. 2. Edited by David M. Hay. Minneapolis: Fortress.

Rulmu, Callia. 2010. "Between Ambition and Quietism: The Socio-Political Background of 1 Thessalonians 4:9–12." *Biblica* 91:393–417.

Russell, R. 1988. "The Idle in 2 Thess 3.6–12: An Eschatological or a Social Problem?" *New Testament Studies* 34:105–19.

Sailors, Timothy B. 2000. "Wedding Textual and Rhetorical Criticism to Understand the Text of 1 Thessalonians 2.7." *Journal for the Study of the New Testament* 80:81–98.

Schellenberg, Ryan. 2018. "Subsistence, Swapping, and Paul's Rhetoric of Generosity." *Journal of Biblical Literature* 137:215–34.

Schmithals, Walter. 1960. "Zur Abfassung und ältesten Sammlung der paulinischen Hauptbriefe." *Zeitschrift für die neutestamentliche Wissenschaft* 51:225–45.

———. 1964. "Die Thessalonicherbriefe als Briefkomposition." Pages 295–315 in *Zeit und Geschichte: Dankesgabe an Rudolf Bultmann zum 80. Geburtstag*. Edited by Erich Dinkler and Hartwig Thyen. Tübingen: Mohr Siebeck.

———. 1965. *Paulus und die Gnostiker: Untersuchungen zu den kleinen Paulusbriefen*. Hamburg-Bergstedt: Herbert Reich.

———. 1972. *Paul and the Gnostics*. Translated by J. E. Steely. Nashville: Abingdon.

Schnelle, Udo. 1986. "Der erste Thessalonicherbrief und die Entstehung der paulinischen Anthropologie." *New Testament Studies* 32:207–24.

Schrader, Karl. 1836. *Der Apostel Paulus*. Vol. 5. Leipzig: C. E. Kollmann.

Schubert, Paul. 1939. *Form and Function of the Pauline Thanksgiving*. Berlin: A. Töpelmann.

Scott, Robert. 1909. *The Pauline Epistles: A Critical Study*. Edinburgh: T&T Clark.

Smith, Jay E. 2001. "1 Thessalonians 4:4: Breaking the Impasse." *Bulletin for Biblical Research* 11:65–105.

Smith, Murray. 2013. "The Thessalonian Correspondence." Pages 269–301 in *All Things to All Cultures: Paul among Jews, Greeks and Romans*. Edited by Mark Harding and Alanna Nobbs. Grand Rapids: Eerdmans.

Sollamo, Raija. 1995. *Repetition of the Possessive Pronouns in the Septuagint*. Atlanta: Scholars Press.

Stefanidou-Tiveriou, Theodosia. 2010. "Social Status and Family Origin in the Sarcophagi of Thessalonikē." Pages 151–88 in *From Roman to Early Christian Thessalonikē: Studies in Religion and Archaeology*. Edited by Laura Salah Nasrallah, C[haralampos] Bakirtzes, and Steven J. Friesen. Cambridge, MA: Harvard University Press.

Still, Todd D. 1999. *Conflict at Thessalonica: A Pauline Church and Its Neighbors*. Journal for the Study of the New Testament Supplement Series 183. Sheffield: Sheffield Academic.

Stowers, Stanley K. 2001. "Does Pauline Christianity Resemble a Hellenistic Philosophy?" Pages 81–102 in *Paul beyond the Judaism/Hellenism Divide*. Edited by Troels Engberg-Pedersen. Louisville: Westminster John Knox.

Tellbe, Mikael. 2001. *Paul between Synagogue and State: Christians, Jews, and Civic Authorities in 1 Thessalonians, Romans, and Philippians*. Coniectanea Biblica: New Testament Series 34. Stockholm: Almqvist & Wiksell.

Thomas, Christine M. 2010. "Locating Purity: Temples, Sexual Prohibitions, and 'Making a Difference' in Thessalonikē." Pages 109–32 in *From Roman to Early Christian Thessalonikē: Studies in Religion and Archaeology*. Edited by Laura Salah Nasrallah, C[haralampos] Bakirtzes, and Steven J. Friesen. Cambridge, MA: Harvard University Press.

Thomas, Robert L. 1978. "1–2 Thessalonians." Pages 227–337 in *The Expositor's Bible Commentary*. Vol. 11. Edited by F. E. Gaebelein. Grand Rapids: Zondervan.

Trilling, Wolfgang. 1972. *Untersuchungen zum zweiten Thessalonischerbrief*. Leipzig: St. Benno.

———. 1980. *Der zweite Brief an die Thessalonicher*. Evangelisch-katholischer Kommentar zum Neuen Testament 14. Zurich: Benziger.

———. 1987. "Die beiden Briefe des Apostels Paulus an die Thessalonicher: Eine Forschungsübersicht." Pages 3365–403 in *Aufstieg und Niedergang der römischen Welt: Geschichte und Kultur Roms im Spiegel der neueren Forschung*. Part 2, *Principat*, 25.4. Edited by H. Temporini and W. Haase. New York: de Gruyter.

Turner, N. 1965. *Grammatical Insights into the New Testament*. Edinburgh: T&T Clark.

vom Brocke, Christoph. 2001. *Thessaloniki: Stadt des Kassander und Gemeinde des Paulus*. Wissenschaftliche Untersuchungen zum Neuen Testament 2/125. Tübingen: Mohr Siebeck.

Wanamaker, Charles A. 1990. *The Epistles to the Thessalonians*. New International Greek Testament Commentary. Grand Rapids: Eerdmans.

Weima, Jeffrey A. D. 2000. "'But We Became Infants among You': The Case for ΝΗΠΙΟΙ in 1 Thess 2.7." *New Testament Studies* 46:547–64.

———. 2012. "'Peace and Security' (1 Thess 5.3): Prophetic Warning or Political Propaganda?" *New Testament Studies* 58:331–59.

———. 2014. *1–2 Thessalonians*. Baker Exegetical Commentary on the New Testament. Grand Rapids: Baker Academic.

Weiss, Johannes. 1959. *Earliest Christianity: A History of the Period A.D. 30–150.* Vol. 1. Translated and edited by Fredrick C. Grant. New York: Harper & Brothers.

West, J. C. 1914. "The Order of 1 and 2 Thessalonians." *Journal of Theological Studies* 15:66–74.

White, Joel R. 2013. "'Peace and Security' (1 Thessalonians 5.3): Is It Really a Roman Slogan?" *New Testament Studies* 59:382–95.

Wiles, Gordon P. 1974. *Paul's Intercessory Prayers: The Significance of the Intercessory Prayer Passages in the Letters of St. Paul.* Society for New Testament Studies Monograph Series 24. Cambridge: Cambridge University Press.

Winter, Bruce W. 1994. *Seek the Welfare of the City: Christians as Benefactors and Citizens.* First-Century Christians in the Graeco-Roman World. Grand Rapids: Eerdmans.

Wrede, Wilhelm. 1903. *Die Echtheit des zweiten Thessalonicherbriefes untersucht.* Leipzig.

Wright, N. T. 2013. *Paul and the Faithfulness of God.* Minneapolis: Fortress.

Yamauchi, Edwin M. 1973. *Pre-Christian Gnosticism.* Grand Rapids: Eerdmans.

———. 1983. "Pre-Christian Gnosticism Reconsidered a Decade Later." Pages 187–249 in *Pre-Christian Gnosticism: A Survey of the Proposed Evidences.* Grand Rapids: Baker.

Index of Subjects

Index of Modern Authors

Index of Scripture and Ancient Sources